TARGET IAS

MISSION UPSC-IAS EXAM
with New Syllabus for Prelims & Main Exams

Dr. P.K. Agrawal
IAS (Retd.)

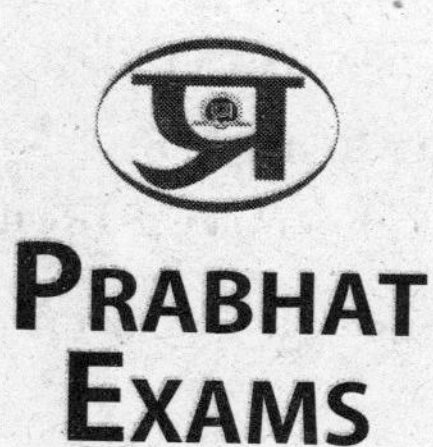

Publisher
PRABHAT EXAMS
Imprint of Prabhat Prakashan Pvt. Ltd.
4/19 Asaf Ali Road, New Delhi–110 002
Ph. 23289555 • 23289666 • 23289777 • Helpline/ 7827007777
e-mail: prabhatbooks@gmail.com • Website: www.prabhatexam.com

Price
Four Hundred Fifty Rupees

ISBN 978-93-5322-809-5

Printed at
SS Japan Arts, Delhi

TARGET IAS
by Dr. P.K. Agrawal IAS (Retd.)

ISBN 978-93-5322-809-5

₹ 450.00

Author's Note

Dear Aspirants,

It is my pleasure to interact with the Civil Services aspirants. I would like you to enrich with my success experience in various civil services like P.C.S. (U.P.), I.R.S. (Income Tax) and I.A.S. (1976).

My old experience is being shared with you with latest trends for the civil services with the help of a team of competent persons to make your I.A.S. Mission successful.

Firstly, the aspirant should have basic knowledge of subjects for preliminary and main examinations. Then you should look at the new syllabus for the Prelims and Main Exams. Syllabus is key to the success in IAS, etc. like the Preamble is the key to open the Constitution. It should be always with you like your friend, philosopher and guide. It is very elaborate covering all aspects of the premier competitive examination of the country. It is like the Ramayana, the Bible or the Quran for you.

Therefore, this book contains the latest syllabi so that you have not to run for it here and there and you can readily refer to it at any time. Concentrate on the syllabus because nothing succeeds like success. You can expand your knowledge after you become successful in IAS, etc. exams. In India, IAS is the best field to serve your society and the country with lot of power and autonomy for experimentation by you.

Thirdly, concentrate your studies on well selected books and notes. Repeat your notes time and again so that you learn them by heart. Practise the answers frequently. Earlier university topper was sure to get into IAS. Now-a- days, candidate with accurate knowledge and exact reproduction gets success. Bacon's saying below is more relevant today;

Reading makes a full man,
Writing an exact man;
Conference a ready man.

Be a ready candidate after jotting down and after discussions with your companions and fellow aspirants or students.

I have tried to give you tips in various ways. But you may adopt according to your way of studies and capacity. Do not leave your chosen track of preparations but add some tips to it to make it more suited to the Civil Services Exams. However, the beginners can follow lot of tips given in this book.

As regards tips for interview, follow the interviews published of successful candidates in UPSC-IAS examination. The first and foremost thing is that you should be well conversant with your background in all its aspects. Be prepared for many related questions on your form filled in for the exam and its critical knowledge. Your inner urge to serve your country and the countrymen should be brought out during the interview without fear and without previous predicaments. Your integrity should also be reflected in the course of interview process. The best way to prepare for interview is through mock sessions among your colleagues and friends specially those who have qualified for the interview and even have given the interview, if available. Otherwise, you can take help of modern I.T. tools including social media to practice for the interview. Earlier, it was only before the mirror.

Aim your target like Arjun with concentration and perseverance. Target is equally achievable by Arjun and Eklavya, by a boy from Jhuggi-Jhopri to the resident of a palace, by the daughter of a rikshapuller and by the daughter of a minister without any favoritism or injustice by UPSC.

My blessings are with you from the stage of preparation for the exams to your appearance before the interview board of the UPSC. Your feedback about the book will help us further to improve the book.

My best wishes to you for the success in the IAS etc. examination.

—Dr. P.K. Agrawal (*IAS Retd.*)

Contents

UNIT-A: Analytical Approach to Crack UPSC-IAS Exams

1 Tips & Strategy for Civil Services Exams Preparation

1. **R&D on Syllabus and Previous Question Papers:** Aspirants are advised to go through the current syllabus (PT & Main) and the previous years' question papers. Classify the syllabus subject-wise, each subject into' topics. A thorough insight of the past question papers will appraise about the portions of the syllabus from where the questions are regularly being asked and secondly, it may also help to understand the nature of the questions being asked. This strategy will constantly guide throughout preparation of the exams. So, they must analyse the question papers and identify the pattern and select the topics which are asked very frequently. Once aspirants have clearly demarcated the topics, the rest of the preparation will be an easy task.
2. **Source Material:** All aspirants are advised not to go through a lot of books, instead rely on one standard book on each topic which deals with the basic concepts. It will not only save time but also enrich aspirants with right concept and factual information. They are also advised to collect required quality books on different topics in advance to save time and to avoid the last minute hurry.
3. **Making Notes**

   Why should aspirants make notes?

   - It makes familiar to the entire syllabus
   - Aspirants' own notes will be of immense help for the revision of the syllabus.
   - It makes them to understand the given topic clearly. As they have to pick up themselves important points and to condense in words and in graphics.
   - Writing down any information by oneself helps to remember it.
   - Aspirants become ***an active reader*** by making notes.
   - When aspirants read their own notes, realize their ***grammatical mistakes.*** And self-corrections help in the exam.
   - It is a good practice for thinking and understanding the given topic.

- Self-making notes ***boost writing speed and develop the skill of precise and correct writing.***
- It helps to avoid going back to voluminous study material time and again.
- It helps aspirants to revise the entire topics in a short period.

How to Make Notes?

There are two types of making notes:

A. **Linear Notes:** In this method, aspirants condense the material they have read and jot down the most relevant points under headings and sub headings. This method is used to make notes after reading a book, newspaper or a magazine.

B. **Pattern Notes:** Here aspirants have to place the main topic at the center of the page and each line radiating from it represents a branch of the main topic. And like wise each branch line can be further divided into sub-branches using a key word or a phrase as per need. It has its own advantages, like

(i) It is more flexible because extra information can be added at any point of time.

(ii) Aspirants can see the entire pattern with important information at one go without actually turning the pages.

(iii) They can indicate the links between different topics more easily.

(iv) It is useful from aspirants' memory point of view as they can keep jotting down the points as and when these crop in their minds.

(v) It is in a shape format, so it is much easier to remember the content of the notes.

The pattern notes has its own disadvantage if there are too many facts and too much of information, as the notes becomes messy and overcrowded.

So the best method is either to adopt a combination of both Linear and Pattern graphic methods or to evolve their own unique pattern of making notes that may help the aspirants in their last minute revisions.

However, for any method of making notes it is essential to prepare into four basic stages:

- one outlining the topic,
- jotting its key points,
- jotting its advantages,
- its disadvantages and finally
- the conclusion.

Moreover, the notes have to be kept handy at all times and in a proper file. Aspirants should start making notes right from the very beginning of the preparation and never treat a set of notes as the final and keep adding important information to it from time to time.

STRATEGIC PLAN FOR EXAMS PREPARATION

The competitive examination comprises two successive stages

(i) Civil Services (Preliminary) Examination (Objective Type) for the selection of candidates for Main Examination; and

(ii) Civil Services (Main) Examination (Written and Interview) for the selection of candidates for the various Services and posts.

A. **Preliminary Examination:** The Examination shall comprise of two compulsory Papers of 200 marks each.

Note: (i) Both the question papers will be of the objective type (multiple choice questions) and each will be of two hours duration.

(ii) The General Studies Paper-II of the Civil Services (Preliminary) Examination will be a qualifying paper with minimum qualifying marks fixed at 33%.

(iii) The question papers will be set both in Hindi and English.

(iv) Details of the syllabi are indicated in Part B of Section III.

B. **Main Examination:** The written examination will consist of the following papers

Qualifying Papers			
Paper	**Subject**	**Topics**	**Marks**
Paper-A	Indian Language	One of the Indian Language to be selected by the candidate from the Languages included in the Eighth Schedule to the Constitution	300 Marks
Paper-B	English		300 Marks

Papers to Be Counted for Merit			
Paper	**Subject**	**Topics**	**Marks**
Paper-I	Essay		250 Marks
Paper-II	General Studies-I	Indian Heritage and Culture, History and Geography of the World and Society	250 Marks
Paper-III	General Studies-II	Governance, Constitution, Polity, Social Justice and International relations: Technology, Economic Development, Bio-diversity, Environment, Security and Disaster Management	250 Marks
Paper-IV	General Studies -III	Technology, Economic Development, Bio-diversity, Environment, Security and Disaster Management	250 Marks
Paper-V	General Studies-IV	Ethics, Integrity and Aptitude	250 Marks

Paper-VI (Optional Subject)	Paper -1	One of the subjects given in optional lists	250 Marks
Paper-VI (Optional Subject)	Paper -2	One of the subjects given in optional lists	250 Marks
Sub-total (Written Marks to be counted for recommendation to interview & Final Merit List)			1750 Marks
Personality Test (Interview)			275 Marks
Grand Total			2025 Marks

CRITERIA TO RECOMMEND NUMBER OF CANDIDATES

For Main and Interview

For Main: UPSC normally calls 12-13 times the number of actual vacancies reported for the corresponding year for Civil Services Mains Exam.

Criteria: If the number of vacancies reported is 1200, UPSC will call 1200 × 12.5 = 15,000 (approx.) candidates for mains exam from the total number of candidates appeared.

For Interview: UPSC will call about twice or 2.5 times the number of candidates of the reported vacancies in coming year.

For example, UPSC called about 3000 candidates for interview, if the number of vacancies reported is 1200, i.e. 2.5 times the number of vacancies. UPSC selects only about 1200 candidates among the top 3000 into the final list for training.

❑ ❑ ❑

2 Strategic Plan for Preliminary Exam Preparation

Trend Analysis: Cut-Off Marks for UPSC Civil Services Prelim Exam

Prelim Result: Year-wise Cut-off Marks					
Year	2015	2016	2017	2018	2019
Cut-Off Marks	107.34/200	116.00/200	105.34/200	98/200	
Percentage	53.67	58.00	52.67	49.00	

Note: UPSC uses the term 'minimum qualifying mark' instead of cut-off.

Prelims Category-wise Cut-off Marks 2018	
Category	**UPSC Prelims Cut off Marks(out of 200)**
General	98
OBC	96.66
SC	84
ST	83.34
PwBD – 1	73.34
PwBD – 2	53.34
PwBD – 3	40
PwBD – 5	45.34

Note: UPSC uses the term 'minimum qualifying mark' instead of cut-off.

Prelims-GS-1 Subject-wise/Year-wise Questions Trend Analysis

The number of questions asked from subjects show wide variations except a few subjects every year as given below in the table.

Subject/Year	2011	2012	2013	2014	2015	2016	2017	2018	2019
Current Events	13	26	28	20	29	27	34	28	22
History	11	17	11	17	14	15	14	15	17
Geography	11	12	9	12	14	7	7	8	14

Polity	12	11	13	11	13	7	22	13	15
Economy	19	13	15	10	13	18	8	16	14
Environment	15	12	13	17	10	18	11	13	11
General Science	19	9	11	13	7	8	4	7	7

WHAT & WHERE FROM TO READ FOR PRELIM EXAM?

Every aspirant must analyse 5 to 10 years previous question papers for both Prelims and Main to understand the trend, nature and pattern of questions asked from each segment of syllabus. On the basis of trend analysis read only those topics of books recommended by IAS toppers and coaching experts covering static portion of syllabus both for Prelims and Main Exams.

Syllabus for Prelim

1. Current events of national and international importance.
2. History of India and Indian National Movement.
3. Indian and World Geography: Physical, Social, Economic Geography of India and the World.
4. Indian Polity and Governance: Constitution, Political System, Panchayati Raj, Public Policy, Rights Issues, etc.
5. Economic and Social Development: Sustainable Development, Poverty, Inclusion, Demographics, Social Sector Initiatives, etc.
6. General issues on: Environmental ecology, Bio-diversity and Climate Change-that do not require subject specialization.
7. General Science.

SOURCES FOR PRELIM EXAM PREPARATION

1. **Current Events:** Important Sources [Follow any one newspaper for news items (preferably The Hindu); one for editorial (best Indian Express); and one Business newspaper only editorials (best is Livemint)].
   - The Hindu & The Indian Express
   - Press Information Bureau (PIB Gist)
   - PRS (Policy Research Studies' articles)
   - IDSA (Institute for Defense Studies and Analysis) articles
   - Yojana and Kurukshetra (selective articles)
   - Lok Sabha and Rajya Sabha Debates
2. **History**

   Modern India
   - NCERT – Class 8th (New) – 'Our Pasts – III'
   - NCERT – Class 12th 'Modern India' (OLD)
   - Tamil Nadu Edition – Class 12th
   - Bipan Chandra

Medieval India

- NCERT – Class 7th (New) –'Our Pasts – II'
- NCERT – Class 11th 'Medieval India' (OLD) – Satish Chandra
- Tamil Nadu Edition – Class 11th

Ancient India

- NCERT– Class 11th 'Ancient India' (OLD) – R.S. Sharma
- NCERT– Class 12th 'Themes in Indian History – Part I' (NEW) – Chapters 1 to 6
- Tamil Nadu Edition – Class 11th

NOTE: Most part of '**Culture**' section overlaps with Ancient and Medieval History

3. **Geography**
   - NCERT Social Science, Class 6th (New) 'The Earth Our Habitat'
   - NCERT Social Science, Class 7th (New) 'Our Environment'
   - NCERT Social Science, Class 8th (New) 'Resource and Development'
   - NCERT Social Science, Class 9th (New) 'Contemporary India'
   - NCERT Social Science, Class 10th (New) 'Contemporary India-Part II'
   - NCERT – Class 11th (New)
     (i) Fundamentals of Physical Geography
     (ii) India physical environment
   - NCERT – Class 12th (New)
     (i) Fundamentals of Human Geography
     (ii) India – People and Economy
   - Atlas: Oxford School Atlas

   Reference Book: Certificate Physical and Indian Geography – Goh Cheng Leong; OLD NCERT Geography – Class 11th and 12th (if available)
4. **Polity**
   - NCERT – Class 6th to 8th (for basic understanding)
   - NCERT – Class 9th to 12th (for understanding more on democracy and federalism)
   - Indian Polity – M. Laxmikanth
   - Introduction to Indian Constitution – D.D.Basu
   - Commentary on the Constitution of India – Dr. P.K. Agrawal (in English & Bharat ka Samvidhan in Hindi)
5. **Economics**
   - NCERT – Class 12th Macroeconomics
   - NCERT – Class 11th Indian Economic Development
   - NCERT – Class 9th & 10th (for basics)
   - Indian Economy – Ramesh Singh (Selective Chapters)
6. **General Science**
   - The Hindu – Monday Edition (only application based Science & Tech.)
   - NCERT – Class 6th to 10th

- NCERT – Biology – Class 11th (Unit IV & V basic concepts only)
- NCERT – Biology – Class 12th (Chap. 4, 5 and from 7 to 16 except technical details)
- NCERT – Biology – Class 12th (OLD) – Chap. 9 onwards
- NCERT – Physics – Class 11th (Chap. 1, 5 & 8) and Class 12th (Chap. 15 only)
- NCERT – Chemistry – Class 11th (Chap. 1 & 14 only) and 12th (Chap. 14 & 16 only)

7. **Environment**
   - ICSE Board – Environmental studies – Class 10th and 11th
   - NCERT – Geography Books (in 6th to 12th chapters on Environment)
   - downtoearth.org.in (Current affairs)
8. **Social Issues & New Policies/Schemes**
   - India yearbook
   - Yojana and
   - Kurukshetra

❑ ❑ ❑

3 Strategic Plan for Main Exam Preparation

Trend Analysis: Cut-off Marks for UPSC Civil Services Main Exam

Main & Final: Year-wise Cut-off Marks for General Category				
Year	Main Cut-Off (Total-1750)	Main Cut-Off %	Main+Interview Cut-Off (Total-2025)	Main+Interview Cut- Off %
2013	562	32.1	775	38.27
2014	678	38.74	889	43.90
2015	676	38.62	877	43.30
2016	787	44.97	988	48.79
2017	809	46.22	1006	49.67
2018	774	44.22	982	48.49

Note: UPSC uses the term 'minimum qualifying mark' instead of cut-off.

Trend Analysis: Main Optional Subjects Among Candidates

Probability of Optional Subjects Candidates opt for IAS Main Exam

Optional Subjects	Probable Number of Candidates
Public Administration	2000–5000
Geography	2000–4000
History	2000–3000
Sociology	1500–2500
Philosophy	1000–2000
Psychology	800–1200
Anthropology	500–1000
Other subjects along with languages are offered by specialized graduates	1–300

Success Rate of Candidates with the Following Optional Subjects in 2016 IAS Main Exam

A. Literature of the Following Languages			
Optional Subject	No. of Candidates Appeared in Main	No. of Candidates Recommended for Interview	Success Rate Percentage
Assamese Lit.	5	2	40
Punjabi Lit.	19	5	26.3
Gujarati Lit.	42	7	16.7
Kannada Lit.	84	14	16.7
Marathi Lit.	42	7	16.7
English Lit.	40	6	15
Urdu Lit.	29	4	13.8
Tamil Lit.	225	29	12.9
Sanskrit Lit.	122	10	8.2
Malayalam Lit.	67	5	7.3
Pali Lit.	255	18	7.1
Telugu Lit.	147	9	6.1
Hindi Lit.	974	56	5.7
Manipuri Lit.	22	1	4.5
Maithili Lit.	25	1	4
Arabic Lit.	1	0	0
Bengali Lit.	5	0	0
Dogri Lit.	1	0	0
Konkani Lit.	1	0	0
Odia Lit.	4	0	0
Persian Lit.	10	0	0
Sindhi Lit.	1	0	0

B. Optional Subjects other than Literature			
Optional Subject	No. of Candidates Appeared in Main	No. of Candidates Recommended for Interview	Success Rate Percentage
Agriculture	220	41	18.6
Medical Sciences	98	16	16.3
Animal Husbandry & Veterinary Sciences	65	8	12.3
Economics	326	37	11.3
Psychology	1061	116	10.9
Anthropology	345	37	10.7
Public Administration	3301	337	10.5
Management	13	1	7.7
Physics	239	16	6.7
Political Science & International Relations	1320	85	6.4
Geography	4049	236	5.8
Sociology	1555	89	5.7
Chemistry	124	7	5.6
Geology	36	2	5.6
History	3870	212	5.5
Electrical Engineering	74	4	5.4
Law	365	19	5.2
Mechanical Engineering	96	5	5.2
Botany	312	14	4.5
Philosophy	2092	84	4
Zoology	484	18	3.7
Civil Engineering	35	1	3.9
Mathematics	277	8	2.9
Statistics	14	0	0

Success Rate of Candidates with the Following Optional Subjects in 2015 IAS Main Exam

Subjects of the following disciplines			
Optional Subject	No. of Candidates Appeared in Main	No. of Candidates Recommended for Interview	Percentage of Success Rate
Medical Science	235	55	23.4
Animal Husbandry & Veterinary Science	52	12	23.1
Economics	269	51	19
Law	246	42	17.1
Agriculture	122	20	16.4
Commerce & Accountancy	188	28	14.9
Management	167	24	14.4
Geology	28	4	14.4
Zoology	228	29	12.7
Botany	104	12	11.5
Political Science & International Relations	1107	121	10.9
Chemistry	104	11	10.6
Civil Engineering	47	5	10.6
Sociology	2490	230	9.2
Philosophy	1116	99	8.9
History	2090	174	8.3
Psychology	1163	92	7.9
Geography	4351	314	7.2
Mathematics	325	23	7.1
Physics	266	17	6.4
Anthropology	579	38	6.3
Statistics	16	1	6.3
Electrical Engineering	126	8	6.3
Public Administration	7077	359	5.1
Mechanical Engineering	64	3	4.7

Percentage-wise Success Rates for Candidates with Optional Subjects (2010–2015)

Literature of the Following Languages						
Optional Subject	**2010**	**2011**	**2012**	**2013**	**2014**	**2015**
Bodo Literature	100	0	0	NA	NA	NA
Dogri Literature	100	0	0	0	NA	0
Sindhi Literature (Devanagari script)	100	NA	0	0	0	33.3
Sindhi Literature (Arabic script)	100	NA	NA	NA	66.7	50
English Literature	26.7	15.1	21.9	16.7	9.1	9.5
Telugu Literature	24.6	8.2	11	4.3	10.7	9.1
Manipuri Literature	18.2	22.2	0	5	23.5	20
Tamil Literature	16.3	13.4	25	10.7	14.7	21.5
Marathi Literature	15.6	15.8	15.4	3.8	12	6.7
Malayalam Literature	14.6	27.3	15.2	8.7	10.8	7.7
Maithili Literature	14.6	10.1	14.7	10.7	14.7	12.3
Kannada Literature	14.4	24.7	13	12	10.6	10.3
Urdu Literature	8.5	40.9	22.2	17.9	19.4	4.9
Gujarati Literature	7.4	16.9	14.5	12.5	13.8	3.7
Sanskrit Literature	7.3	11.8	11.4	5.6	10	6.4
Hindi Literature	3.9	13.1	11.7	4.2	5.4	2.8
Punjabi Literature	2.6	16.7	10	11.1	6.6	11.5
Odia Literature	0	7.1	0	10	0	28.6
Bengali Literature	0	20	0	16.7	33.3	16.7
Santhali Literature	0	33.3	33.3	100	0	100
Assamese Literature	0	25	37.5	0	0	0

Percentage-wise Success Rates for Candidates with Optional Subjects (2010–2015)

Subjects of the following disciplines						
Optional Subject	**2010**	**2011**	**2012**	**2013**	**2014**	**2015**
Medical Science	18.8	23.4	23.4	16.4	19.9	23.4
Management	14.3	5.6	14.4	13.8	11.4	14.4
Anthropology	12	13.2	6.6	11.8	11	6.3
Sociology	10.5	8.2	9.2	9.1	10.6	9.2
Animal Husbandry and Veterinary Science	10.1	10	23.1	15.6	14.3	23.1

Physics	9.9	9.6	6.4	8.8	9.3	6.4
Public Administration	9.2	7.9	5.1	6.2	5.3	5.1
Geography	8.6	7.6	7.2	5.6	7.3	7.2
Geology	8.3	10	14.3	6.7	3.6	14.4
Psychology	8.2	10.5	7.9	9.8	15.8	7.9
Law	8	8	17.1	24.3	17	17.1
Political Science and IR	7.6	9.7	10.9	6.1	6.3	10.9
Commerce and Accountancy	7.3	6.9	14.9	7.5	10.3	14.9
Mathematics	7.2	8.3	7.1	6.1	10	7.1
Economics	6.6	5.6	19	20.2	12.1	19
Chemistry	6.5	8.9	10.6	7.1	7.1	10.6
Mechanical Engineering	5.8	6.8	4.7	6.7	6.3	4.7
Zoology	5.5	7.1	12.7	9.8	11.4	12.7
Electrical Engineering	5.3	5.3	6.3	11.5	7.8	6.3
History	4.8	8.5	8.3	7.7	6.5	8.3
Philosophy	4.3	8.2	8.9	7.9	7	8.9
Botany	3.4	6.7	11.5	14	0	11.5
Civil Engineering	1.7	3.4	10.6	13	7.7	10.6
Agriculture	1.5	12.1	16.4	9.1	10.8	16.4
Statistics	0	5.3	6.3	16.7	16.7	6.3

Notes

- As per data given in the above table, medical science has been the most consistent performer among all the subjects.
- Some of the literatures which have shown very high percentage (up to 100%) due to very less number of candidates with those subjects.
- Mark 'NA', indicates no candidates had opted for that optional subject that year.

Conclusion

From above trend analysis and rational approach, an aspirant can conclude that a particular optional subject for candidate **X** is not necessarily the best scoring as it is for candidate **Y**. So, candidates should always select optional subjects applying rational approach based on syllabus of the subject, personal background/interest, performance in the subject during postgraduate examination, time availability, quality study materials, etc.

SOURCES FOR MAIN EXAM PREPARATION

General Studies Paper I

A. Indian Heritage & Culture, History

Sources:

- NCERT XI
- NIOS notes on culture
- NCERT Ancient History
- The Wonder That was India – A L Basham
- NCERT Medieval Indian History
- IGNOU material
- History of Medieval India – Satish Chandra
- India's Struggle for Independence – Bipan Chandra
- India After Independence – Bipan Chandra
- NCERT XII: Politics in India after Independence
- Mastering Modern World History – Norman Lowe
- NCERT XII: Indian Society
- NCERT XII: Social Change and Development in India
- Indian Culture, Art and Heritage – Dr. P.K. Agrawal

B. **Geography of the World and Society**

Sources:

- Certificate Physical and Human Geography – G C Leong
- NCERT XI: Fundamentals of Physical Geography
- NCERT XI: India: Physical Environment
- NCERT XII: India: People and Economy
- Geography of India – Majid Husain
- World Geography – Majid Husain
- Status of Forests Report
- Orient BlackSwan School Atlas

General Studies Paper II

A. **Governance, Constitution, Polity, Social Justice**

Sources:

- Indian Polity – M Laxmikanth
- NCERT XI: Indian Constitution at Work
- Introduction to the Constitution of India – D D Basu
- Constitution of India Bare Act – Dr. P.K. Agrawal
- Punchhi Commission Report
- Constitution Commission (NCRWC)
- Finance Commission Report
- 2nd Arc Report
- Five Year Plan Documents

B. International Relations

Sources:

- ♦ NCERT XII: Political Science: World Politics
- ♦ India's Foreign Policy – Rajiv Sikri

General Studies Paper III

A. **Technology, Economic Development, Biodiversity, Environment**

Sources:

- ♦ Indian Economy – Ramesh Singh
- ♦ NCERT XI: India's Economic Development
- ♦ NCERT XII: Geography India People and Economy
- ♦ Budget
- ♦ Economic Survey
- ♦ Science and Technology – Spectrum

C. **Security and Disaster Management**

Sources:

- ♦ Annual Report of the Ministry of Home Affairs
- ♦ Internal Security & Disaster Management – Ashok Kumar
- ♦ IGNOU material Security & Disaster Management

General Studies Paper IV

Ethics, Integrity & Aptitude

Sources: Ethics, Integrity and Aptitude for Civil Services Main Examination – G Subba Rao and P N Roy Chowdhury

4 How to Choose Main Exam Optional Subject?

Aspirants need to select an optional subject in which they are comfortable to score high in UPSC Mains. The level of comfort depends on many factors like the – knowledge of the subject, availability of books and other study materials, availability of time, scope of study-mates discussion, recent trends of marks, the level of difficulty as per the syllabus and previous question papers etc. If the subject they had in graduation or postgraduation is available in the list of subjects given, the same option will turn out as a comfortable option. All others look for an optional subject which can be finished in a time-bound manner without encroaching upon the time for GS preparation.

Selecting an overlapping optional subject with General Studies is a good strategy to save the time required to study an optional subject not mentioned as per GS syllabus. This case is not universally applicable. For example, Rachat Raj, UPSC 2013 Rank 3, scored exceptionally well with Zoology optional. There are also many who made it to the top with optional subjects like Medical Science. None of these optional subjects overlap with GS syllabus as subjects like History or Geography or Political Science and International Relations do. So aspirants should neither take an optional just for the sole reason of GS overlapping nor just based on advice from coaching institute gurus for the sake of commercial interests behind promoting each optional subject. Moreover, aspirants will have to be smart and mature enough to analyse the advice and come to conclusion on their own. The reason is that each and every optional subject is equally scoring. The real test of academic excellence is in the optimal subject only. One should not resort to short-cuts, made easy, or selected topics in the optimal subject but he or she should have indepth study in all facets of the subject. The candidate is supposed to give a balanced view point or any view point which is factually and logically sound and convincing. Some optional subjects might not turn high-scoring in some years because of scaling effects, but there is no universal trend or theory regarding any optional subject.

There are three important factors every aspirant must consider before selecting optional subject:

(i) Time available,
(ii) The effort required and
(iii) The possibility of maximum marks.

The Advice to Think Over

1. Aspirants should not take an overlapping optional if they are not strong in it, because it can be a counterproductive.
2. If aspirants have limited time (i.e. less than 4 months), they must not take an optional subject which requires extensive preparation.
3. A scoring overlapping optional subject with vast nature of syllabus, which requires extensive preparation, can be adopted, if aspirants have the following:
   - Background of the subject
   - Previous exposure in the subject, or
   - There is adequate time left.

   Otherwise, select an optional paper which requires less time for a decent level of preparation.
4. There are many hardworking candidate who start preparation 1-3 years before the Main exam and are able to finish quality textbooks of any optional subject. But they must be careful on compromising GS marks for optional preparation as it can also turn suicidal, and hence not advised to do so.

Optional Subjects List for UPSC Main Exam

1. Agriculture	2. Animal Husbandry and Veterinary Science	3. Anthropology	4. Botany	5. Chemistry
6. Civil Engineering	7. Commerce & Accountancy	8. Economics	9. Electrical Engineering	10. Geography
11. Geology	12. History	13. Law	14. Management	15. Mathematics
16. Mechanical Engineering	17. Medical Science	18. Philosophy	19. Physics	20. Political Science & International Relations
21. Psychology	22. Public Administration	23. Sociology	24. Statistics	25. Zoology
Literature of the following languages				
1. Assamese	2.Bengali	3. Bodo	4. Dogri	5. Gujarati
6. Hindi	7. Kannada	8. Kashmiri	9. Konkani	10. Maithili
11. Malayalam	12. Manipuri	13. Marathi	14. Nepali	15. Odia
16. Punjabi	17. Sanskrit	18. Santhali	19. Sindhi	20. Tamil
21. Telugu	22. Urdu	23. English		

❑❑❑

What & How to Read for Main Exam Preparation?

- Aspirants are advised before reading on any topic, go through the questions asked in the previous exams on the given topic of the syllabus and jot down them with some more probable additions. This will help them forming an idea about the kind of study material they need to be studied for writing answer of such frequently asked questions (faqs) in coming exam.
- It is always wise to be selective on standard reading material advised by IAS toppers, because reading from too many sources can only confuse them.
- Sometimes notes from seniors in college or university or from friends preparing for IAS exam can be quite good option better than notes from the coaching institutions/centres.
- It is important for aspirants that studying for Civil Service exam involves '*purposeful reading*.' It means they must focus on the given topic to prepare the possible questions and making bullet points for their possible answers from the topic.
- After this approach to reading, try to read logically and link all the points to construct a probable answer to the questions by elaborating on those points.
- Try to correct your knowledge of the subject to the recent trends in public life.
- This strategy of reading can help aspirants in preparing the short notes that can be revised periodically.
- This approach to reading will help to retain the salient points of the topic in their memory, improve grip over the topic and make them more confident about the subject.
- Moreover, the above approach and strategy will make the aspirants more confident on clearing Prelims and writing brilliant answers in the Mains exams.

❑❑❑

How to Write Essay for Civil Services Main Exam?

The Essay Paper is one of the UPSC Civil Services Main Exam papers carrying 250 marks counted for merit formulation of candidates. In this paper, candidates will have to write two essays each for 125 marks with a word count of 1000–1200 in 3 hours. Candidates have the choice to select one topic from each of the two sections providing four topics in each one. Hence, the candidates must prepare and attempt this paper with the same seriousness as all other papers in GS Main and learn the art of writing the essay as per topic requirement.

The candidates are advised to keep in mind certain steps while writing the essay paper in the main exam, like:

A. Read All the Topics Thoroughly Section-wise

The most important step in the process of writing essay for IAS Main exam is to choose one out of four topics from each section on which candidates can write better. While selecting the topics, candidates should make sure that they know the most about the chosen topics out of the given sections. What not to select:

- A sensitive or controversial topic like, Sabarimala temple in Kerala.
- A topic which is too complex in meaning and concept. This can work against the candidates' thought process and so the composition of essay.

B. How to Proceed after Selecting the Topics?

After the selection of topics, candidates should not start writing straight away. It is important to think for some time and note down the headings, subheadings, and points of information for different paragraphs of the body of essay. This is important because only then candidates can write their points in the required sequence. For example, if they are supposed to write about India's relations with her neighbours, they need to write the historical facts and events in the beginning. The reason is that, suppose candidates start writing on the topic, and realise only at the end that they have forgotten to mention an important point, then it would be too late to add it because of a space crunch. Therefore, it helps if candidates write their rough points in the beginning.

Once the candidates have the points in sequence on rough spaces, they can start writing without the fear of forgetting any important points. While writing, they must adhere to a good structure. The structure of a good essay is as follows:

(i) Introduction in brief
(ii) Historical information
(iii) Main issue/problem/subject
(iv) Current scenario related to the topic
(v) Positive and negative aspects
(vi) Reforms required
(vii) Conclusion

C. Add-on Points

- Relevant quotes/sayings by famous personalities
- Relevant government schemes and policies
- Any accurate figures or numbers

Examples of few previous essay topics could be taken to figure out the complexities inherent in these essays.

1. Should a moratorium be imposed on all fresh mining in tribal areas of the country?
2. Preparedness of our society for India's global leadership role.
3. From traditional Indian Philanthropy to the Gates-Buffett model—a natural progress or a paradigm shift?

The first essay, 'should a moratorium be imposed on all fresh mining in tribal areas of the country', throws open a difference of opinion and expects the candidates to solve the riddle of development on one hand and preservation of tribal culture, on the other. On one hand, we are bound by developmental responsibilities to find out newer prospects for industrialisation based on cheap and amply available raw materials to boost our production for the elimination of poverty and hunger that in turn improve the living standard. The challenge of improving the living standard of two-thirds of the population can only be overcome by exploring the possibilities of rapid industrialisation. The second five year plan was the envision of Pandit Jawaharlal Nehru—a great visionary, statesman and one of the founding fathers of our nation. Hence, it becomes all more necessary to mine the mineral-rich places that are often near plateaus and hilly areas. However, it is to be kept in mind that these places are inhabited by our primitive tribes. They represent the rare heritage of our ancient culture, values and practices that have gradually diminished to become endangered today and are on the verge of starvation. Preserving them and their interests is our national, moral and humane responsibility.

Moreover, they have nothing to do with our ambitious developmental projects as the fruits of development hardly reach them. Hence, confronted with this sophisticated situation, a mature, balanced, intelligent and innovative approach is needed to tackle both these critical and important issues in equal measure. At the same time, significant attention has to be paid while expressing opinion in support of or against any of these two needs, as these are very delicate and sensitive issues. Hence, the need of the hour is to take what Buddha preached a middle path or Aristotle's golden mean of the two, that is, granting the permission of mining to only those areas where the mobilisation and displacement of these naturally habituated tribes is low and where they could be provided similar alternate habitat to feel at home even after their displacement.

Though, our previous experiences of displacement failed to meet our expectations and the interests of these tribes, but we can learn and identify the possible areas of their vulnerability out of those experiences. Three categories can be identified: (1) Special case, where tribals have a unique habitat with no alternate option, (2) Where the displacement options are available along with some cultivable land, (3) Where they agree to adapt to the mainstream development-borne life style, for example, few areas of northeastern states and (4) Where they can be associated in the mining process through employment or giving them shares or annuity in the industrial entity. Regions falling under the first category would not be suitable for mining considerations while the other two cases may allow mining but with utmost care and precaution. Therefore, it can be concluded that a clear cut order banning all fresh mining activities in triba areas of the country shall be in contravention to our development strategy which forms the basis of our planning and policies. Thus, careful consideration should be given to argue and conclude a middle path that is best suited along with empathy for the poor and the deprived people. A candidate having sound knowledge in the above domain can easily fetch marks ranging from 100–140.

The 2nd Essay: 'Preparedness of our society for India's global leadership role', is something that can be anticipated as a topic preferred by all types of students, including the students of history, sociology, public administration, literature and philosophy All the students have enough space to accommodate their ideas and reveal a newe dimension to it. Thus, this essay provides immense scope. A survey found that this essay is preferred by over 80% of the students as it helps them in identifying and connecting their studies and understanding of India. Moreover, the selection of this essay require one to have a deep understanding of Indian society and its progress along with the vision of India as a global leader. Since the very ancient times, the prosperity, spirituality well-being and welfare-based governance of India made it renowned worldwide a the 'World guru' or the 'World leader'. The societal structure of India, with more than 5000-year old recorded history, can be divided into ancient, medieval, modern and contemporary periods. During all these periods, the Indian society witnessed development in three dimensions, namely, (1) spiritual, (2) psychic or attitudinal and (3) physical. Physically, a developed society is known to be that which fulfils the basic amenities of its people, provides them a decent standard of life and empower them with prosperity. The fast moving cars, aeroplanes, space shuttle, computers machines, mobile and internet-based satellite communication, etc. facilitating the humankind nowadays reflects our physical growth in a good light. Nowadays, plenty of success stories of the Indians are there in the field of literature, science, technolog etc. Mentally, the viewpoint of young generation seems far better and coherent than that of older generations. Thus, in terms of mental aspects a significant leap is taken by the human society. The features of a spiritually advanced society are its openness, liberal thinking and universalistic aptitude that reflect highest degree of human rationality and scientific temper instead of superstition, bigotry and old conventions. In such a society, people have feelings of brotherhood within themselves, considering themselves part of a united family, and associate themselves with one universal God. The age-old values of '*Vasudhaiva Kutumbakam*' and '*sarvam khalvidam brahma*' etc. reflects the prevalence of such spiritual practices in ancient India.

A society incorporating all the three dimensions in a balanced state can only claim to be an all-round developed society. As the physical and psychic levels of development, with each and every developmental effort, involve a very critical risk of evolving their negative counterparts also. For example, the development of a fast moving car at physical level also brings with it the simultaneous risk of severe accidents. Similarly at the psychic level, though plenty of Global Prizes are won every year along with publication of new researches and innovations, but there has been rise in case of various mental disorders also. In present times, negative tendencies such as frustrations, anxieties and suicide attempts have increased manifolds. Hence, it can be seen that the physical and psychic levels of development carry them their negative counterparts also. Only, the spiritual development does not have any negativity associated with it. Therefore, these three levels are linked together in a complex relationship, which have to be brought to exist in harmony to give the true sense of a developed society.

Since the ancient times, Indian society is said to practice spirituality that was followed with a strong foundation even in the medieval time. Refined with higher standards of values, ethics and morality, the social consciousness was characterised with confidence. People believed in themselves and psychically the society was strong. The people were able to meet their needs and requirements and physically too the society had abundant wealth to take care of its people. The living standard of people was remarkably good and they were satisfied with it.

The medieval period in Indian society during the period of Delhi Sultanate and the Mughals witnessed a little deterioration in the physical well-being of its people, but overall the society was able to manage the intricate balance amongst the three levels.

However, a great deal of harms to the interest of people in India and its societal structure was done in the modern period during the period of European invasion that resulted into British rule and colonisation of India. This was done in two levels—physical level and psychic level. Physically, the Britishers followed the policy of 'Drain of Wealth' and put all their efforts to exploit, extract and export Indian wealth to England. To suit their selfish interests, they exploited the very structure of Indian economy, trade, commerce and occupation of the people without even caring about the grave consequences that followed in the form of long-term destruction of the Indian agriculture and industry. Psychically too they were able to inflict damage to the attitude of the society to such an extent that Indians lost faith and belief in their values. This caused a remarkable loss to the Indian society and it needs time to heel and revive the society.

Hence, the contemporary Indian society is comprised of people who underwent physical and psychic exploitation for over two and half centuries. However, even the alien intrusions could not destabilise them from spirituality. Hence, during all these periods of crisis the base of Indian society in the form of spirituality remained intact.

Post-independence, a strong foundation laid by the visionary leadership of Mahatma Gandhi, Pandit Nehru, Ballabh Patel, Dr. Ambedkar, etc. led to the present form of governance based on modern principles of democracy, village upliftment socialism and secularism. Our Constitution very well incorporates all these principles and enjoys the privilege of being one of the largest written constitutions in the world.

The solid foundations laid by our Constitution have resulted in providing a strong base to the Indian society to become self-reliant in food grain production and most of its basic needs. In the present scenario, the country is widely recognised as one of the fastest growing economy in the world and emerging as a leader on many fronts. Even the U. S. President Obama acknowledged that 'When India speaks, the World listens'.

In the 1960s, followed by a series of famines, when our late Prime Minister Smt. Indira Gandhi went to USA to seek help for food grains and other economic needs, she was made to wait half an hour in the presidential corridor to meet the U. S. President. In the present scenario, the situation has changed to such a level that the U. S. President Mr. Obama came to India and sought employment for its people. Today, India is playing a leadership role in international organisations including ASEAN, SAARC, G-20, BASIC, IBSA, etc. Moreover, India has been given an observer status in other organisations like G-8, SCO, EU, etc. which portrays the significant role India plays, its participation and the respect gains by it in the International Forums. India adopted the harmonious and peaceful coexistence principles of Non-Aligned Movement (NAM) based on India's ancient value system of 'Sarva Jan Hitaya Cha' and 'Vashudhaiv Kutumbakam'. It evolved as a result of Indian societal structure and has provided an alternative to the polarised world that followed immature, dictatorial and sentimental principles of polarisation during the second World War. India played a significant role in the formation of the UN even before it achieved independence. Many of the UN institutions are based on India's age-old principles of humanism and universalism of which India is also the founding member.

Thus, physically India is able to revive itself within a very short span of time after independence. Presently, India has registered itself as the second fastest growing economy of the world. This has led to a boost in the psychological status of Indian people reflecting growing social awareness, confidence in the society and respect world over. Nowadays, Indians have regained the sense of belief and pride in being an Indian. This reflects a great sign of improvement the Indian society is going through.

The economic development, prosperity of the people and international position held by India and its people show the readiness of Indian society for betterment in all spheres of life. The living standard of Indian society has improved in all these fronts. Few social problems such as poverty, unemployment, mass scale hunger, malnourishment, ignorance, illiteracy, and other forms of iniquities that still exist in the present society can be eliminated in future with good development push, successful functioning democracy, education, good governance and due contribution by the people. All these developments indicate that India would be able to regain its status of global leader in the time to come. As it is the only country with a social set-up having a harmonious balance in all the three aforementioned fundamental pillars that form the basis of an ideal society.

A relatively good essay could be turned out by elaborating few of these aspects combined with logical arguments on a relevant topic. This essay becomes an obvious choice as a student well versed in these basic aspects of society, could get marks in the range of 100 to 145.

The third essay topic: 'From traditional Indian Philanthropy to the Gates-Buffett model—a natural progress or a paradigm shift?' is more of a philosophical tone. To attempt this essay one should have adequate knowledge of the differences that lie in the Indian practice of 'paropkara' and the contemporary western practice of 'philanthropy'. Thereafter, one is assumed to provide comments on whether philanthropy in practice today is a natural progress or a Paradigm shift?

Before taking a position, the essayist should elaborate upon these two practices then should logically conclude the topic. The concept of philanthropy in India was called as 'Paropkara', that is, 'Par' + 'Upkara' which means 'service to others'. Therefore, the philanthropy was considered as service or duty to perform whether one had enough wealth or little wealth. This is inbuilt in all religions. The people distributing their money or wealth would consider themselves indebted to person receiving their money and never viewed themselves obliging to the needy or the beneficiary. Raja Harishchandra, Bharathari, Raja Bhoja, Ashoka, etc. are some examples of the kings who testify this system of philanthropy that was prevalent in India since the time immemorial.

In present times, philanthropy in practice is a western adaptation. Influenced by this system, most of the Indian wealthy people, who have become billionaire very recently, are following the western philanthropists, like Bill, Warren Buffett and Milinda Gates, etc. The widespread fame and recognition that comes with this practice motivates these multi billionaires. Thus, most of the Indian philanthropists in their eagerness to transform themselves as modern western men get drawn into this westernisation. This is not bad.

However, the Indian philanthropy by the corporates has been now given an institutional recognition by the Indian law whereas the companies have to share/ spend their little profit (upto 2%) under the new scheme CSR (Corporate social responsibility).

Modernisation does not mean westernisation and is instead a mindset based on the principles of democracy, socialism, equality, secularism and freedom and universalism. Hence, the practice of philanthropy nowadays by Indians who recently turned rich cannot be called as a natural development but a paradigm shift.

However they can still do a lot under the corporate social responsibility (CSR) framework. This is a balanced way between the two as they dedicate their hard earned wealth for the purpose of education of the down-trodden or to fill up few gaps of the modern Indian society with their corporate planning and implementation acumen like Azim Prem Ji of WIPRO and Narayan Murthi of INFOSYS.

Now, enough light has been thrown on core of the issues and one can always make use of his/her vision and understanding to further elaborate on the topic. One can put relevant facts and figures in a meaningful way to make it more substantive. Hence, this essay requires more of a philosophical knowledge than factual knowledge or something learnt from books. A well-written essay on this topic can fetch marks in the range of 100–140.

Thus, we can see that main examination nowadays has become very competitive similar to the situations that we undergo in our daily walk of life in the present scenario. A comprehensive understanding of Indian society, its culture, people, practices and philosophies is a must for an individual who wants to compete in the exam. Writing on some of these topics or on similar issues and getting oneself evaluated is the best way to prepare for essay writing. The importance of essays should not be taken lightly as these could be decisive in changing the rank and portfolio of a candidate and making it to the final list of successful candidates.

Some sources for Essay writing

1. Essay for Civil Services Examination.

—Dr. B. Ramaswamy

2. Nibhandh Mahasagar.

—Dr. P.K. Agrawal

❑❑❑

How to Write an Appropriate Answer for Civil Services Main Exam?

There are two important factors involved in evaluating an answer to fetch good marks:

(i) Understanding the question completely,

(ii) Sticking to the words limit.

Understanding a question fully, aspirants must know that questions asked in Main Exams have keywords. Every question is framed on a 'topic' with a 'directive'.

For example,

Q. "Gandhian strategy of non-violence and satyagraha had its own limitations". Examine.

In the above question,

Topic of the question: 'limitations of Gandhian strategy of non-violence and satyagraha.'

Directive for the Answer: 'Examine'.

If anyone gives an 'explanation' to this answer how Gandhian strategy had limitations and affected freedom struggle, the examiner will give less than average marks. Instead, the directive guides the aspirants for the *examination* of the statement to look into topic in detail, to understand it, inspect it, investigate it and establish issues and facts related to topic. Aspirants are advised to explain why these issues and facts are important and what implications they have with contemporary incidents if words limit permits.

Alternate Directive for Answer on the Same Topic: 'Critically Examine'.

In addition to previous directive aspirants are advised to give both positive and negative related to topic followed by a balanced conclusion for the satisfaction of examiner.

Likewise UPSC often gives many other directives in its questions and each demand a precise answer. For examples, 'Examine', 'Comment', 'Analyze', 'Evaluate', 'Discuss', 'Critically Examine', Critically Comment', 'Critically Analyze' and 'Assess', etc.

❑❑❑

8 Tips for Interview Preparation

The Civil Services main exam candidates are interviewed. Although the interview is of 275 marks, but for final selection, it is very important. In the interview, if the candidate performs well, he may be able to achieve 60-70%, he can capture a seat in the final race.

In interview, more than the candidate's knowledge and general aptitude, his understanding towards the world, India and his point of view are given importance. It is also a test how likely a candidate is to become a public servant.

The board is generally supportive. However, the candidate should answer patiently and carefully. He should start his interview by introducing himself. For this, the candidate should prepare beforehand his each and every small or big interest or disinterest very carefully. Mock interviews with friends as well as joining any coaching classes are also beneficial.

Another important point in the interview is that the candidate should answer politely but firmly in his views. It is commonly believed that a candidate should be sensitive and responsive because you will be appointed as a public officer, and how responsible you are towards the public – such points are judged by the members in the interview.

All the board members are experienced in their fields. Therefore, the answers should be precise and to the point. If you don't know the answer to a question, you should apologise than to equivocate.

In the interview, the candidates should answer confidently but, yes, over-confidence should be avoided. Over-confidence can be detrimental to your selection. For the interview, please pay attention to your dress. Men should choose neat, clean and formal clothes to wear. Salwar, suits or saris would be better choice for women candidates.

Hindi-literate candidates are generally skeptical about the fact that preference is given to English-medium candidates. If a member of the board asks questions in English, then humbly take permission to answer in Hindi. There is nothing wrong in this.

Observing the past performance, the board has called you for an interview. Therefore, there should be no confusion or doubt in your mind over the language while preparing for an interview.

Interview Preparation

The interview is the most important in any competitive examination. Verbal communication is an integral part of it. Persons who take the interview are well qualified, experienced and have specialised in their respective fields. They have specific tasks to examine the ability of candidates. In the interview, they focus on those things:

His interest; dedication towards work; personality; ability to work with the team; general knowledge; testing of common sense; competitive ability and intelligence. The competitor's ability is judged on all the above-mentioned parameters.

Personality

The personality of a person is a combination of inner and outer qualities, like person's nature, attraction, presentation, manner of conversation, presentation of questions-answers, knowledge of a subject, methodology, revealing the character, courage and enthusiasm, etc. A few aspects of personality, such as the skin colour are decided by God but the other qualities can be developed and improved because it is important to strive for an impressive personality that make you a winner in an interview.

The candidate should have a keen interest in the position and field he is applying for. Success will be in doubt only if your interest isn't projected or it appears that you have come due to some compulsion. So, prepare very well.

General Knowledge and Common Sense

In an interview, these two are very helpful keys. There is a difference between general knowledge and common sense. You have knowledge of the facts but if you don't have the proper ability to use the knowledge, then it is futile. Common sense can help you answer questions on topics that you may not have studied earlier. Such study can be developed by practice. If you have good general knowledge, you can create a lasting impression in the interview.

Designation as per Capability

Try to develop the qualities as per the designation. For example, administrative job, technical job, judicial job, financial institute jobs are special jobs where the responsibilities and duties are different. So, in general, all those positions have a few necessary, common points but from another point of view, those special jobs need some special qualities, which you should try to develop within yourself.

Remember

Here is the list of a few things that should be taken care of while giving the interview. If you don't behave accordingly, it will have a harmful effect:

- Don't enter the interview room without permission.
- Don't wave your hands to greet.
- Sit on the chair after taking permission.
- Ensure to thank after receiving the permission to sit.

- Don't interrupt between the conversations of members in the interview, even if the things are related to you.
- Don't place your files or briefcase on the table, in front of interviewers.
- Neither enter the room nor leave the room too hastily. It shows your nervousness. Enter or leave the room decently.
- Don't speak until the question has been finished.
- In your answer, don't jibe about any person, institution or political party.
- Don't reveal anxiety in front of the interview members.
- If you don't know the exact facts about the question, tell the interviewers clearly.
- Don't beat about the bush, as they have complete knowledge on the subjects.
- Don't exaggerate your topic.
- Don't argue using irrelevant logic.
- Use handkerchief in the interview to muffle your cough or sneeze.
- Don't get into religious debates. Talk in terms of humanity only.
- If the question cannot be understood by you, use "pardon me, please" and ask the question again, but please don't reply to the questions without understanding them.
- Use "Shriman" or "Sir" while communicating.
- Don't use words that appear flattering.
- Perform with decency and courtesy.
- Avoid any gesture of indifference or negativity.
- Calm your mind and answer with intelligence.

True Facts

- In the conversation, whatsoever you say, must be clear to others. Otherwise the message will be meaningless.
- Message should be based on your experience and views should show your confidence and maturity.
- Speaking is an art that can be mastered with use of technical gadgets, with practice.
- So, be firm on your ideas while at the interview. You can look at the previous records and prepare yourself accordingly.
- Shakespeare said, "Brevity is the soul of wit." Therefore, keep everything you say in brief.
- Pay attention to two things in precis writing – 1) all the essential elements should be included; 2) it should be limited to one-third of the words of the passage.
- Your thoughts on the topic, originality of imagination and knowledge level and the ability to interpret are tested in the interview. That's why, the topic should be chosen very carefully even your hobby.
- Use your sense of humour only if you have full command over it.
- Appropriate and positive body language impacts twice on the interviewer. So, use it to your advantage.

Analyse the Person Interviewing You

The very first essential qualification required for success in the interview is "educational qualification". But besides this, there is something else that can be helpful. Facing the interviewers is one of them. Try to mould yourself according to the mood of the interviewers. Usually, we like the person whose behaviour is similar to that of us. This is true in the matter of interview too.

Sit in the interview, formally, in the same way as the interviewer. Try the same conversational tone similar to the pitch of sound and words which are in practice. In terms of behaviour, such small gestures can take you a long way in maintaining relationships.

You must take care of the mood of the person who is taking interview, because the person who is in command would want the next person to be in the same mood. It should not be that one person is serious and the other is overly excited. In this situation, your excitement can get the better of you or vice versa. However, the only thing is to be alert while giving the interview. Experts call it "facing", which means to capture the mood and tone of the person before you. In other words, hold the other's pulse at the right time and at the right speed.

You in the Interview Room

Interview is the last but most significant exam in Civil Services as it plays an important role in the process of selection. The board of interview members tests the overall personality of the candidate in the interview. Members of the board want to ensure that the huge responsibility of administration is being placed on the shoulders of an able person having a suitable personality, so that there are no problems in future.

Before going for the interview of civil services, identify your own weakneses honestly, like nervousness, overexcitement, and hassle, and avoid lying. In the interview, the board members already have a copy of the resumé of the candidate but still they ask questions based on it. Therefore, questions related to your resumé should be prepared very well. The key test is primarily for specific information, but a few questions from GS and GK must be answered very carefully.

After a conversation with successful candidates, it has been found that they were very nervous when they went before the interview board. Always try to avoid getting nervous. But the initial nervousness was evaporated once the candidate started answering with his background of sound and knowledge and firmed up views.

Sometimes, the candidates even start shivering which represents their weak personality at the interview. In bewilderment, they do not speak what they want to say and instead speak what they don't want to. Sometimes, this is noticed by the board and the head of the board may say, "You may leave now." That's why, avoid to be in a hassle as much as you can.

Haste or over excitement is very dangerous in an interview. Candidates often make mistakes because of their nervousness. For example, before listening to the complete question, they start answering. It is a sign of being uncivilised. The candidate should listen carefully to the person who asks the question and answer it properly. Answers should be well revised and thought of before replying.

Don't try to lie in the interview. It has been observed that when a candidate is asked a question for which he doesn't know the answer properly, he tries to cover it up by lying. This is absolutely wrong and unacceptable to the board. Don't ever try to fool them because they are older and superior to you, and as regards knowledge and intelligence, they are better than you.

If you don't know the answer, tell the board politely and seek their forgiveness. Sometimes it may happen that the board will tell you the appropriate answer. Listen to them carefully and even if you have any doubts, do not raise any counter-question. The board is there to interview you, not to teach you.

After all this, questions and answers session takes place. Usually they start with your resumé. While going for an interview, when the candidate is asked about his resumé, he must be mindful of it, such as, a person's birthday is on October 2nd, so in the Indian history, how does this day matter? When the candidate is trying to give the answer to this question, it becomes a way to asking new questions. In this way, the board tests your personality.

Likewise, a person born in Rajgir in Nalanda district, Bihar can be asked questions that could relate to Nalanda University, Buddhism and Jainism.

The answers to these questions should never be wrong. The wrong answer to any question can trap you into many other questions because the people who are sitting in front of you are far more experienced.

Candidates are asked a few questions from the elective subject. Such questions are the same as are useful in a man's life. As in-depth knowledge of the subject has been tested earlier in the main exam, here the questions on the topic are critical in terms of your job, society and nation. Therefore, revision of the subject is a must, and, moreover, you have to see its relevance to society, the nation and public life vis-a-vis your job as well.

Now, GK and GS questioning session takes place. The recent events in the region in question can be asked – how the events took place, their impact on the society and on the nation? What are your personal views on such events? What are its repercussions? How these repercussion can be handled? Extra questions are asked to evaluate your views.

The answers to such questions should be given carefully and very clearly, so that the board members are satisfied.

An important and final question in the interview is regarding your designation and the problems related to it. Suppose, you are an officer of a district, and any leader, MP, MLA or minister comes to you with a problem, and for some in reason, he abuses you, hits you, what will you do in such a situation? Would you act in the same way or resolve the issue differently? The answers to such questions should be carefully deliberated on.

Similarly, suppose you are the DM of a district. Floods, earthquakes, epidemics, drought, and famines may occur there. Then how would you deal with such situations? Answer these questions thoughtfully and patiently because such questions help the board members test your intelligence, patience, presence of mind and your diligence while dealing with a particular problem.

The purpose of the board through these questions is to measure your capability and not to tease or hassle you. So, answer them with due care and patience. Overlook the comment on your answers by the board members. These are just to test your patience or perseverance during the interview.

In front of the interview board, you should be answering diligently. It is not important that the questions or answers given here are complete or the best. The candidates should prepare them in their own way and the answers can be changed. Here, our sample questionnaire is just meant to provide you with an introduction of interview process.

Interview Process

When the name of the candidate is announced, he slowly opens the door of the room and seeks permission to enter:

Ma'am/Sir, may I come in? (As per person in chair)

After getting permission, the candidate enters the room. It may be possible that the permission may be slightly delayed. Don't make a fuss in such a situation. It is advisable to wait a little. Sometimes, the interview board does this to judge the candidate. The purpose behind this is to check the patience level and the etiquette of the candidate.

From entry to exit, the candidate is under close scrutiny by the board members. So, it is better to evaluate each moment and every step with great care. Exiting the room is also one of the parts of the interview. So, maintain your behaviour while exiting the interview room. Just as you need permission before entering the room, similarly you must humbly say "thank you", Sir/Madam before leaving and place the chair at its proper place, without making any noise.

Be careful while opening and shutting the door of the room. There should be no noise at all. Try to maintain a reasonable distance after the interview from the interview room if you want to talk with someone.

Sample Interview–1

Amit Prakash has been called for an interview. He is sitting outside with other candidates. The peon calls out to him and he walks towards the room. He waits near the door, takes permission, and then enters the room.

Amit Prakash bows down and greets the members and stands in front of the table.

Interviewer: Please be seated.

Amit Prakash: Thank you, Sir. (Thanks and sits on the chair).

After lastly wards, the interview is being conducted as we described earlier.

Lastly:

Interviewer: Thank you, Mr. Amit Prakash. You may go now.

Amit Prakash: Thank you, Sir.

Amit Prakash stands up, greets all the interviewers and leaves the room.

Sample Interview–2

Question: Tell us about yourself.

Ans: Sir, my name is Rajesh. My father Shri Suresh Kumar Verma works in the electricity board. I have done my B.Sc. from University of Delhi. I hope and believe that with my hard work and dedication, I am the perfect and the suitable candidate for this designation.

Question: What is the goal of your life?

Ans: Sir, every human being dreams of a respectable designation and to have all the luxuries of the world. I am no different from them, but I would like to achieve this through my hard work, devotion, loyalty and output.

Question: What is the meaning of success in your life?

Ans: Success depends on an individual's hard work, dedication and efforts. I believe that if you achieve your goal, you are successful. Everyone has different goals with different meaning of success.

Question: What type of people do you dislike?

Ans: Sir, those who go back on their own words or avoid their duties. Shall try to amend such individuals. If they are not amenable to suggestions, I shall maintain distance from such individuals.

Question: Nowadays, English dominates. Our youth is accepting English language and emulating the English culture. What is your opinion?

Ans: Sir, today our country is blindly following English language and foreign culture, and, in the process, is forgetting our own culture. Today's youth feels that the foreign language and literature is the best. Foreign lifestyle is impacting our country more than ever before, and we are drifting away from our own. This should in my opinion, is wrong.

Question: Is learning and understanding from other language be considered wrong?

Ans: Sir, learning from others can't be wrong. We should learn from others but should always take care that the knowledge is based on our own background. The roots of our culture are strong and it has many features as well. It is a great civilisation and is more ancient than others. Other ancient civilisation and culture have either been destroyed or forgotten with time, but our civilisation and culture are still alive. So, our lifestyle should be based on those superior elements.

Question: Our country is the land of saints and sages. Can the welfare of the society be achieved through the path of devotion? What do you think?

Ans: Our country is a country of saints and sages, who have always given guidance to the whole world. But it is also true that devotion alone can't rid us from the problem of the real world. But yes, this can help in solving problems. Tulsidas, Kabirdas, Surdas and other saints adopted the path of devotion, and lit the lamps of duty, knowledge and spirituality, which are even today the leading beacons of light

Question: What is your opinion concerning 'reservations'?

Ans: The issue of 'reservation' is very difficult. It is necessary because some sections of our society are backward. They may have talent but they don't get enough opportunities. Through reservation, such situations can be improved but it should be within some limits as decided in the Constitution. So, reservation should also be in accordance with the Constitution instead of individual selfishness of the politicians based on vote bank.

Question: Do you agree that for equal work, lower wages should be offered to women as compared to men?

Ans: Sir, I don't agree with lower pay for women for equal work. It is mentioned in our Constitution that everyone should get equal pay for equal work.

Question: What is a Bridge Loan?

Ans: Companies often expand their capital through launching new shares and debentures. Companies take more than 3 months to raise capital after issuing shares. In this time period, companies borrow money from the banks for the interim period and continue their work. Thus, such loans are called "bridge loans".

Question: What does the term 'Poverty' mean?

Ans: Poverty generally is a state below the minimum living standards. According to the Planning Commission, for rural areas, the per head consumption should be 2,400 calories, and for urban areas, it is 2,100 calories. When the consumption falls below this level, it is called 'poverty'.

Question: What are Gross Domestic Product (GDP) and Gross National Product?

Ans: GDP is the monetary value of all finished goods and services produced within a country's borders in a specific time period. Though GDP is calculated on an annual basis, it can be calculated on a quarterly basis as well.

GNP is the total value of all final goods and services produced within a nation in a particular year, (i.e. GDP) plus income earned by its citizens (including the income of those located abroad), minus the income of non-residents located in the country.

Question: What do you understand by the term 'National Income'?

Ans: It refers to the total net value of all goods and services produced within a nation over a specified period of time, representing the sum of wages, profits, rents, interest and pension payments to the residents of the nation.

The formula for calculating Net National Income is: Consumption + Investment + Government spending + Net Exports (calculated by subtracting imports from exports) + Net Foreign Factor Income – Indirect Taxes – Depreciation.

Question: It is said that the Indian economy is a mixed economy. What do you think?

Ans: A mixed economy is the coexistence of public and private sectors. In the development period, post-Independence, this policy was adopted to accomplish the target of socialism. Throughout, the government has invested around 45% of capital of the public sector, giving pace with economic planning, but still the avenues of production and resources are the monopoly of the private sector (about 80%). Despite liberalisation, the Indian economy is poised towards a capitalist economy.

Question: Briefly describe what "Renaissance" means.

Ans: "Renaissance" means "Rebirth" or "Reawakening". It was the period in Europe from the 14th to the 17th Century, when there was surge of interest in and production of great works of art and literature. It is known as the 'Golden Era' in the field of art, literature, painting, etc.

Expectations from the Candidates

Earlier, we have discussed those points that should be considered by the candidate in the process of an interview. Now, consider the second aspect – what does the interviewer consider about the candidate?

Selection of a candidate depends on what the interviewer wants in the candidate. From entering the interview room to exiting it, the interviewer observes the candidate very carefully.

The interviewer tests the candidate's character, intelligence, patience, alertness, temperament, ability of thinking, intensive study of the individual family situation, etc. The interviewer reads the eagerness of the candidate to learn new facts.

The interviewer takes special care of the identical academic career of the candidate (in which he/she is capable to pursue it as a career). During the conversation, the interviewer tries to find out what element the candidate is hiding. Interviewers like true and honest candidates.

They focus on the fact how capable the candidate is in expressing and how he is behaving. Interviewers prefer the candidates who are obedient, responsible, mellow and soft-spoken but confident. Besides these, the candidates should be healthy too.

Candidate, whose ambition is to get high rank and devote himself to the country, would be given preference by the selectors. They don't like over-smartness at all. They investigate how much the candidate is active and alert and how visionary he/she is. Which question marks the candidate apprehensive and which one keeps his mind stable, are deeply inspected during the interview.

Interviewers don't like timid candidates. They notice how the candidate adjusts himself to different circumstances. They prefer candidates who are serious towards work. They prefer candidates with good habits. The interviewers don't like candidates who are blunt and talkative.

The interviewers notice if the candidate has the ability to understand the words or not. They also check his presence of mind.

Interviewers also take care of the comfort of the candidates during the interview. Interviewers inspect the candidates' qualification and capacity. Candidates should also be well aware of various languages. Interviewers observe the following features in the candidates while selection – (1) Intelligence, Understanding; (2) Confidence;

(3) Expression of ideas; (4) Behaviour; (5) His ability to understand the terms; (6) Academic life; (7) Clothing; (8) Health.

Tips for a Successful Interview

Hard work is the key to success. When you work diligently and sincerely, you will surely get good results. After studying, everyone wants to do work but few people would be chosen for the job. There are some keys which help you achieve success in any field. If you want to be successful in an interview, then follow a few simple things:

Keep a Track of Time

Punctuality is very important in life. Make it a habit of reaching before time. This will help you to become successful. If you get some time before the interview, use it to converse with other candidates regarding the background of interview panel and prepare yourself accordingly.

Focus on Appearance

Focus on your dress for the interview. Clothes should be clean and well ironed, which fit the occasion. Young women should not wear messy hair or leave long hair untied. They should be neatly tied up so as to avoid tucking them behind their ears.

Go with Good Preparation

Before going for the interview, know well about the related designation or services. Do take an extra copy of all the documents and certificates with you. The same certificate should be given as is being asked for. Don't panic here. Before the interview, do not think of extra things; think only about the possible questions, so that when the interviewer asks the question, you can respond without any hesitation.

Listen carefully to the interviewer. At the time of the interview, always remain focussed. Listen carefully to the question. You don't need to ask it again. By doing so, the impact on them gets affected. Sometimes people start answering before the question is finished because of overenthusiasm. This leaves a negative impact on the interview board. Therefore, answer them confidently and with ease. Don't get nervous. If you are well prepared, you will surely get fine results.

Don't tell 'Lies'

Don't try to avoid the question or tell the panel clearly if you don't know the exact answer, instead of trying to make them believe that you know a lot about the question. In such situations, there is a little hope of selection.

Your Expression

Be calm during the interview. Don't move your hands nor wipe the sweat repeatedly. Having a smile on the face would be effective.

Don't be Loud

During the interview, don't respond so loudly or so softly that the interviewers cannot hear you properly. Answer the questions in a gentle tone with due spontaneity. As far as possible, speak in limited words. Give a chance to the interviewer to speak, don't interrupt. Be to yourself.

All Should Be Addressed

When four or more persons are present in the interview panel, then many questions will be asked. It would be nice, if you answer politely and address them all but looking at the member who has put the question.

Don't Argue

Don't argue during the interview. Doing so doesn't show your confidence and knowledge. You can make the interviewer believe in you through confidence and humility. So, avoid debates or arguments. Accept the point of view of the interviewer if it is convincing and thank him for the same.

General Tips to Follow During IAS Exam Preparation

SOME HELPFUL GUIDELINES

The body and the mind both work towards ensuring that you succeed in the examinations. Exercising the mind is as important as is exercising your body. A few tips are given here that would help you in exercising your mind and brain so that it is sharp and alert.

Prepare yourself to exercise your brain. Exercising the brain is much different from that of the body. Games like chess were developed in our country. These games help in developing and sharpening the brain to a great extent. However, one does not always have access to chess nor does everyone play the game. But there are other games that one can play in order to exercise the mind. To begin with, one may solve the crossword puzzles or may play the computer game, Solitaire. If these also do not interest you, you may just carry out the arithmetical calculations, i.e. the simple addition, subtraction, multiplication and division.

There is also another easier way to exercise the brain. Try to recollect and memorise poetry or a joke at least once a week. This would definitely shape up your brain and strengthen it as well. Try to experiment with something new to sharpen your brain. You should also sometimes think like a child. Children are so full of energy, positive attitude and curiosity. When one adapts to these, one gets to know a lot more things without any hesitation or fear.

Many successful people also insist on day-dreaming. This helps you in your thinking capabilities. Do not limit yourself to being a single person. Think from various other angles as well. This gives you the opportunity to think about all the pros and cons of a single situation and many other alternatives as well.

Let Go the Fear of the Examination

It is a common feeling of anxiety or nervousness for the examinations amongst the students. Thoughts like 'Had I read a little more'; 'Would I be able to answer?' and many such things occupy the mind. Such pressures in small amounts would rather prove beneficial for the candidate due to the adrenalin flow in the body, making the candidate a little more cautious and alert in his approach.

Slight anxiety is quite natural for the aspirants, but the moment it goes a little to the higher side, it could create problems for a person. It could create a sphere of isolation where the person loses his calm and is not able to differentiate between the good and the bad. He might also lose his concentration. This also impacts the student's performances as he is now not able to concentrate on the questions, leave alone the correct and reasonable answers. However, there are many ways to overcome the fear of the examinations which when exercised would help the candidates concentrate better on their goals.

Before the Examinations

Do try to finish off the syllabus beforehand. The revisions should also be done at least a day before. Studying till the last moment may cause anxiety. Ways to keep calm and free the mind should be adopted. People have their own ways to do so. Some people resort to exercising, some hum a few tunes, and others take a lukewarm shower. Such ways to keep calm are quite helpful when practised on the day of the examination or a day before. These methods help in retaining all that you have studied and enhance your confidence.

Lack of directions to the examination hall may also cause anxiety. So, get to know about the route and direction to the examination hall in advance preferably one day before so as not to create last-moment confusions. Fix up transport which is reliable and under your control. It is always advisable to read and understand the instructions beforehand. Clarify the same with friends in case of doubts. Have a proper sound sleep before the examination.

During the Examination

'I do not know anything'. One may have such thoughts in case of less or no preparation by the candidate. However, one may also have such thoughts even when he is completely prepared for the examinations. People often are quite anxious, that makes them lose concentration. The following methods, when adopted, may yield better results for the candidate:

- Reach the examination hall well ahead of the scheduled time.
- Take deep breaths once you reach the centre. Sit straight while you do so.
- Try to concentrate or focus on any immovable object or the wall in front of you.
- Think positive and repeat the same in your mind. 'I have come here to clear the examination' and such thoughts should prevail. My duty is to attempt paper. Result is in the hand of God.

  "कर्मन्येवाधिकारस्ते मा फलेषु कदाचन"
- Read the questions carefully. In case you get nervous again, in course of the examination, repeat the processes mentioned above again. Answer even part of question correctly.
- Lay down your strategies for answering the paper carefully. Decide on the questions that should be answered first.

- Leave those questions whose answers you are unable to recollect at first go. Attempt them at the end. By that time, your memory will be activated due to positive handling of other questions.

Ways to Improve Memory Power

The best way to retain anything is to aide it with proper meaning and object. Giving it proper examples and names would also help in retaining the facts for a longer period of time. It is also scientifically proven that understanding the facts helps in retaining it in the memory for a long time rather than just mugging it up.

Cramming things without knowing about them does not help. Instead, learn the literal and the actual meaning of the facts, and then proceed towards understanding the value of the facts and their importance in the human lives. Learn the impact it creates. This way you will be able to retain things for long.

Points to Remember

- Your answers should be in such a way that it creates an impression of you having understood the problems faced by the general public. Remember, you would be working for the general public itself. So, you cannot ignore their problems.
- Do not take any decision under any pressure or influence. Listen to all the advice given, but do what is best for the people. Act upon your own judgements.
- It is well known that the UPSC is a tough examination. So, rise above any diversions and work in a smart way to achieve your goal.
- Carry out your revisions as many times as possible. The Preliminary examinations test your understanding of the subject as well as your ability to retain the facts and figures. Hence, a regular reading habit of general knowledge books, magazines, competitive books of the previous year, especially the year book of economics of 'Pratiyogita Darpan' and such other publications are very important.
- Carry out self-memory tests while revising the chapters. Try to recall the facts in the chapters and try to complete them at a glance at a fast pace. In case you are not able to recall all the facts, then an in-depth study of the particular fact is necessary.
- Pay proper attention to General Awareness and those parts in CSAT, where you feel difficulty in answering the questions.
- History, Public Administration, Indian Economics, Indian Polity are subjects that fetch good scores. Your proper hold on these subjects is very important. You need to have an in-depth knowledge in these subjects.
- Do keep your mind calm the evening before the examination. Have a sound sleep and get up early with positive energy and the determination to reach the stars.

- Keep all the requisites for the examination ready a day before. Keep the admit card with you. Other things like ball pen and your watch and any such other necessary things should also be kept ready. Reach the examination hall one and half hour in advance at least on the first day.
- Do not get involved in any gossip or unnecessary discussions with your friends at the examination centre. There could be possibilities of such talks turning out to be disappointing for you.
- In case you are able to go through any magazine at the centre, then go to a corner and read it again with a calm mind. If you still have time, go through your own short notes again. These will help you in avoiding any negative feeling coming to you and distract you from getting involved in unnecessary discussions. However, if you feel uneasy and nervous, then sit calm and take deep breaths. This will help you relax. In any case, don't read anything at last half an hour before the start of examination. That will add more confusion.
- Carry a bottle of water along with you to the examination centre. If needed, add glucose to it as well. Many times, people feel nervous inside the hall and the mouth dries up. Though this can be tackled with a cool mind, a bottle of water surely helps. The candidate might also not be able to go out for drinking water owing to insufficient time for answering the questions. So, try to carry your own personal bottle.
- Beware of negative marking. Do not attempt to answer the question you are totally unaware of. If you are in doubt about a question as to which of the two alternatives is correct, you can go for intelligent guessing.
- There is no negative marking in the Logical Reasoning section of CSAT. Hence, go for all the questions in this section.
- The candidate may have problems in understanding the questions in Hindi as these are the verbatim translation of the English questions. In doubt, the candidate should refer to the question in English to understand its core meaning rather than waiting to get it clarified from the inspector.
- Read the instructions carefully in Paper-I, General Studies in the Preliminary examinations. The general structure of the questions is that there is a fact and three to four points associated with the fact. You need to specify which of these hold true. So, you need to study all the points carefully.
- Paper II comprises of questions based on passages. Read the passages carefully and answer the questions. Your answers should strictly be from the passages itself. Taking the large number of questions into consideration, it is advisable to answer these properly as these could score much for you.
- The questions on reasoning and based on pictorial diagrams need to be given proper time for better understanding and analysis.

- One must also pay attention to questions on arithmetical ability and mental ability questions. Don't be over awed. These are simple arithmetical problems which you had solved during your schooling.
- One should give importance to the eight questions based on English intended to test the candidate's understanding of the subject and the grammar.
- In questions where you need to present your decision, proper care should be taken that the decisions are at par with those provided under the Preamble and are justifiable to the people and the country. It should also be so as to be promoting development in the country.
- Do not even attempt any unfair means during examination. Do not try to help or take help from the co-examinee.
- UPSC is keen to test your integrity as corruption has become our all pervading problem. Therefore, one has to be careful while answering questions during written examination as well as during interview as questions on intellectual and moral integrity will be crafted in a very intelligent way even through some case studies or incidents.

TIME MANAGEMENT FOR IAS EXAM

It is said that until we plan our time, we cannot manage anything else. This is even relevant when we talk about something. Thinking over it again and again and studying rigorously and continuously for definite time will be a habit and it will shape your perspective and character. A civil servant, who is always under work pressure, has to understand the importance of time. Hence, the selection process deliberately makes the candidates to give best of their time management skills.

Time management helps the candidates in two ways, firstly, during the preparation and secondly, during the exam. Time keeps moving, it does not stop for anyone. Just as we cannot hold the sand in our fist, we cannot stop time from passing. That's why we require time management.

Time management refers to reaching the clearly defined goals within the stipulated time. Both of these are interrelated. If there is no goal, there is no time management and if there is no time management, it's difficult to achieve success.

Set a routine for yourself. But it doesn't mean that you prepare a time table and display it on the wall or table and forget to follow it. In that case, you will be far from reaching your goal. It is important to be focussed and to implement a routine. This is a key factor of time management.

Time Table

- Include all daily routine work in time table.
- Assign proper time for each work.
- Wake up early in the morning positively.
- Make sure you sleep for at least 6 hours.

- Instead of studying all subjects on a single day, allot days for each subject.
- Remember, whatever you study, you must understand it well.
- The main intention of a time table is to make your study systematic and regular. Therefore, keep this in mind while preparing the time table.
- It is necessary to keep your mind fresh. You need entertainment for that. Schedule a time for entertainment. Due to some reason, if your routine is disturbed, don't get upset. Once it is normal, start following your time table and fill in the lost time.
- Prepare a schedule for the next day in advance. This will save your time.
- Decide about your priorities, what to do first and what to do later. This should be decided after giving it a serious thought.
- Time for television, internet, social websites should be decided strictly. We don't realise the time wasted in these activities. Avoid checking online updates and status frequently. This will not only waste your time but also lose your concentration. It will have an ill effect on your efficiency. Less you devote to these diversions, better it is.
- Pay keen attention to your physical health. It is important to exercise for half-an-hour daily, such as outdoor games, exercise, yogasanas, pranayam, visit of nature or walking. Set a time for this so that your wealth does not falter or fail you during crucial days of examinations.
- Some candidates divide time in three ways; for newspaper or magazine reading, for subject study (4-5 hours) and revision (at least for one hour). However, candidates, may fix their own time schedule based on their readyness and gaps to be filled in.

Things to Remember

- The one who wastes time, time spoils his life. Hence, make use of time properly.
- People say we never get anything before the right time. Try to live in the present and go with flow.
- Utilise time correctly and use the opportunity properly to gain victory.
- Your mind can have only one thought at a time, which could be positive or negative. But you have to convert your negative thoughts into positive, and you can do everything.
- Use time management tools, such as mobile phones, calendar or chart, etc. You should stop being idle.
- Don't waste your time in waiting for opportunities, have faith in yourself and do your work.
- If you keep your set of clothes ready for the next day in the night itself, then you will save time in the morning.
- Prepare a list of things you need while you go shopping. Most of our time is wasted in such activities. Make a list and bring all necessary things at one go.

- Students should know their priorities – how much time they need for studies and how much they can spend on other activities. Divide the syllabus into three parts: the best preparation, satisfactory preparation and less preparation part.
- Include solving the unsolved papers in your routine. Read and understand the topics well before making the notes. Try to divide the topic in small parts and assign a heading to all parts. Notes should always be short and full of facts.
- English-medium candidates face difficulty in Hindi and Sanskrit whereas Hindi-medium candidates find English difficult. Therefore, make it a habit to refer to English and Hindi dictionaries.
- Your clean and neat writing will impress the examiner. So, try to improve your handwriting. Write words in different style to bring in improvement in writing. Keep a pencil and paper with you while reading so as to note down important points to remember.
- Set a time limit for the preparation of each topic. It's not necessary to remember the whole chapter. Select the frequently asked questions from it and prepare them thoroughly.
- Read aloud and write the portions which require more preparation. While studying, you should take a break of 3-4 minutes after every 30-60 minutes, so that you don't feel tired.
- Trying to improve handwriting in higher classes will consume a lot of time and you have to write very fast in these classes. Hence, it is advised that you practise good handwriting from the beginning itself.
- The best memory tonic is to study after a sound sleep. Less sleep causes lowered efficiency.
- Decide which subject requires less preparation or more preparation. Stay away from meeting friends and making phone calls. Tell them about your fixed breaks and ask them to contact only at that time.
- If you don't understand something, don't hesitate to ask-be it a coaching class or school your senior, father or friend, to solve your problems. You can also refer to Google sometime when there is no other source and time left is minimum.
- Solve each other's problems in a group. Learn to study in a group. Many a time, students go into depression due to lack of self-confidence. This affects their studies. Therefore, it is important to have self-confidence.
- Many students get exam phobia due to stress. Try out some relaxation techniques to overcome stress. Affinity and guidance can cure exam phobia.
- Many students consume medicines for improving memory. However, these could be dangerous. Some medicines contain alcohol. Though it relaxes one's mind, dependence on this can result in problems of kidney and lungs. Be sure that your memory will be activated when it is best needed.

- Don't organise celebrations and entertainment programmes during exam time. These will distract students. During exams, reduce the use of television and radio.
- Completing the course in a small amount of time is difficult and because of this, you cannot understand many things. It is important to overcome these problems before exams. Start preparation 3-4 months in advance.
- Check that there is no public road or loud noise close to the study room and that people don't pass by this room too often. It's tough to stop other activities when the exam is approaching. But you can reduce those and use the time saved for studies. You can switch on to radio songs to avoid outside noise.
- Sit in a chair while studying. The room should have ample ventilation and light. The other family members should visit the room at times and appreciate your studies. Visit of children will be incentive for your studies to refresh your mind and heart.
- Keep your goal high. If you aim for 100%, only then you will score 80-90%. Usually students make a mistake of leaving some chapters as they are difficult. Be positive and overcome your weaknesses.
- Find your weak areas and solve those. Take help of tutor or coaching classes or your ex-teacher to solve difficult problems of science or mathematics.
- For essay paper, you should continuously keep in touch with the latest happenings so that you can give a constructive suggestion at the end. But in essay paper, one should focus on the topic accurately. If you digress, you may score very poor marks like an administrator, who has no freedom to go beyond the main point within limited time and resources. Ideas in essay should be arranged like pearls in necklace and expression should be exact and effective.
- Students should stay away from family tensions and responsibilities while exams are going on. Be in constant touch with your friends, so that you can ask them about doubts as and when necessary. After reading a topic, write it in your words. The best way to remember anything is to revise it.
- Reach the exam centre at least-an-hour before so that there is no problem in searching your roll number. Be calm on your seat 10-15 minutes before the exam.
- A timetable is necessary for planned preparation. More than that, it's important to follow it religiously.
- In order to be fit, it is necessary to exercise. Dedicate some time for exercise after studying early in the morning. After studying for two to three hours, take some time out to freshen up. During this time, you can relax, watch TV or go for a walk.
- You should develop a habit of studying early in the morning not only during exam but also on other days. Since the mind is fresh and vacant in the morning hours, you can remember well. You should dedicate these hours to some selective subjects.

- ♦ If you devote all your time to studies after school/college, then take a nap after your lunch. Then study for some hours. In the evening, you can spend time with your friends and entertain yourself through discussions on current topics.
- ♦ Many students have a habit of studying late in the night. However, experts opine that memory cells are not active during night as much as they are in the day. The 8-hour study of night is equal to 3-hour study of the day.
- ♦ Some students keep notes in their laptops etc. But the traditional method is still better as it trains your handwriting which is the medium for IAS etc. exams.

INSPIRING THOUGHTS

1. Winners don't do different things, they do things differently.

   —Shiv Khera
2. If you fool me once, shame on you. If you fool me twice, shame on me.
3. Freedom without discipline leads to destruction.
4. Study as if you will live forever. Live as if you will die tomorrow.

   —Mahatma Gandhi
5. It is much better to deserve an honour and not get it, rather than not deserve it and yet get it.

   —Mark Twain
6. A smooth sea never made a skilful mariner.
7. Some books should be tasted, some devoured, but only a few should be chewed and digested thoroughly. **—Sir Francis Bacon**
8. The critic is one who knows the price of everything and the value of nothing.

   —Oscar Wilde
9. Trifles make perfection and perfection is no trifle.

   —Miche Langelo
10. No risk, no gain.

    —Ray Kroc (McDonald's Founder)
11. The easier way may actually be the tougher way.
12. Even a stopped watch gives the right time twice in a day.
13. Ways to create a good viewpoint: (i) Change focus, look for positivity, (ii) Make a habit of doing it now, (iii) Develop a conviction of gratitude, (iv) Get into a continuous educational programme.
14. Never leave for tomorrow what you can do today.

    —Benjamin Franklin
15. When you are good to others, you are good to yourself.

    — Benjamin Franklin

16. Stay away from bad company.
17. Learn to admire things that are necessary.
18. Bigger the hurdle, bigger the opportunity.
19. Trifles can make a big difference and to be big is no small matter.
20. Every opportunity comes but once in life.
21. Hurdles are such dreadful things which you notice only when you deviate from your aim.
22. The world does not appear the way it is, but the way we are.
23. We must keep an open mind, not an empty mind.
24. Always remember the 8 'Ps': Purpose, principle, planning, preparation, practice, perseverance, patience and pride.
25. Not taking any risk is in itself the biggest risk.

—Erica Jong

HOW TO WIN FRIENDS AND PEOPLE?

1. Don't criticize, condemn or complain.
2. Give honest and sincere appreciation.
3. Become genuinely interested in other people.
4. Remember that a person's name is to that person the sweetest and most important sound in any language.
5. Be a good listener. Encourage others to talk about them.
6. Talk in terms of the other person's interests.
7. Make the other person feel important and do it sincerely.
8. The only way to get the best of an argument is to avoid it.
9. Show respect for the other person's opinion. Never say, "You are wrong."
10. If you are wrong, admit it quickly and emphatically.
11. Begin in a friendly way.
12. Get the other person saying 'Yes, Yes' immediately.
13. Let the other person do a great deal of the talking.
14. Try honestly to see things from the other person's point of view.
15. Be sympathetic to the other person's ideas and desires.
16. Talk about your own mistakes before criticizing the other person.
17. Ask questions instead of giving direct orders.
18. Let the other person save face.
19. Praise the slightest improvement and praise every improvement. Be hearty in your approbation and lavish in your praise.
20. Give the other person a fine reputation to live up to.
21. Use encouragement. Make the fault seem easy to correct.
22. Make the other person happy about doing the thing you suggest.
23. Let the other person feel that the idea is his or hers.
24. A true friend never gets in your way unless you happen to be going down.
25. Friendship is a single soul dwelling in two bodies.

❑❑❑

10 Other Career Options

I have observed that the aspirants, who come from the middle class, lower middle class or from economically weak background, remain very tense and confused. They have many apprehensions about their success, i.e., if they are not selected in the Civil Services, what will happen to them, what they will do then, how they will face their families,how they will lead their lives etc. Some of them take so much tension that they become the victims of anxiety and possessiveness.They feel that if they do not become an I.A.S, their lives will be useless, and after that there will be no other aim to pursue in their lives.

These aspirants think so, because they have not planned for any other suitable career option, apart from the Civil Services. I agree with the fact that it is necessary for an aspirant to possess the dedication, perseverance, devotion and concentration; but one should possess a another career option also to avoid this type of tension, depression, speculation and confusion. If you possess another career option, or you know that you have the eligibility and employability to earn a respectable living and lead a good life even in the adverse conditions, when you are actually not selected in the Civil Services; then definitely you will feel calm and relaxed.

I want to make it clear in this regard that, having another career option is not compulsory for doing the preparations of the Civil Services examination, and there are numerous examples of the aspirants who have done the preparations of this examination considering it as their only career option, and they have been successful too; but it is a wise decision to have another career option and employability, keeping in mind the uncertainty and cut-throat competition for getting selected in the Civil Services. Therefore, it is better to remain free from such a useless tension and pressure, and do the preparations in a natural manner. If you prepare for Civil Services exams, you will definitely lend up in any other second category of which will be good enough if you compose its status in the society vis-a-vis common people in India. Therefore don't get disheartened if you can not make to the IAS etc. final list. You are a young educated person. Country and your family need you equally in other jobs or capacity.

You must have heard the saying,"Try for the best, prepare for the worst".

Therefore, to keep a career option in mind is a better way to handle such a situation. Let us discuss some of the career options to lead a good life, in case you do not get selected in the Civil Services. This strategy is also known as a 'backup plan'. Remember the famous proverb,"Don't put all eggs in one basket". So you should not limit your efforts to just one career option, you should look for another career option instead, which suits your interests, expectations and abilities. Some of the suggested career options for such aspirants are given below:

(I) **Other competitive exams of UPSC:** According to their eligibility and aptitude, the aspirants of Civil Services can appear in the following examinations also, which are conducted every year by the Union Public Service Commission:

- (i) Indian Forest Service
- (ii) Indian Engineering Service
- (iii) Indian Statistical Service
- (iv) Indian Economic Service
- (v) Central Medical Service
- (vi) Central Police Force, Assistant Commandant

All the above mentioned examinations are Group 'A' services of Government of India, which are extremely prestigious and challenging career options and have similar pay package as IAS etc. More number of people have risen to the top bracket in the country from non-IAS category.

(II) **Examinations of State Public Service Commission(s):** The public service commission of various states of India conduct the examinations for the various Gazetted/Non-Gazetted posts of Group 'A' and Group 'B' also, apart from conducting their own State Civil Service Examinations. Besides, the Public Service Commission of various states issue the advertisements for the other posts too from time to time. I am sure that you can prepare for your home state Civil Services Examination (P.C.S) along with the Civil Services preparations. I too had done the preparations for the Uttar Pradesh P.C.S., along with the preparations of the Civil Services. Generally, the syllabus of the State Civil Services examination contains one paper of the Official Language of that state. The State Civil Service successful candidates (PCS) now get into IAS much faster than before. And they are always in the forefront of the administration.

(III) **Other different competitive examinations:** In addition to the above mentioned Public Service Commission, the various board/commission of the Central and State Governments also conduct various examinations:

- (i) Parliament of India (Joint Recruitment Cell)
- (ii) CGL Examination of SSC
- (iii) Delhi Subordinate Services Selection Board
- (iv) Railway Recruitment Board
- (v) State Bank of India and Institute of Banking Personnel Selection. (IBPS)

These competitive examinations provide a respectable career option. Interestingly, these examinations too offer the subjects, like general knowledge, English, reasoning and mathematics, which are more or less similar to that of UPSC C-SAT.

(IV) **Other career options:** The other attractive career options for the aspirants, who are preparing their backup plan, are as following:

(i) UGC-NET-JRF (teaching and research work): It is a very respectable career. You can clear NET-JRF in Hindi Literature in the first attempt and get its fellowship, and do the M.Phil also from any University. There is fabulous payment of stipends during research work and in teaching thereafter.

(ii) Media and Mass Communication

(iii) Advertisement and Public Relation

(iv) Radio and T.V.

(v) Interpretation and Translation

(vi) You can be an entrepreneur and start your own business.In this way, you will give employment to others, and can play a role in the nation building.

(vii) Another emerging career option is Social Work. By joining a good NGO or doing part-time job in this sector, you will earn some money as well as you can contribute in the development of the society. In order to gain a social experience, many aspirants do the social-work during the period they get after giving the mains exam and before appearing in the interview.

(V) **Further studies through the distance learning mode:** Some of the aspirants while doing the Civil Services Examination preparations or after completing their preparations, continue their further studies through the distance education mode. It has three benefits: firstly, you will be able to improve your profile in the years, which are otherwise considered as gap years; secondly, you can get a help in your Optional Subject or G.S. and thirdly, after attaining the degree/diploma, the chances of your employability and the level of your confidence will increase.

The Indira Gandhi National Open University offers the best course options in the distance education mode.All the more,the study material of IGNOU courses is is excellent. I It can help you to a great extent in the preparations of your optional subject.

Besides IGNOU, you can do further studies through the distance learning mode from the State Open Universities also.

In addition to the above courses, you can do some recognized computer courses, like P.G. Diploma in Computer Applications (PGDCA) and DOEACC.

Keep your main and primary focus area. I have informed you about these alternate career/ study options, so that you can understand that, 'beyond the stars are even more worlds'.Your life should never halt or stop, even if you fail in a particular examination on a particular day. Moving ahead continuously following the mantra of 'Keep going-Keep going' is the essence of life. In this context, the following poem of Hindi poet Gopal Das 'Niraj' is very relevant for the youths:

“ O thee who stealthily shed tears!
Who waste these pearls of their eye!
If some dreams cease to be Life doesn't end, it doesn't die

What's a dream? Just a dew-drop,
On your eye, amidst a siesta deep,
And its dissipation is as if,
Youth is woken-up mid-sleep,
O thee who make their lives moist
Who bathe, but don't immerse, why!
If some water flows out and away Monsoon
doesn't end, it doesn't die.

So what if the beads scattered,
The problem is resolved per se,
If your tears are auctioned off,
Then your penance is complete.
O thee who spend their days glum!
who sew their torn shirts and cry,
If some lamps get extinguished,
the porch stays, it doesn't die.

Nothing gets lost here,
The book changes its cover,
Like the night peels moonlight,
In the morn to be sun-ray lover.
O thee who change clothes and come,
who go, but in new pomp and style,
If lost is the moon you thought a toy,
childhood doesn't end, it doesn't die.

Many, many pots n pails have broken,
Not a crease on the well's face of muscle.
Many, many boats have sunk,
The shore has the same hustle-bustle.
O thee who extend the darkness,
Who reduce the life of light,
Fall may try, and then try,
The orchard lives, it doesn't die.

The gardener pillaged the garden,
Flower's fragrance couldn't be stolen.
Even storms tried playing with it,
But window of dust would remain open.
O thee who embrace hatred, who throw dirt on every guy,
Even if some faces are upset the mirror stays, it doesn't die.

❑❑❑

UNIT-B: Recruitment Process of UPSC Civil Services/ IAS Exams

Important Information & Instructions

1. **Candidates to Ensure their Eligibility for the Examination:** The Candidates applying for the examination should ensure that they fulfill all eligibility conditions for admission to examination. Their admission to all the stages of the examination will be purely provisional subject to satisfying the prescribed eligibility conditions. Mere issue of e-Admit Card to the candidate will not imply that his/her candidature has been finally cleared by the Commission. The Commission takes up verification of eligibility conditions with reference to original documents only after the candidate has qualified for Interview/ Personality Test.
2. **How to Apply:** Candidates are required to apply Online by using the website [**https://upsconline.nic.in**]. Detailed instructions for filling up online applications are available on the above mentioned website. Brief Instructions for filling up the "Online Application Form" given in **Appendix-II**.
   2.1 Candidate should have details of one Photo ID Card viz. Aadhaar Card/ Voter Card/PAN Card/Passport/Driving Licence/Any other Photo ID Card issued by the State/Central Government. The details of this Photo ID Card will have to be provided by the candidate while filling up the online application form. The candidates will have to upload a scanned copy of the Photo ID whose details have been provided in the online application by him/her. This Photo ID Card will be used for all future referencing and the candidate is advised to carry this Photo ID Card while appearing for Examination/Personality Test.
3. **Last Date for Receipt of Applications:** The online Applications can be filled up to ..., 20... till 6:00 PM. The eligible candidates shall be issued an e-Admit Card three weeks before the commencement of the examination. The e-Admit Card will be made available in the UPSC website [https://upsconline.nic.in] for downloading by candidates. No Admit Card will be sent by post.
4. **Penalty for Wrong Answers:** Candidates should note that there will be penalty (negative marking) for wrong answers marked by a candidate in the Objective Type Question Papers.

5. **Facilitation Counter for Guidance of Candidates:** In case of any guidance/information/clarification regarding their applications, candidature, etc. candidates can contact UPSC's Facilitation Counter near gate 'C' of its campus in person or over Telephone No. 011-23385271 011-23381125/ 011-23098543 on working days between 10.00 hrs and 17.00 hrs.
6. **Mobile Phones Banned:**
   (a) The use of any mobile phone (even in switched off mode), pager or any electronic equipment or programmable device or storage media like pen drive, smart watches, etc. or camera or bluetooth devices or any other equipment or related accessories either in working or switched off mode capable of being used as a communication device during the examination is strictly prohibited. Any infringement of these instructions shall entail disciplinary action including ban from future examinations.
   (b) Candidates are advised in their own interest not to bring any of the banned items including mobile phones/pagers to the venue of the examination, as arrangement for safe-keeping cannot be assured.
7. Candidates are advised not to bring any valuable/costly items to the venue of the examination, as safe-keeping of the same cannot be assured. Commission will not be responsible for any loss in this regard.
   F. No. ...: Preliminary Examination of the Civil Services Examination for recruitment to the Services and Posts mentioned below will be held by the Union Public Service Commission on ...(Day) ... (Month), 202... in accordance with the Rules published by the Department of Personnel & Training in the Gazette of India Extraordinary dated ..., ..., 202...

❑❑❑

2 Services and Posts

(i) Indian Administrative Service.
(ii) Indian Foreign Service.
(iii) Indian Police Service.
(iv) Indian P & T Accounts & Finance Service, Group 'A'.
(v) Indian Audit and Accounts Service, Group 'A'.
(vi) Indian Revenue Service (Customs and Central Excise), Group 'A'.
(vii) Indian Defence Accounts Service, Group 'A'.
(viii) Indian Revenue Service (I.T.), Group 'A'.
(ix) Indian Ordnance Factories Service, Group 'A' (Assistant Works Manager, Administration).
(x) Indian Postal Service, Group 'A'.
(xi) Indian Civil Accounts Service, Group 'A'.
(xii) Indian Railway Traffic Service, Group 'A'.
(xiii) Indian Railway Accounts Service, Group 'A'.
(xiv) Indian Railway Personnel Service, Group 'A'.
(xv) Post of Assistant Security Commissioner in Railway Protection Force, Group 'A'
(xvi) Indian Defence Estates Service, Group 'A'.
(xvii) Indian Information Service (Junior Grade), Group 'A'.
(xviii) Indian Trade Service, Group 'A'.
(xix) Indian Corporate Law Service, Group 'A'.
(xx) Armed Forces Headquarters Civil Service, Group 'B' (Section Officer's Grade).
(xxi) Delhi, Andaman & Nicobar Islands, Lakshadweep, Daman & Diu and Dadra & Nagar Haveli Civil Service, Group 'B'.
(xxii) Delhi, Andaman & Nicobar Islands, Lakshadweep, Daman & Diu and Dadra & Nagar Haveli Police Service, Group 'B'.
(xxiii) Pondicherry Civil Service, Group 'B'.
(xxiv) Pondicherry Police Service, Group 'B'.

The number of vacancies to be filled on the result of the examination is expected to be approximately ... which include ... vacancies reserved for Persons with Benchmark Disability Category, i.e. ... vacancies for candidates of (a) blindness and low vision; ... Vacancies for (b) deaf and hard of hearing; ... Vacancies for (c) locomotor disability including cerebral palsy, leprosy cured, dwarfism, acid attack victims and muscular dystrophy; and ... Vacancies for (e) multiple disabilities from amongst persons under clauses (a) to (c) including deaf-blindness.

The final number of vacancies may undergo change after getting firm number of vacancies from Cadre Controlling Authorities. Reservation will be made for candidates belonging to Scheduled Castes. Scheduled Tribes, Other Backward Classes, the Economically Weaker Sections and Persons with Benchmark Disability in respect of vacancies as may be fixed by the Government.

As per the decision taken by the Government for increasing the access of unemployed to job opportunities, the Commission will publicly disclose the scores of the candidates (obtained in the Written Examination and Interview/Personality Test) through the public portals. The disclosure will be made in respect of only those willing candidates who will appear in the Interview/Personality Test for the Civil Service Examination and are not finally recommended for appointment. The information shared through this disclosure scheme about the non-recommended candidates may be used by other public and private recruitment agencies to appoint suitable candidates from the information made available in the public portal.

Candidates will be required to give their options at the time of Interview/ Personality Test, while downloading the e-Summon Letter from the Commission's website for the interview. A candidate may opt out of the scheme also and in that case his/her details will not be published by the Commission.

Besides sharing of the information of the non-recommended willing candidates of this examination, the Commission will not assume any responsibility or liability for the method and manner in which information related to such candidates is utilized by public/private organizations.

❑❑❑

3 Services Suitable for Persons with Benchmark Disability

A list of Services Identified suitable for Persons with Benchmark Disability along with the Physical Requirements and Functional Classifications:

Sl. No.	Name of the Service	Category(ies) for which Identified	Functional Classification	Physical Requirements
1.	Indian Administrative Service (IAS)	(i) Locomotor disability including Cerebral Palsy, Leprosy Cured, Dwarfism, Acid Attack Victims	OA, OL, BA, BH, MW, OAL, Cerebral Palsy, Leprosy Cured, Dwarfism, Acid Attack Victims	S, ST, W, SE, H, RW, C
			BLA, BLOA, BL	S, SE, H, RW, C
		(ii) Blindness and Low Vision	LV	MF, PP, S, ST, W, L,C, RW, H, KC, BN
			B	MF, PP, S, ST, W, L,C, RW, (in braille/software), H, KC, BN
		(iii) Deaf and Hard of Hearing	FD, HH	PP, S, ST, W, L, C, RW, KC, BN
		(iv) Multiple disability including only above three sub-categories	1. Low vision + HH	MF, PP S, ST, W, L, C, RW, H, KC, BN, SE

			2.	OA + Low vision	MF, PP, S, ST ,W, L, C, RW, H, KC, BN, SE
				OL + Low vision	
				Leprosy cured + Low vision-	
				Acid Attack Victims + Low Vision	
			3.	OL + Blindness	MF, PP, S, ST, W, L, C, RW (In Braille/ Software),
				Dwarfism + Blindness	
			4.	OA + HH	MF, PP, S, ST, W, L, C, RW, H, KC, BN, SE
				OL + HH	
				OL + Deaf	
				Leprosy Cured + HH	
				Acid attack victims + HH	
				Dwarfism + Deaf	
				Dwarfism + HH	
			5.	OA + Low vision + HH	MF, PP, S, ST, W, L, C, RW, H, KC, BN, SE
				OL + Low vision + HH	
				Leprosy cured + Low vision + HH	
				Acid attack victims + Low vision + HH	
				Dwarfism + Low vision + HH	

2.	Indian Foreign Service (IFS)	(i) Locomotor disability including Dwarfism and Acid Attack Victims	OA, OL, OAL	S, ST, W, RW, C, MF
		(ii) Visual Impairment	LV	SE, RW
		(iii) Hearing Impairment	PD	H
		(iv) Multiple disability including only above three sub-categories	All mentioned in above rows	All mentioned in above rows
3.	Indian Revenue Service (Customs and Central Excise Gr. A)	(i) Locomotor Disability	One Arm (OA), One Leg (OL),	S, ST, W, SE, RW, C
			One Arm One Leg (OAL)	
			Both Legs (BL)	S, SE, RW, C
			Cerebral Palsy	S, W, SE, RW, C
			Leprosy Cured	S, ST, W, SE, RW, C
			Dwarfism	S, ST, W, SE, RW, C
			Acid Attack Victims	S, ST, W, SE, RW, C
			Muscular Dystrophy	S, SE, RW, C
		(ii) Visual Imp airment	Low Vision	MF, PP, L, KC, BN, ST, W, H, RW, C
			Blindness	MF, PP, L, KC, BN, ST, W,
		(iii) Hearing Impairment	Hard of Hearing	MF, PP, L, KC, BN, ST, W, H, RW, C
			Deaf	MF, PP, L, KC, BN, ST, W, RW, C

4.	Indian P and T Accounts and Finance Service Gr. 'A'	(i) Locomotor Disability	OA, OL, OAL, Cerebral Palsy, Leprosy Cured, Dwarfism, Acid Attack Victims	S, W, SE, RW, C, BN, ST, H, L, KC, MF, PP
			BA, BH	S, W, SE, RW, C, BN, ST, H, KC
			BL, MW	S, SE, RW, C, BN, H, L, KC, MF, PP
		(ii) Visual Impairment	Blindness	S, W, C, BN, ST, H, L, KC, MF, PP, RW (in Braille/ software)
			Low Vision	S, W, RW, C, BN, ST, H, L, KC, MF, PP
		(iii) Hearing Impairment	Deaf and Hard of Hearing	S,W, SE, RW, C, BN, ST, L, KC, MF, PP
5.	Indian Audit and Accounts Service, Gr. 'A'	(i) Locomotor Disability including Leprosy Cured, Dwarfism, Acid Attack Victims	One leg affected (R or L), or one arm affected (R or L) Leprosy Cured (LC), Dwarfism (DW), Acid Attack	S, ST, W, BN, SE, RW, C
		(ii) Hard of Hearing	Hard of Hearing (HH)	As above
		(iii) Multiple Disabilities [2 or more disabilities among (i) and (ii) above]	All mentioned in above [(i) and (ii) above]	As above
6.	Indian Defence Accounts Service, Gr. 'A'	(i) Locomotor Disability including Leprosy Cured, Dwarfism and Acid Attack Victims	One Arm (OA), One Leg (OL),	S, ST, W, BN, SE, RW, C, MF, PP, L, KC, H
		(ii) Visual Impairment	Low Vision (LV)	As above
		(iii) Hearing Impairment	Hard of Hearing (HH)	As above

		(iv) Multiple Disabilities amongst the above three categories	(i) OA, LV (ii) OL, LV (iii) OA, HH (iv) OL, HH	As above
7.	Indian Revenue Service (IT), Gr. 'A'	(i) Locomotor Disability	One Arm (OA) One Leg (OL)	S, ST, W, SE, RW, C
			Both Legs (BL)	S, SE, RW, C
			Cerebral Palsy	S, W, SE, RW, C
			Leprosy Cured	S, ST, W, SE, RW, C
			Dwarfism	S, ST, W, SE, RW, C
			Acid Attack Victims	S, ST, W, SE, RW, C
			Muscular Dystrophy	S, SE, RW, C
		(ii) Visual Impairment	Low Vision	MF, PP, L, KC, BN, ST, W, H, RW, C
			Blindness	MF, PP, L, KC, BN, ST, W, H, C
		(iii) Hearing Impairment	Hard of Hearing	MF, PP, L, KC, BN, ST, W, H, RW, C
			Deaf	MF, PP, L, KC, BN, ST, W, RW, C
		(iv) Multiple Disabilities	Amongst persons under clauses (i) to (iii) above including deaf-blindness in the posts identified for each disabilities.	S, C, MF
8.	Indian Ordnance Factories Service	(i) Locomotor Disability including Cerebral Palsy, Leprosy Cured, Dwarfism Acid Attack Victims, Muscular Dystrophy.	OL, OA	S, M, RW, SE, H, C, MF

		(ii) Visual Impairment	LV (Low Vision)	S, M, RW, SE, H, C, MF
		(iii) Hearing Impairment	HH (Hard of Hearing)	S, M, RW, SE, H (Speaking), C, MF
		(iv) Multiple disabilities [Amongst (i) to (iii) above]	All mentioned in above rows	S, M, RW, SE, H, C, MF
9.	Indian Postal Service, Gr. 'A'	(i) Locomotor Disability including Cerebral Palsy, Leprosy Cured, Dwarfism, Acid Attack Victims and Muscular Dystrophy.	OA, OL Cerebral Palsy, Leprosy Cured, Dwarfism, Acid Attack Victims	S, ST, W, BN, RW, SE, H, C
		(ii) Blindness and Low Vision	LV	S, ST, W, BN, RW, SE, H, C
		(iii) Deaf and Hard of Hearing	HH	S, ST, W, BN, RW, SE, H, C
		(iv) Multiple Disabilities from amongst persons under clauses (i) to (iii) including deaf-blindness in the posts identified for each disabilities	LV, HH, OA, OL, Cerebral Palsy, Leprosy Cured, Dwarfism, Acid Attack Victims	S, ST, W, BN, RW, SE, H, C
10.	Indian Civil Accounts Service	(i) Locomotor Disability including Cerebral Palsy	One Arm (OA)	S, ST, W, SE, H, RW, C, MF, PP, L, KC, BN
			One Leg (OL)	S, SE, H, RW, C, MF, PP, L
			Both Arm (BA)	S, ST, W, SE, H, C, KC, BN
			Both Legs (BL)	S, SE, H, RW, C, MF, PP, L

			Both Hands (BH)	S, ST, W, SE, H, C, KC, BN
			Muscular Weakness (MW)	S, SE, H, RW, C, MF
			One Arm One Leg (OAL)	S, SE, H, RW, C, MF, PP, L
			Both Legs & Arms (BLA)	S, SE, H, RW, C
			Both Legs One Arm (BLOA)	S, SE, H, RW, C, MF, PP, L
			Leprosy Cured	S, ST, W, SE, H, RW, C, MF, PP, L, KC, BN
			Dwarfism	S, ST, W, SE, H, RW, C, MF, PP, L, KC, BN
			Acid Attack Victims	S, ST, W, SE, H, RW, C, MF, PP, L, KC, BN
		(ii) Blindness and Low Vision	Low Vision (LV)	S, ST, W, H, RW, C, MF, PP, L, KC, BN
		(iii) Deaf and Hard of Hearing	Hard of Hearing	S, ST, W, SE, RW, C, MF, PP, L, KC, BN
11.	Indian Railways Accounts Service	(i) Locomotor Disability	OA, OL, OAL, BL, Leprosy	S, ST, BN, W, SE, MF, C, RW, H
		(ii) Visual Impairment	Low Vision (LV)	S, ST, BN, W, SE, MF, C, RW, H
		(iii) Hearing Impairment	HH	S, ST, BN, W, SE, MF, C, RW, H (Acceptable with Hearing Aids)
12.	Indian Railways Personnel Service	(i) Locomotor Disability	OA, OL, Leprosy Cured, Acid	S, ST, BN, W, SE, MF, C, RW, H
		(ii) Visual Impairment	LV	S, ST, BN, W, SE, MF, C, RW, KC, CL, JU, H

		(iii) Hearing Impairment	HH	S, ST, BN, W, SE, MF, C, RW, KC, CL, JU, H, (Acceptable with Hearing Aids)
13.	Indian Railways Traffic	(i) Locomotor Disability	OA, OL, Leprosy Cured, Acid	S, ST, BN, W, SE, MF, C, RW, PP, H
14.	Indian Defence Estates Service,	(i) Locomotor Disability including Dwarfism, Acid Attack Victims, Leprosy Cured, Muscular Dystrophy	OA (One Arm) OL (One Leg)	S, ST, W, SE, RW, C, MF
			BL (Both Legs)	S, SE, RW, C, MF
		(ii) Visual Impairment	LV (Low Vision)	SE, RW
		(iii) Hearing Impairment	HH (Hard of Hearing)	H
		(iv) Multiple disability including only above three categories	All mentioned in above rows	All mentioned in above rows
15.	Indian Information Service, Gr. 'A'	(i) Locomotor Disability including Cerebral Palsy, Leprosy Cured, Dwarfism, Acid Attack Victims, Muscular Dystrophy	BL, BLOA	S, RW, SE, H, C
			BLA	S, SE, H, C
			BA, BH	S, ST, W, SE, H
			OL, OA, MW, OAL	S, ST, W, SE, H, RW, C
		(ii) Blind and Low Vision	LV	MF, PP, L, KC, BN, ST, W, H, RW, C, SE
			B	MF, PP, L, KC, BN, ST, W, H, RW, C, SE
		(iii) Deaf and Hard of Hearing	HH	MF, PP, L, KC, BN, ST, W, H, RW, C
			FD	MF, PP, L, KC, BN, ST, W, RW, C

		(iv) Multiple disabilities from amongst persons under clauses (i) to (iii) above inclu ding deaf blindness in the posts identified for each disabilities	All the above mentioned in categories (i) to (iii) above	
16.	Indian Trade Service, Gr. 'A' (Gr. III)	(i) Locomotor Disability including Cerebral Palsy, Leprosy Cured, Dwarfism, Acid Attack Victims and Muscular Dystrophy	One Leg (OL), One Arm (OA), One Arm One Leg (OAL), Muscular Weakness	S, ST, W, SE, H, RW, C
			Both Legs (BL), Both Legs One Arm	S, SE, H, RW, C
			Both Legs and Arms (BLA)	S, SE, H, C
			Both Arms (BA), Both Hands (BH)	S, ST, SE, H, C
		(ii) Blindness and Low Vision	Low Vision (LV)	MF, PP, L, KC, BN, ST, W, H, RW, C
			Blind (B)	MF, PP, L, KC, BN, ST, W, H, C
		(iii) Deaf and Hard of Hearing	Hard of Hearing (HH)	MF, PP, L, KC, BN, ST, W, H, RW, C
			Fully Deaf (FD)	MF, PP, L, KC, BN, ST, W, RW, C
17.	Indian Corporate Law Service, Group 'A'	(i) Locomotor Disability	One Arm (OA),	SE, RW, C, M, S, BN, ST, H
			One Leg (OL),	SE, RW, C, M, S, BN, ST, H
			One Arm and One Leg (OAL),	SE, RW, C, M, S, BN, ST, H
			Both Legs (BL),	SE, RW, C, M, S, BN, H
			Leprosy Cured (LC),	SE, RW, C, M, S, BN, ST, H
			Dwarfism (DW),	SE, RW, C, M, S, BN, ST, H

			Acid Attack Victims (AAV),	SE, RW, C, M, S, BN, ST, H
			Muscular Dystrophy (MDy)	SE, RW, C, M, S, BN, ST, H
		(ii) Visual Impairment	Low Vision (LV),	SE, RW, C, M, S, BN, ST, H
		(iii) Hearing Impairment	Deaf (D),	SE, RW, C, M, S, BN, ST
			Hard of Hearing (HH)	SE, RW, C, M, S, BN, ST, H
		(iv) Multiple Disabilities	Multiple Disabilities (MD), [2 or more disabilities among (i) to (iii)]	SE, RW, C, M, S, BN
18.	Armed Forces Headquarters Civil Service, Gr. 'B' (Section Officers' Grade)	(i) Locomotor Disability including Cerebral Palsy, Leprosy Cured, Dwarfism, Acid Attack	OA, OL, MW, OAL, Cerebral Palsy, Leprosy Cured, Dwarfism, Acid Attack	S, ST, W, BN, MF, SE, RW, H, C
			BLOA, BL	S, SE, H, RW, C
		(ii) Blindness and Low Vision	B	S, ST, W, BN, MF, RW (in Braille/ software), H, C
			LV	S, ST, W, BN, MF, RW, H, C
		(iii) Deaf and Hard of Hearing	FD, HH	S, ST, W, BN, MF, SE, RW, C
19.	Delhi, Andaman and Nicobar Islands, Lakshadweep, Daman and Diu and Dadra and Nagar Haveli Civil Service, Gr. 'B'	(i) Locomotor disability including Cerebral Palsy, Leprosy Cured,	OA, OL, BA, BH, MW, OAL, Cerebral Palsy, Leprosy Cured, Dwarfism, Acid Attack Victims	S, ST, W, SE, H, RW, C
		Dwarfism, Acid Attack Victims	BLA, BLOA, BL	S, SE, H, RW, C
		(ii) Blindness and Low Vision	LV	MF, PP, S, ST, W, L, C, RW, H, KC, BN

			B	MF, PP, S, ST, W, L, C, RW (in Braille/software), H, KC, BN|
		(iii) Deaf and Hard of Hearing	FD, HH	PP, S, ST, W, L, C, RW, KC, BN
20.	Pondicherry Civil Service, Gr. 'B'	(i) Locomotor Disability including Cerebral Palsy, Leprosy Cured, Dwarfism, Acid Attack Victims	OA, OL, BA, BH, MW, OAL, CP, LC, DW, AAV	S, ST, W, SE, H, RW, C
			BLA, BLOA, BL	S, SE, H, RW, C
		(ii) Blindness and Low Vision	LV	MF, PP, S, ST, W, L, C, RW, H, KC, BN
			B	MF, PP, S, ST, W, L, C, RW (in Braille/software), H, KC, BN
		(iii) Deaf and Hard of Hearing	FD, HH	PP, S, ST, W, L, C, RW, KC, BN

*For details about Functional Classification and Physical Requirements, para 8 of this Notice may please be referred.

❑❑❑

Centres of Civil Services (Preliminary & Main) Examination

CENTRES OF EXAMINATION

(A) Centres of Civil Services (Preliminary) Examination

AGARTALA	GORAKHPUR	PANAJI (GOA)
AGRA	GURGAON	PATNA
AJMER	GWALIOR	PORT BLAIR
AHMEDABAD	HYDERABAD	PRAYAGRAJ (ALLAHA BAD)
AIZAWL	IMPHAL	PUDUCHERRY
ALIGARH	INDORE	PUNE
ANANTPUR (ANDHRA PRADESH)	ITANAGAR	RAIPUR
AURANGABAD	JABALPUR	RAJKOT
BANGALURU	JAIPUR	RANCHI
BAREILLY	JAMMU	SAMBALPUR
BHOPAL	JODHPUR	SHILLONG
BILASPUR	JORHAT	SHIMLA
CHANDIGARH	KOCHI	SILIGUDI
CHENNAI	KOHIMA	SRINAGAR
COIMBATORE	KOLKATA	THANE
CUTTACK	KOZHIKODE (CALICUT)	THIRUVANANTHA-PURAM
DEHRADUN	LUCKNOW	TIRUCHIRAPALLI
DELHI	LUDHIANA	TIRUPATI
DHARWAD	MADURAI	UDAIPUR

DISPUR	MUMBAI	VARANASI
FARIDABAD	MYSORE	VELLORE
GANGTOK	NAGPUR	VIJAYAVADA
GAYA	NAVI MUMBAI	VISHAKHAPATNAM
GHAZIABAD	GAUTAM BUDDH NAGAR	WARANGAL

(B) Centres of Civil Services (Main) Examination

AHMEDABAD	DELHI	PATNA
AIZAWL	DISPUR (GUWAHATI)	PRAYAGRAJ (ALLAHABAD)
BANGALURU	HYDERABAD	RAIPUR
BHOPAL	JAIPUR	RANCHI
CHANDIGARH	JAMMU	SHILLONG
CHENNAI	KOLKATA	SHIMLA
CUTTACK	LUCKNOW	THIRUVANANTHA-PURAM
DEHRADUN	MUMBAI	VIJAYAWADA

The Centres and the date of holding the examination as mentioned above are liable to be changed at the discretion of the Commission. Applicants should note that there will be a ceiling on the number of candidates allotted to each of the Centres, except Chennai, Dispur, Kolkata and Nagpur. Allotment of Centres will be on the "first-apply-first allot" basis, and once the capacity of a particular Centre is attained, the same will be frozen. Applicants, who cannot get a Centre of their choice due to ceiling, will be required to choose a Centre from the remaining ones. Applicants are, thus, advised that they may apply early so that they could get a Centre of their choice. NB: Notwithstanding the aforesaid provision, the Commission reserves the right to change the Centres at its discretion if the situation demands. All the Examination Centres for Civil Services (Preliminary), Examination, 20… will cater to examination for Persons with Benchmark Disability in their respective Centres. Candidates admitted to the examination will be informed of the time table and place or places of examination. The candidates should note that no request for change of Centre will be entertained.

5 Eligibility Conditions

NATIONALITY

(1) For the Indian Administrative Service, the Indian Foreign Service and the Indian Police Service, a candidate must be a citizen of India.

(2) For other services, a candidate must be either:

   (a) a citizen of India, or
   (b) a subject of Nepal, or
   (c) a subject of Bhutan, or
   (d) a Tibetan refugee who came over to India before 1st January, 1962 with the intention of permanently settling in India, or
   (e) a person of Indian origin who has migrated from Pakistan, Burma, Sri Lanka, East African countries of Kenya, Uganda, the United Republic of Tanzania, Zambia, Malawi, Zaire, Ethiopia and Vietnam with the intention of permanently settling in India.

Provided that a candidate belonging to categories (b), (c), (d) and (e) shall be a person in whose favour a certificate of eligibility has been issued by the Government of India.

A candidate in whose case a certificate of eligibility is necessary, may be admitted to the examination but the offer of appointment may be given only after the necessary eligibility certificate has been issued to him/her by the Government of India.

AGE LIMITS

(a) A candidate must have attained the age of 21 years and must not have attained the age of 32 years on the 1st of August, 2019 i.e., he must have been born not earlier than 2nd August, 1987 and not later than 1st August, 1998. Necessary action to make corresponding changes in respective Rules/Regulations pertaining to various services is being taken separately.

(b) The upper age-limit prescribed above will be relaxable:

   (i) up to a maximum of five years if a candidate belongs to a Scheduled Caste or a Scheduled Tribe;
   (ii) up to a maximum of three years in the case of candidates belonging to Other Backward Classes who are eligible to avail of reservation applicable to such candidates;

(iii) up to a maximum of three years in the case of Defence Services Personnel, disabled in operations during hostilities with any foreign country or in a disturbed area and released as a consequence thereof;

(iv) up to a maximum of five years in the case of ex-servicemen including Commissioned Officers and ECOs/SSCOs who have rendered at least five years Military Service as on 1st August, 2019 and have been released;

  (a) on completion of assignment (including those whose assignment is due to be completed within one year from 1st August, 2019 otherwise than by way of dismissal or discharge on account of misconduct or inefficiency; or

  (b) on account of physical disability attributable to Military Service; or

  (c) on invalidment.

(v) up to a maximum of five years in the case of ECOs/SSCOs who have completed an initial period of assignment of five years of Military Service as on 1st August, 2019 and whose assignment has been extended beyond five years and in whose case the Ministry of Defence issues a certificate that they can apply for civil employment and that they will be released on three months' notice on selection from the date of receipt of offer of appointment.

(vi) up to a maximum of 10 years in the case of

  (a) blindness and low vision;

  (b) deaf and hard of hearing;

  (c) locomotor disability including cerebral palsy, leprosy cured, dwarfism, acid attack victims and muscular dystrophy;

  (d) autism, intellectual disability, specific learning disability and mental illness; and

  (e) multiple disabilities from amongst persons under clauses (a) to (d) including deaf-blindness.

(vii) up to a maximum of five years if a candidate had ordinarily been domiciled in the State of Jammu and Kashmir during the period from the 1st day of January, 1980 to the 31st day of December, 1989.

Note I: Candidates belonging to the Scheduled Castes and the Scheduled Tribes and the Other Backward Classes who are also covered under any other clauses of Rule 6(b) above, viz. those coming under the category of Ex-servicemen, persons domiciled in the State of J & K , Persons of Benchmark Disabilities, viz.

(a) blindness and low vision;

(b) deaf and hard of hearing;

(c) locomotor disability including cerebral palsy, leprosy cured, dwarfism, acid attack victims and muscular dystrophy;

(d) autism, intellectual disability, specific learning disability and mental illness; and

(e) multiple disabilities from amongst persons under clauses (a) to (d) including deaf-blindness etc., will be eligible for grant of cumulative age-relaxation under both the categories.

Note II: The details of Functional Classification (FC) and Physical Requirements (PR) of each service is indicated in this Notice which are identified and prescribed by the respective Cadre Controlling Authorities (CCAs) as per the provisions of Section 33 and 34 of the Rights of Persons with Disabilities Act, 2016. Only those category(ies) of disability(ies) mentioned in the Notice shall apply for the examination under Persons with Benchmark Disability (PwBD) categories.

Therefore, the candidates belonging to the Persons with Benchmark Disability categories are advised to read it carefully before applying for the examination.

Note III: The term Ex-servicemen will apply to the persons who are defined as Ex-servicemen in the Ex-servicemen (Re-employment in Civil Services and Posts) Rules, 1979, as amended from time to time.

Note IV: The age concession under para 3(II)(iv) and (v) will be admissible to Ex-servicemen, i.e. a person who has served in any rank whether as combatant or non-combatant in the Regular Army, Navy and Air Force of the Indian Union and who either has been retired or relieved or discharged from such service whether at his/her own request or being relieved by the employer after earning his or her pension.

Note V: Notwithstanding the provision of age relaxation under para 3 (b)(vi) above, candidates of Persons with Benchmark Disability will be considered to be eligible for appointment only if he/she (after such physical examination as the Government or appointing authority, as the case may be, may prescribe) is found to satisfy the requirements of physical and medical standards for the concerned Services/Posts to be allocated to the Persons with Benchmark Disability by the Government. Save as provided above, the age-limits prescribed can in no case be relaxed.

The date of birth, accepted by the Commission is that entered in the Matriculation or Secondary School Leaving Certificate or in a certificate recognized by an Indian University as equivalent to Matriculation or in an extract from a Register of Matriculates maintained by a University which extract must be certified by the proper authority of the University or in the Higher Secondary or an equivalent examination certificate. These certificates are required to be submitted only at the time of applying for the Civil Services (Main) Examination. No other document relating to age like horoscopes, affidavits, birth extracts from Municipal Corporation, Service records and the like will be accepted.

The expression Matriculation/Higher Secondary Examination Certificate in this part of the Instruction include the alternative certificates mentioned above.

Note 1: Candidate should note that only the date of birth as recorded in the Matriculation/Secondary Examination certificate or an equivalent certificate on the date of submission of application will be accepted by the Commission, and no subsequent request for its change will be considered or granted.

Note 2: Candidates should also note that once a date of birth has been claimed by them and entered in the records of the Commission for the purpose of admission to an Examination, no change will be allowed subsequently or at any other Examination of the Commission on any grounds whatsoever.

Note 3: The candidate should exercise due care while entering their date of birth in the online Application Form for the Preliminary Examination. If on verification at any subsequent stage, any variation is found in their date of birth from the one entered in their matriculation or equivalent Examination certificate, disciplinary action will be taken against them by the Commission under the Rules.

MINIMUM EDUCATIONAL QUALIFICATIONS

The candidate must hold a degree of any of Universities incorporated by an Act of the Central or State Legislature in India or other educational institutions established by an Act of Parliament or declared to be deemed as a University Under Section-3 of the University Grants Commission Act, 1956, or possess an equivalent qualification.

Note I: Candidates who have appeared at an examination the passing of which would render them educationally qualified for the Commission's examination but have not been informed of the result as also the candidates who intend to appear at such a qualifying examination will also be eligible for admission to the Preliminary Examination.

All candidates who are declared qualified by the Commission for taking the Civil Services (Main) Examination will be required to produce proof of passing the requisite examination along with their application (i.e. Detailed Application Form-I) for the Main Examination, failing which such candidates will not be admitted to the Main Examination. Such proof of passing the requisite examination should be dated earlier than the due date (closing date) of Detailed Application Form-I of the Civil Services (Main) Examination.

Note II: In exceptional cases the Union Public Service Commission may treat a candidate who does not have any of the foregoing qualifications as a qualified candidate provided that he/she has passed examination conducted by the other Institutions, the standard of which in the opinion of the Commission justifies his/her admission to the examination.

Note III: Candidates possessing professional and technical qualifications which are recognised by the Government as equivalent to professional and technical degree would also be eligible for admission to the examination.

Note IV: Candidates who have passed the final professional M.B.B.S. or any other Medical Examination but have not completed their internship by the time of submission of their applications for the Civil Services (Main) Examination, will be provisionally admitted to the Examination provided they submit along with their application a copy of certificate from the concerned authority of the University/ Institution that they had passed the requisite final professional medical examination.

In such cases, the candidates will be required to produce at the time of their interview original Degree or a certificate from the concerned competent authority of the University/Institution that they had completed all requirements (including completion of internship) for the award of the Degree.

NUMBER OF ATTEMPTS

Every candidate appearing at the examination, who is otherwise eligible, shall be permitted six attempts at the examination:

(a) Provided that this restriction on the number of attempts will not apply in the case of

(b) Scheduled Castes and Scheduled Tribes candidates who are otherwise eligible,

(c) Provided further that the number of attempts permissible to candidates belonging to Other Backward Classes, who are otherwise eligible, shall be nine. The relaxation will be available to the candidates who are eligible to avail of reservation applicable to such candidates,

(d) Provided further that candidates of Persons with Benchmark Disability will get as many attempts as are available to other candidates who do not belong to Persons with Benchmark Disability of his or her community, subject to the condition that a candidate of Persons with Benchmark Disability belonging to the General Category shall be eligible for nine attempts. Necessary action to make corresponding changes in respective Rules/regulations pertaining to various services is being taken separately. The relaxation will be available to the candidates of Persons with Benchmark Disability who are eligible to avail of reservation applicable to such candidates.

Notes:

(I) An attempt at a Preliminary Examination shall be deemed to be an attempt at the Civil Services Examination.

(II) If a candidate actually appears in any one paper in the Preliminary Examination, he/she shall be deemed to have made an attempt at the Examination.

(III) Notwithstanding the disqualification/cancellation of candidature, the fact of appearance of the candidate at the examination will count as an attempt.

RESTRICTIONS ON APPLYING FOR THE EXAMINATION

(a) A candidate who is appointed to the Indian Administrative Service or the Indian Foreign Service on the results of an earlier examination and continues to be a member of that service will not be eligible to compete at this examination. In case such a candidate is appointed to the IAS/IFS after the Preliminary Examination of Civil Services Examination, 2019 is over and he/she continues to be a member of that service, he/she shall not be eligible to appear in the

Civil Services (Main) Examination, 2019 notwithstanding his/her having qualified in the Preliminary Examination, 2019.

Also provided that if such a candidate is appointed to IAS/IFS after the commencement of the Civil Services (Main) Examination, 2019 but before the result thereof and continues to be a member of that service, he/she shall not be considered for appointment to any service/post on the basis of the result of this examination viz. Civil Services Examination, 2019.

(b) A candidate who is appointed to the Indian Police Service on the results of an earlier examination and continues to be a member of that service will not be eligible to opt for the Indian Police Service in Civil Services Examination, 2019.

PHYSICAL STANDARDS

Candidates must be physically fit according to physical standards for admission to Civil Services Examination, 20... as per guidelines given in Appendix-III of Rules for Examination published in the Gazette of India Extraordinary dated ..., ..., 202....

Fee

Candidates (excepting Female/SC/ST/Persons with Benchmark Disability Candidates who are exempted from payment of fee) are required to pay fee of ₹ .../- (Rupees ... only) either by remitting the money in any Branch of State Bank of India or by using Visa/Master/RuPay Credit/Debit Card or by using Internet Banking of SBI. Applicants who opt for "Pay by Cash" mode should print the system generated Pay-in-slip during part II registration and deposit the fee at the counter of SBI Branch on the next working day only. "Pay by Cash" mode will be deactivated at 11.59 P.M. of ..., ..., 202... i.e. one day before the closing date; however applicants who have generated their Pay-in-Slip before it is deactivated may pay at the counter of SBI Branch during banking hours on the closing date. Such applicants who are unable to pay by cash on the closing date i.e. during banking hours at SBI Branch, for reasons whatsoever, even if holding valid pay-in-slip will have no other offline option but to opt for available online Debit/Credit Card or Internet Banking payment mode on the closing date i.e. till 18:00 Hours of ..., ..., 202....

For the applicants in whose case payments details have not been received from the bank they will be treated as fictitious payment cases and a list of all such applicants shall be made available on the Commission website within two weeks after the last day of submission of online application.

These applicants shall also be intimated through e-mail to submit copy of proof of their payment to the Commission at the address mentioned in the e-mail. The applicant shall be required to submit the proof within 10 days from the date of such communication either by hand or by speed post to the Commission. In case, no response is received from the applicants their applications shall be summarily rejected and no further correspondence shall be entertained in this regard.

All female candidates and candidates belonging to Scheduled Caste/Scheduled Tribe/ Persons with Benchmark Disability categories are exempted from payment of fee. No fee exemption is, however, available to OBC/EWS candidates and they are required to pay the prescribed fee in full. Persons with Benchmark Disability are exempted from the payment of fee provided they are otherwise eligible for appointment to the Services/Posts to be filled on the results of this examination on the basis of the standards of medical fitness for these Services/Posts (including any concessions specifically extended to the Persons with Benchmark Disability). A candidate of Persons with Benchmark Disability claiming fee concession will be required by the Commission to submit along with their Detailed Application Form - I, a certified copy of the Certificate of Disability from a Government Hospital/Medical Board in support of his/her claim for belonging to Persons with Benchmark Disability.

NB: Notwithstanding, the aforesaid provision for fee exemption, a candidate of Persons with Benchmark Disability will be considered to be eligible for appointment only if he/she (after such physical examination as the Government or the Appointing Authority, as the case may be, may prescribe) is found to satisfy the requirements of physical and medical standards for the concerned Services/Posts to be allocated to candidates of Persons with Benchmark Disability by the Government.

Note I: Applications without the prescribed Fee (Unless remission of Fee is claimed) shall be summarily rejected.

Note II: Fee once paid shall not be refunded under any circumstances nor can the fee be held in reserve for any other examination or selection.

Note III: If any candidate who took the Civil Services Examination held in 2018 wishes to apply for admission to this examination, he/she must submit his/her application without waiting for the results or an offer of appointment.

Note IV: Candidates admitted to the Main Examination will be required to pay a further fee of Rs. 200/- (Rupees Two hundreds only).

HOW TO APPLY?

(a) Candidates are required to apply online using the website http://www.upsconline.nic.in. Detailed instructions for filling up online applications are available on the above mentioned website. The applicants are advised to submit only single application; however, if due to any unavoidable situation, if he/she submits another/multiple applications, then he/she must ensure that application with the higher RID is complete in all respects like applicants' details, examination centre, photograph, signature, Photo ID, fee etc. The applicants who are submitting multiple applications should note that only the applications with higher RID (Registration ID) shall be entertained by the Commission and fee paid against one RID shall not be adjusted against any other RID.

(b) All candidates, whether already in Government Service, Government owned industrial undertakings or other similar organizations or in private employment should submit their applications direct to the Commission.

Persons already in Government Service, whether in a permanent or temporary capacity or as work charged employees other than casual or daily rated employees or those serving under the Public Enterprises are however, required to submit an undertaking that they have informed in writing to their Head of Office/Department that they have applied for the Examination. Candidates should note that in case a communication is received from their employer by the Commission withholding permission to the candidates applying for/appearing at the examination, their application will be liable to be rejected/candidature will be liable to be cancelled.

Note 1: While filling in his/her Application Form, the candidate should carefully decide about his/her choice of centre for the Examination. If any candidate appears at a centre other than the one indicated by the Commission in his/her Admission Certificate, the papers of such a candidate will not be evaluated and his/her candidature will be liable to cancellation.

Note 2: The Persons with Benchmark Disabilities in the categories of blindness, locomotor disability (both arm affected – BA) and cerebral palsy will be provided the facility of scribe, if desired by the person. In case of other category of Persons with Benchmark Disabilities as defined under Section 2(r) of the RPWD Act, 2016, the facility of scribe will be allowed to such candidates on production of a certificate to the effect that the person concerned has physical limitation to write, and scribe is essential to write examination on behalf, from the Chief Medical Officer/Civil Surgeon/Medical Superintendent of a Government Health Care institution as per proforma at Appendix – IV. The candidates have discretion of opting for his/her own scribe or request the Commission for the same.The details of scribe i.e. whether own or the Commission's and the details of scribe in case candidates are bringing their own scribe, will be sought at the time of filling up the application form online. Suitable provisions in Online Application have been made.

Note 3: The qualification of the Commission's scribe as well as own scribe will not be more than the minimum qualification criteria of the examination. However, the qualification of the scribe should always be matriculate or above.

Note 4: The Persons with Benchmark Disabilities in the category of blindness, locomotor disability (both arm affected – BA) and cerebral palsy will be allowed Compensatory Time of twenty minutes per hour of the examination. In case of other categories of Persons with Benchmark Disabilities, this facility will be provided on production of a certificate to the effect that the person concerned has physical limitation to write from the Chief Medical Officer/Civil Surgeon/Medical Superintendent of a Government Health Care institution as per proforma at Appendix – IV.

Note 5: Candidates appearing in Civil Services (Preliminary) Examination, 2019 will be required to indicate information such as (a) detail of Centres for Civil Services (Main) Examination and Indian Forest Service (Main) Examination (b) Optional subject to be selected for the examination, (c) Medium of examination for Civil Services (Main) Examination, (d) Medium of Examination for Optional Subject if he/she chooses any Indian Language as the Medium of Examination for

Civil Services (Main) Examination and (e) compulsory Indian Language for Civil Services (Main) Examination at the time of the filling up online application itself.

Note 6: Candidates are not required to submit alongwith their applications any certificate in support of their claims regarding Age, Educational Qualifications, Scheduled Castes/Scheduled Tribes/Other Backward Classes/Economically Weaker Sections and Persons with Benchmark Disability etc. which will be verified at the time of the Main examination only. The candidates applying for the examination should ensure that they fulfill all the eligibility conditions for admission to the Examination. Their admission at all the stages of examination for which they are admitted by the Commission viz. Preliminary Examination, Main (Written) Examination and Interview Test will be purely provisional, subject to their satisfying the prescribed eligibility conditions. If on verification at any time before or after the Preliminary Examination, Main (written) Examination and Interview Test, it is found that they do not fulfill any of the eligibility conditions; their candidature for the examination will be cancelled by the Commission. If any of their claims is found to be incorrect, they may render themselves liable to disciplinary action by the Commission in terms of Rule 14 of the Rules for the Civil Services Examination, 202... reproduced below:

A candidate who is or has been declared by the Commission to be guilty of:

(i) Obtaining support for his candidature by the following means, namely:
- (a) offering illegal gratification to; or
- (b) applying pressure on; or
- (c) blackmailing, or threatening to blackmail any person connected with the conduct of the examination; or

(ii) impersonation; or

(iii) procuring impersonation by any person; or

(iv) submitting fabricated documents or documents which have been tampered with; or

(v) uploading irrelevant photos in the application form in place of actual photo/ signature.

(vi) making statements which are incorrect or false or suppressing material information; or

(vii) resorting to the following means in connection with his candidature for the examination, namely:
- (a) obtaining copy of question paper through improper means;
- (b) finding out the particulars of the persons connected with secret work relating to the examination;
- (c) influencing the examiners; or

(viii) being in possession of or using unfair means during the examination; or

(ix) writing obscene matter or drawing obscene sketches or irrelevant matter in the scripts; or

(x) misbehaving in the examination hall including tearing of the scripts, provoking fellow examinees to boycott examination, creating a disorderly scene and the like; or

(xi) harassing or doing bodily harm to the staff employed by the Commission for the conduct of their examination; or

(xii) being in possession of or using any mobile phone, (even in switched off mode), pager or any electronic equipment or programmable device or storage media like pen drive, smart watches etc. or camera or bluetooth devices or any other equipment or related accessories either in working or switched off mode capable of being used as a communication device during the examination; or

(xiii) violating any of the instructions issued to candidates along with their admission certificates permitting them to take the examination; or

(xiv) attempting to commit or, as the case may be, abetting the commission of all or any of the acts specified in the foregoing clauses; may in addition to rendering himself liable to criminal prosecution, be liable:

(a) to be disqualified by the Commission from the Examination for which he is a candidate; and/or

(b) to be debarred either permanently or for a specified period:

(i) by the Commission, from any examination or selection held by them;

(ii) by the central government from any employment under them; and

(c) if he is already in service under Government to disciplinary action under the appropriate rules:

Provided that no penalty under this rule shall be imposed except after:

(i) giving the candidate an opportunity of making such representation in writing as he may wish to make in that behalf; and

(ii) taking the representation, if any, submitted by the candidate within the period allowed to him into consideration.

Last Date for Online Submission of Applications

The Online Applications can be filled up to ...th ..., 202... till 6:00 P.M. after which the link will be disabled. Detailed instructions regarding filling of online application is available at Appendix-II.

CORRESPONDENCE WITH THE COMMISSION

The Commission will not enter into any correspondence with the candidates about their candidature except in the following cases:

(i) The eligible candidates shall be issued an e-Admit Card three weeks before the commencement of the examination. The e-Admit Card will be made available on the UPSC website [www.upsc.gov.in] for downloading by candidates. No Admit Card will be sent by post. If a candidate does not receive his e-Admit Card or any other communication regarding his/her candidature for the examination three weeks before the commencement of the examination, he/she should at once contact the Commission. Information in this regard can also be obtained from the Facilitation Counter located in the Commission's Office either in person or over phone Nos. 011-23381125/011-23385271/011-23098543. In case no communication is received in the Commission's Office from the candidate regarding non-receipt of his/her e-Admit Card at least 3 weeks before the examination, he/she himself/herself will be solely responsible for non-receipt of his/her e-Admit Card. No candidate will ordinarily be allowed to take the examination unless he/she holds an e-Admit Card for the examination. On downloading of e-Admit Card, check it carefully and bring discrepancies/errors, if any, to the notice of UPSC immediately.

The candidates should note that their admission to the examination will be purely provisional based on the information given by them in the Application Form. This will be subject to verification of all the eligibility conditions by the UPSC.

The mere fact that an e-Admit Card to the Examination has been issued to a candidate, will not imply that his/her candidature has been finally cleared by the Commission or that entries made by the candidate in his/her application for the Preliminary examination have been accepted by the Commission as true and correct. Candidates may note that the Commission takes up the verification of eligibility conditions of a candidate, with reference to original documents, only after the candidate has qualified for Civil Services (Main) Examination. Unless candidature is formally confirmed by the Commission, it continues to be provisional.

The decision of the Commission as to the eligibility or otherwise of a candidate for admission to the Examination shall be final.

Candidates should note that the name in the Admit Card in some cases, may be abbreviated due to technical reasons.

(ii) In the event of a candidate downloading more than one Admit Card from the Commission's website, he/she should use only one of these Admit Card for appearing in the examination and report about the other(s) to the Commission's Office.

(iii) Candidates are informed that as the Preliminary Examination is only a screening test, no marks sheets will be supplied to successful or unsuccessful candidates and no correspondence will be entertained by the Commission, in this regard.

(iv) Candidates must ensure that their emails IDs given in their online application are valid and active.

Important: All communications to the Commission should invariably contain the following particulars.

1. Name and year of the examination.
2. Registration ID (RID)
3. Roll Number (if received)
4. Name of candidate (in full and in block letters)
5. Complete postal address as given in the application.

N.B. I. Communication not containing the above particulars may not be attended to.

N.B. II. Candidates should also note down their RID number for future reference. They may be required to indicate the same in connection with their candidature for the Civil Services (Main) Examination.

❑❑❑

6 Reservation Criteria

RESERVATION FOR THE PERSONS WITH BENCHMARK DISABILITIES

The eligibility for availing reservation against the vacancies reserved for the Persons with Benchmark Disabilities shall be the same as prescribed in "The Rights of Persons with Disabilities Act, 2016 (RPwD Act, 2016)". The candidates of Multiple Disabilities will be eligible for reservation under category (e) - Multiple Disabilities only of Section 34(1) of RPwD Act, 2016 and shall not be eligible for reservation under any other categories of disabilities i.e. (a) to (d) of Section 34(1) of RPwD Act, 2016 on account of having 40% and above impairment in any of these categories of PwBD.

Provided further that the Persons with Benchmark Disabilities shall also be required to meet special eligibility criteria in terms of Functional Classification and Physical Requirements (abilities/disabilities) (FC&PR) consistent with requirements of the identified service/post as may be prescribed by its cadre controlling authority at note-II of Para-1 of this Notice.

The physical requirement and functional classification can for example be one or more of the following:

Code	Physical Requirements	Code	Functional Classification
S	Sitting	OH	Orthopaedically Handicapped
ST	Standing	VH	Visually Handicapped
W	Walking	HH	Hearing Handicapped
SE	Seeing	OA	One Arm
H	Hearing/Speaking	OL	One Leg
RW	Reading and Writing	BA	Both Arm
C	Communication	BH	Both Hands
MF	Manipulation by Finger	MW	Muscular Weakness

PP	Pushing & Pulling	OAL	One Arm One Leg
L	Lifting	BLA	Both Legs and Arms
KC	Kneeling and Crouching	BLOA	Both Legs One Arm
BN	Bending	LV	Low Vision
M	Movement	B	Blind
JU	Jumping	PD	Partially Deaf
CL	Climbing	FD	Fully Deaf
		BL	Both Legs
		D	Dwarfism
		CP	Cerebral Palsy
		LC	Leprosy Cured
		AAV	Acid Attack Victims
		MD	Multiple Disabilities

Note: The above list is subject to revision.

BENEFIT OF COMMUNITY RESERVATION

A candidate will be eligible to get the benefit of community reservation only in case the particular caste to which the candidates belong is included in the list of reserved communities issued by the Central Government. The candidates will be eligible to get the benefit of the Economically Weaker Section reservation only in case the candidate meets the criteria issued by the Central Government and in possession of such eligibility certification. If a candidate indicates in his/her application form for Civil Services (Preliminary) Examination that he/she belongs to General category but subsequently writes to the Commission to change his/her category to a reserved one, such request shall not be entertained by the Commission. Further, once a candidate has chosen a reserved category, no request shall be entertained for change to other reserved category viz. SC to ST, ST to SC, OBC to SC/ST or SC/ST to OBC, SC to EWS, EWS to SC, ST to EWS, EWS to ST, OBC to EWS, EWS to OBC. No reserved category candidates other than those recommended on General Merit shall be allowed to change his/her category from Reserved to Unreserved or claim the vacancies (Service/Cadre) for UR category after the declaration of final result by UPSC.

Further no Persons with Benchmark Disabilities (PwBD) candidate of any subcategory thereunder shall be allowed to change his/her sub-category of disability.

While the above principle will be followed in general, there may be a few cases where there was a gap of not more than 3 months between the issuance of a Government Notification enlisting a particular community in the list of any of the reserved communities and the date of submission of the application by the candidate. In such cases the request of change of community from general to reserved may be considered by the Commission on merit. In case of a candidate unfortunately becoming physically disabled during the course of the examination process, the candidate should produce valid document showing him/her acquiring a disability to the extent of 40% or more as defined under The Rights of Persons with Disabilities Act, 2016 to enable him/her to get the benefits of PwBD reservation.

CERTIFICATES FOR GETTING BENEFITS

Candidates seeking reservation/relaxation benefits available for SC/ST/OBC/EWS/PwBD/Ex-servicemen must ensure that they are entitled to such reservation/relaxation as per eligibility prescribed in the Rules/Notice. They should also be in possession of all the requisite certificates in the prescribed format in support of their claim as stipulated in the Rules/Notice for such benefits, and these certificates should be dated earlier than the due date (closing date) of the application of Civil Services (Preliminary) Examination, 202.... Provided further that EWS Candidates can submit their Income and Asset Certificate (certificate of eligibility) at the time of submission of online Detailed Application Form (DAF-I). The Income and Asset Certificate must be dated earlier than 1st August, 202....

Withdrawal of Applications

NO request for withdrawal of candidature received from a candidate after he/she has submitted his/her application will be entertained under any circumstances.

(...)
JOINT SECRETARY
UNION PUBLIC SERVICE COMMISSION

❑❑❑

7 Plan and Scheme of Exams (Appendix-I)

SECTION-I: PLAN OF EXAMINATIONS

1. The competitive examination comprises two successive stages:
   (i) Civil Services (Preliminary) Examination (Objective Type) for the selection of candidates for Main Examination; and
   (ii) Civil Services (Main) Examination (Written and Interview) for the selection of candidates for the various Services and posts.
2. The Preliminary Examination will consist of two papers of Objective type (multiple choice questions) and carry a maximum of 400 marks in the subjects set out in sub-section (A) of Section II. This examination is meant to serve as a screening test only; the marks obtained in the Preliminary Examination by the candidates who are declared qualified for admission to the Main Examination will not be counted for determining their final order of merit. The number of candidates to be admitted to the Main Examination will be about twelve to thirteen times the total approximate number of vacancies to be filled in the year through this examination. Only those candidates who are declared by the Commission to have qualified in the Preliminary Examination in the year will be eligible for admission to the Main Examination of that year provided they are otherwise eligible for admission, to the Main Examination.

Note I: The Commission will draw a list of candidates to be qualified for Civil Services (Main) Examination based on the criterion of minimum qualifying marks of 33% in General Studies Paper-II of Civil Services (Preliminary) Examination and total qualifying marks of General Studies Paper-I of Civil Services (Preliminary) Examination as may be determined by the Commission.

Note II: There will be negative marking for incorrect answers (as detailed below) for all questions except some of the questions where the negative marking will be inbuilt in the form of different marks being awarded to the most appropriate and not so appropriate answer for such questions.

(i) There are four alternatives for the answers to every question. For each question for which a wrong answer has been given by the candidate, one-third (0.33) of the marks assigned to that question will be deducted as penalty.

(ii) If a candidate gives more than one answer, it will be treated as a wrong answer even if one of the given answers happen to be correct and there will be same penalty as above for that question.

(iii) If a question is left blank i.e. no answer is given by the candidate, there will be no penalty for that question.

3. The Main Examination will consist of written examination and an interview test. The written examination will consist of 9 papers of conventional essay type in the subjects set out in sub-section (B) of Section II out of which two papers will be of qualifying in nature. Also see Note (ii) under Para I of Section II (B) Marks obtained for all the compulsory papers (Paper-I to Paper-VII) and Marks obtained in Interview for Personality Test will be counted for ranking..

3.1 Candidates who obtain such minimum qualifying marks in the written part of the Main Examination as may be fixed by the Commission at their discretion, shall be summoned by them for an interview for a Personality Test, vide sub-section 'C' of Section II. The number of candidates to be summoned for interview will be about twice of the number of vacancies to be filled. The interview will carry 275 marks (with no minimum qualifying marks).

3.2 Marks thus obtained by the candidates in the Main Examination (written part as well as interview) would determine their final ranking. Candidates will be allotted to the various Services keeping in view their ranks in the examination and the preferences expressed by them for the various Services and posts.

SECTION-II: SCHEME AND SUBJECTS FOR THE PRELIMINARY & MAIN EXAMINATIONS

A. Preliminary Examination

The Examination shall comprise of two compulsory Papers of 200 marks each.

Notes:

(i) Both the question papers will be of the objective type (multiple choice questions) and each will be of two hours duration.

(ii) The General Studies Paper-II of the Civil Services (Preliminary) Examination will be a qualifying paper with minimum qualifying marks fixed at 33%.

(iii) The question papers will be set both in Hindi and English.

(iv) Details of the syllabi are indicated in next Chapter 8.

B. Main Examination

The written examination will consist of the following papers:

Qualifying Papers			
Paper	**Subject**	**Topics**	**Marks**
Paper-A	Indian Language	One of the Indian Language to be selected by the candidate from the Languages included in the Eighth Schedule to the Constitution	300 Marks
Paper-B	English	-	300 Marks

Papers to Be Counted for Merit			
Papers	**Subject**	**Topics**	**Marks**
Paper-I	Essay		250 Marks
Paper-II	General Studies-I	Indian Heritage and Culture, History and Geography of the World and Society	250 Marks
Paper-III	General Studies-II	Governance, Constitution, Polity, Social Justice and International relations	250 Marks
Paper-IV	General Studies-III	Technology, Economic Development, Bio-diversity, Environment, Security and Disaster Management	250 Marks
Paper-V	General Studies-IV	Ethics, Integrity and Aptitude	250 Marks
Paper-VI (Optional Subject)	Paper-1	One of the subjects given in optional lists	250 Marks
Paper-VI (Optional Subject)	Paper-2	One of the subjects given in optional lists	250 Marks
Sub-total (Written Marks to be counted for recommendation to interview & Final Merit List)			1750 Marks
Personality Test (Interview)			275 Marks
Grand Total			2025 Marks

Candidates may choose any one of the optional subjects from amongst the list of subjects given in para 2 below:

Note:

(i) The papers on Indian languages and English (Paper A and Paper B) will be of Matriculation or equivalent standard and will be of qualifying nature. The marks obtained in these papers will not be counted for ranking.

(ii) Evaluation of the papers, namely, 'Essay', 'General Studies' and Optional Subject of all the candidates would be done simultaneously along with evaluation of their qualifying papers on 'Indian Languages' and 'English' but the papers on Essay, General Studies and Optional Subject of only such candidates will be taken cognizance who attain 25% marks in 'Indian Language' and 25% in English as minimum qualifying standards in these qualifying papers.

(iii) The paper A on Indian Language will not, however, be compulsory for candidates hailing from the States of Arunachal Pradesh, Manipur, Meghalaya, Mizoram, Nagaland and Sikkim.

(iv) The paper A on Indian Language will not, however, be compulsory for Candidates belonging to Persons with Benchmark Disabilities (only Hearing Impairment sub-category) provided that they have been granted such exemption from 2nd or 3rd language courses by the concerned education Board/ University. The candidate needs to provide an undertaking/self declaration in this regard in order to claim such an exemption to the Commission.

(v) Marks obtained by the candidates for the Paper I-VII only will be counted for merit ranking. However, the Commission will have the discretion to fix qualifying marks in any or all of these papers.

(vi) For the Language medium/literature of languages, the scripts to be used by the candidates will be as under:

Language	Script
Assamese	Assamese Bengali
Bengali	Bengali
Gujarati	Gujarati, Hindi Devanagari
Kannada	Kannada
Kashmiri	Persian
Konkani	Devanagari
Malayalam	Malayalam
Manipuri	Bengali
Marathi	Devanagari
Maithilli	Devanagari

Language	Script
Nepali	Devanagari
Odia	Odia
Punjabi	Gurumukhi
Sanskrit	Devanagari
Sindhi	Devanagari or Arabic
Telugu	Telugu
Urdu	Persian
Bodo	Devanagari
Dogri	Devanagari
Santhali	Devanagari or Olchiki

Note: For Santhali language, question paper will be printed in Devanagari script; but candidates will be free to answer either in Devanagari script or in Olchiki.

List of Optional Subjects for UPSC Main Exam

1. Agriculture	2. Animal Husbandry and Veterinary Science	3. Anthropology	4. Botany	5. Chemistry
6. Civil Engineering	7. Commerce & Accountancy	8. Economics	9. Electrical Engineering	10. Geography
11. Geology	12. History	13. Law	14. Management	15. Mathematics
16. Mechanical Engineering	17. Medical Science	18. Philosophy	19. Physics	20. Political Science & International Relations
21. Psychology	22. Public Administration	23. Sociology	24. Statistics	25. Zoology

Literature any one of the following languages				
1. Assamese	2. Bengali	3. Bodo	4. Dogri	5. Gujarati
6. Hindi	7. Kannada	8. Kashmiri	9. Konkani	10. Maithili
11. Malayalam	12. Manipuri	13. Marathi	14. Nepali	15. Odia
16. Punjabi	17. Sanskrit	18. Santhali	19. Sindhi	20. Tamil
21. Telugu	22. Urdu	23. English		

Note:

(i) The question papers for the examination will be of conventional (essay) type.

(ii) Each paper will be of three hours duration.

(iii) Candidates will have the option to answer all the question papers, except the Qualifying Language Papers, Paper-A and Paper-B, in any one of the languages included in the Eighth Schedule to the Constitution of India or in English. Notwithstanding this, the Candidate will have the choice to write the Optional Papers in English also if candidates opt to write Paper I-V except the Qualifying Language Papers, Paper-A and Paper-B, in any one of the language included in the Eighth Schedule to the Constitution of India.

(iv) Candidates exercising the option to answer Papers in any one of the languages included in the Eight Schedule to the Constitution of India mentioned above may, if they so desire, give English version within brackets of only the description of the technical terms, if any, in addition to the version in the language opted by them. Candidates should, however, note that if they misuse the above rule, a deduction will be made on this account from the total marks otherwise accruing to them and in extreme cases; their script(s) will not be valued for being in an unauthorized medium.

(v) Candidates should note that if any irrelevant matter/signages/marks etc. are found written in the answer script(s), which would not be related to any question/answer and/or would be having the potential to disclose the candidate's identity, the Commission will impose a penalty of deduction of marks from the total marks otherwise accruing to the candidate or will not evaluate the said script(s) on this account.

(vi) The question papers (other than the literature of language papers) will be set in Hindi and English only.

(vii) The details of the syllabi are set out in Part B of Section III.

General Instructions for Preliminary & Main Examinations

(i) Candidates must write the papers in their own hand. In no circumstances will they be allowed the help of a scribe to write the answers for them. The Persons with Benchmark Disabilities in the categories of blindness, locomotor disability (both arm affected – BA) and cerebral palsy will be provided the facility of scribe, if desired by the person. In case of other category of Persons with Benchmark Disabilities as defined under section 2(r) of the RPWD Act, 2016, the facility of scribe will be allowed to such candidates on production of a certificate to the effect that the person concerned has physical limitation to write, and scribe is essential to write examination on behalf, from the Chief Medical Officer/Civil Surgeon/Medical Superintendent of a Government Health Care institution as per proforma at Appendix – V.

(ii) The candidates have discretion of opting for his/her own scribe or request the Commission for the same. The details of scribe i.e. whether own or the Commission's and the details of scribe in case candidates are bringing their own scribe, will be sought at the time of filling up the application form online as per proforma at Appendix - VI.

(iii) The qualification of the Commission's scribe as well as own scribe will not be more than the minimum qualification criteria of the examination. However, the qualification of the scribe should always be matriculate or above.

(iv) The Persons with Benchmark Disabilities in the category of blindness, locomotor disability (both arm affected – BA) and cerebral palsy will be allowed Compensatory Time of twenty minutes per hour of the examination. In case of other categories of Persons with Benchmark Disabilities, this facility will be provided on production of a certificate to the effect that the person concerned has physical limitation to write from the Chief Medical Officer/ Civil Surgeon/ Medical Superintendent of a Government Health Care institution as per proforma at Appendix – V.

Note 1: The eligibility conditions of a scribe, his/her conduct inside the examination hall and the manner in which and extent to which he/she can help the PwBD candidate in writing the Civil Services Examination shall be governed by the instructions issued by the UPSC in this regard. Violation of all or any of the said instructions shall entail the cancellation of the candidature of the PwBD candidate in addition to any other action that the UPSC may take against the scribe.

Note 2: The criteria for determining the percentage of visual impairment shall be as follows:

Better Eye Best Corrected	Worse Eye Best Corrected	Per Cent Impairment	Disability Category
6/6 to 6/18	6/6 to 6/18	0%	0
	6/24 to 6/60	10%	0
	Less than 6/60 to 3/60	20%	I
	Less than 3/60 to No Light Perception	30%	II (One eyed person)
6/24 to 6/60 Or Visual field less than 40 up to 20 degree around centre of fixation or heminaopia involving macula	6/24 to 6/60	40%	III a (low vision)
	Less than 6/60 to 3/60	50%	III b (low vision)
	Less than 3/60 to No Light Perception	60%	III c (low vision)
Less than 6/60 to 3/60 Or Visual field less than 20 up to 10 degree around centre of fixation	Less than 6/60 to 3/60	70%	III d (low vision)
	Less than 3/60 to No Light Perception	80%	III e (low vision)
Less than 3/60 to 1/60 Or Visual field less than 10 degree around centre of fixation	Less than 3/60 to No Light Perception	90%	IV a (Blindness)
Only HMCF Only Light Perception	Only HMCF Only Light Perception	100%	IV b (Blindness)
No Light Perception	No Light Perception		

Note 3: The concession admissible to blind/low vision candidates shall not be admissible to those suffering from Myopia.

(v) The Commission has discretion to fix qualifying marks in any or all the subjects of the examination.

(vi) If a candidate's handwriting is not easily legible, a deduction will be made on this account from the total marks otherwise accruing to him.

(vii) Marks will not be allotted for mere superficial knowledge.

(viii) Credit will be given for orderly, effective and exact expression combined with due economy of words in all subjects of the examination.

(ix) In the question papers, wherever required, SI units will be used.

(x) Candidates should use only International form of Indian numerals (i.e. 1, 2, 3, 4, 5, 6 etc.) while answering **question papers**.

(xi) Candidates will be allowed the use of Scientific (Non-Programmable type) Calculators at the conventional (Essay) type examination of UPSC. Programmable type calculators will however not be allowed and the use of such calculators shall tantamount to resorting to unfair means by the candidates. Loaning or interchanging of calculators in the Examination Hall is not permitted.

It is also important to note that candidates are not permitted to use calculators for answering objective type papers (Test Booklets). They should not therefore bring the same inside the Examination Hall.

C. Interview Test

1. The candidate will be interviewed by a Board who will have before them a record of his career. He will be asked questions on matters of general interest. The object of the interview is to assess the personal suitability of the candidate for a career in public service by a Board of competent and unbiased observers. The test is intended to judge the mental caliber of a candidate. In broad terms this is really an assessment of not only his intellectual qualities but also social traits and his interest in current affairs. Some of the qualities to be judged are mental alertness, critical powers of assimilation, clear and logical exposition, balance of judgement, variety and depth of interest, ability for social cohesion and leadership, intellectual and moral integrity.
2. The technique of the interview is not that of a strict cross-examination but of a natural, though directed and purposive conversation which is intended to reveal the mental qualities of the candidate.
3. The interview test is not intended to be a test either of the specialised or general knowledge of the candidates which has been already tested through their written papers. Candidates are expected to have taken an intelligent interest not only in their special subjects of academic study but also in the events which are happening around them both within and outside their own State or Country as well as in modern currents of thought and in new discoveries which should rouse the curiosity of well educated youth.

8 Syllabi for the Examinations

Note: Candidates are advised to go through the Syllabus published in this Section for the Preliminary Examination and the Main Examination, as periodic revision of syllabus has been done in several subjects.

PART A—PRELIMINARY EXAMINATION

Paper I - (200 marks) **Duration: Two hours**

1. Current events of national and international importance.
2. History of India and Indian National Movement.
3. Indian and World Geography: Physical, Social, Economic Geography of India and the World.
4. Indian Polity and Governance: Constitution, Political System, Panchayati Raj, Public Policy, Rights Issues, etc.
5. Economic and Social Development: Sustainable Development, Poverty, Inclusion, Demographics, Social Sector Initiatives, etc.
6. General issues on Environmental ecology, Bio-diversity and Climate Change – that do not require subject specialization.
7. General Science.

Paper II - (200 marks) **Duration: Two hours**

1. Comprehension;
2. Interpersonal skills including communication skills;
3. Logical reasoning and analytical ability;
4. Decision making and problem solving;
5. General mental ability;
6. Basic numeracy (numbers and their relations, orders of magnitude, etc.) (Class X level);
7. Data interpretation (charts, graphs, tables, data sufficiency etc. — Class X level);

Note 1: Paper-II of the Civil Services (Preliminary) Examination will be a qualifying paper with minimum qualifying marks fixed at 33%.

Note 2: The questions will be of multiple choice, objective type.

Note 3: It is mandatory for the candidate to appear in both the Papers of Civil Services (Prelim) Examination for the purpose of evaluation. Therefore a candidate will be disqualified in case he/she does not appear in both the papers of Civil Services (Prelim) Examination.

PART B—MAIN EXAMINATION

The main Examination is intended to assess the overall intellectual traits and depth of understanding of candidates rather than merely the range of their information and memory.

The nature and standard of questions in the General Studies papers (Paper II to Paper V) will be such that a well-educated person will be able to answer them without any specialized study. The questions will be such as to test a candidate's general awareness of a variety of subjects, which will have relevance for a career in Civil Services. The questions are likely to test the candidate's basic understanding of all relevant issues, and ability to analyze, and take a view on conflicting socio-economic goals, objectives and demands. The candidates must give relevant, meaningful and succinct answers.

The scope of the syllabus for optional subject papers (Paper VI and Paper VII) for the examination is broadly of the honours degree level i.e. a level higher than the bachelors' degree and lower than the masters' degree. In the case of Engineering, Medical Science and law, the level corresponds to the bachelors' degree.

Syllabi of the papers included in the scheme of Civil Services (Main) Examination are given as follows:

Qualifying Papers on Indian Languages and English

The aim of the paper is to test the candidates' ability to read and understand serious discursive prose, and to express his ideas clearly and correctly, in English and Indian language concerned.

The pattern of questions would be broadly as follows:

(i) Comprehension of given passages.
(ii) Précis Writing.
(iii) Usage and Vocabulary.
(iv) Short Essays.

Indian Languages

(i) Comprehension of given passages.
(ii) Précis Writing.
(iii) Usage and Vocabulary.
(iv) Short Essays.
(v) Translation from English to the Indian Language and vice-versa.

Note 1: The papers on Indian Languages and English will be of Matriculation or equivalent standard and will be of qualifying nature only. The marks obtained in these papers will not be counted for ranking.

Note 2: The candidates will have to answer the English and Indian Languages papers in English and the respective Indian language (except where translation is involved).

Paper-I

Essay: Candidates may be required to write essays on multiple topics. They will be expected to keep closely to the subject of the essay to arrange their ideas in orderly fashion, and to write concisely. Credit will be given for effective and exact expression.

Paper-II

General Studies-I: Indian Heritage and Culture, History and Geography of the World and Society.

(i) Indian culture will cover the salient aspects of Art Forms, literature and Architecture from ancient to modern times.

(ii) Modern Indian history from about the middle of the eighteenth century until the present-significant events, personalities, issues.

(iii) The Freedom Struggle — its various stages and important contributors/ contributions from different parts of the country.

(iv) Post-independence consolidation and reorganization within the country.

(v) History of the world will include events from 18th century such as industrial revolution, world wars, redrawal of national boundaries, colonization, decolonization, political philosophies like communism, capitalism, socialism etc. — their forms and effect on the society.

(vi) Salient features of Indian Society, Diversity of India.

(vii) Role of women and women's organization, population and associated issues, poverty and developmental issues, urbanization, their problems and their remedies.

(viii) Effects of globalization on Indian society.

(ix) Social empowerment, communalism, regionalism and secularism.

(x) Salient features of world's physical geography.

(xi) Distribution of key natural resources across the world (including South Asia and the Indian sub-continent);

(xii) Factors responsible for the location of primary, secondary, and tertiary sector industries in various parts of the world (including India).

(xiii) Important Geophysical phenomena such as Earthquakes, Tsunami, Volcanic activity, cyclone etc.

(xiv) Geographical features and their location-changes in critical geographical features (including water-bodies and ice-caps) and in flora and fauna and the effects of such changes.

Paper-III

General Studies-II: Governance, Constitution, Polity, Social Justice and International relations.

(i) Indian Constitution—historical underpinnings, evolution, features, amendments, significant provisions and basic structure.

(ii) Functions and responsibilities of the Union and the States, issues and challenges pertaining to the federal structure, devolution of powers and finances up to local levels and challenges therein.

(iii) Separation of powers between various organs dispute redressal mechanisms and institutions. Comparison of the Indian constitutional scheme with that of other countries.

(iv) Parliament and State legislatures—structure, functioning, conduct of business, powers & privileges and issues arising out of these.

(v) Structure, organization and functioning of the Executive and the Judiciary—Ministries and Departments of the Government; pressure groups and formal/informal associations and their role in the Polity.

(vi) Salient features of the Representation of People's Act.

(vii) Appointment to various Constitutional posts, powers, functions and responsibilities of various Constitutional Bodies.

(viii) Statutory, regulatory and various quasi-judicial bodies.

(ix) Government policies and interventions for development in various sectors and issues arising out of their design and implementation.

(x) Development processes and the development industry—the role of NGOs, SHGs, various groups and associations, donors, charities, institutional and other stakeholders.

(xi) Welfare schemes for vulnerable sections of the population by the Centre and States and the performance of these schemes; mechanisms, laws, institutions and Bodies constituted for the protection and betterment of these vulnerable sections.

(xii) Issues relating to development and management of Social Sector/Services relating to Health, Education, Human Resources.

(xiii) Issues relating to poverty and hunger.

(xiv) Important aspects of governance, transparency and accountability, e-governance- applications, models, successes, limitations, and potential; citizens charters, transparency & accountability and institutional and other measures.

(xv) Role of civil services in a democracy. India and its neighborhood-relations.

(xvi) Bilateral, regional and global groupings and agreements involving India and/or affecting India's interests.

(xvii) Effect of policies and politics of developed and developing countries on India's interests, Indian diaspora.

(xviii) Important International institutions, agencies and for-their structure, mandate.

Paper-IV

General Studies-III: Technology, Economic Development, Biodiversity, Environment, Security and Disaster Management

(i) Indian economy and issues relating to planning, mobilization, of resources, growth, development and employment.

(ii) Inclusive growth and issues arising from it. Government Budgeting.

(iii) Major crops-cropping patterns in various parts of the country, different types of irrigation and irrigation systems storage, transport and marketing of agricultural produce and issues and related constraints; e-technology in the aid of farmers.

(iv) Issues related to direct and indirect farm subsidies and minimum support prices; Public Distribution System – objectives, functioning, limitations, revamping; issues of buffer stocks and food security; technology missions; economics of animal-rearing.

(v) Food processing and related industries in India – scope and significance, location, upstream and downstream requirements, supply chain management.

(vi) Land reforms in India.

(vii) Effects of liberalization on the economy, changes in industrial policy and their effects on industrial growth.

(viii) Infrastructure: Energy, Ports, Roads, Airports, Railways etc.

(ix) Investment models.

(x) Science and Technology-developments and their applications and effects in everyday life.

(xi) Achievements of Indians in science and technology; indigenization of technology and developing new technology.

(xii) Awareness in the fields of IT, Space, Computers, robotics, nano-technology, bio-technology and issues relating to intellectual property rights.

(xiii) Conservation, environmental pollution and degradation, environmental impact assessment. Disaster and disaster management.

(xiv) Linkages between development and spread of extremism.

(xv) Role of external state and non-state actors in creating challenges to internal security. Challenges to internal security through communication networks, role of media and social networking sites in internal security challenges, basics of cyber security; money-laundering and its prevention.

(xvi) Security challenges and their management in border areas – linkages of organized crime with terrorism.

(xvii) Various security forces and agencies and their mandate.

Paper-V

General Studies-IV: Ethics, Integrity and Aptitude

This paper will include questions to test the candidates' attitude and approach to issues relating to integrity, probity in public life and his problem solving approach to various issues and conflicts faced by him in dealing with society. Questions may utilise the case study approach to determine these aspects. The following broad areas will be covered:

(i) **Ethics and human interface:** Essence, determinants and consequences of Ethics in-human actions; dimensions of ethics; ethics - in private and public relationships. Human Values - lessons from the lives and teachings of great leaders, reformers and administrators; role of family society and educational institutions in inculcating values.

(ii) **Attitude:** Content, structure, function; its influence and relation with thought and behaviour; moral and political attitudes; social influence and persuasion.

(iii) **Aptitude and foundational values:** For Civil Service, integrity, impartiality and non-partisanship, objectivity, dedication to public service, empathy, tolerance and compassion towards the weaker-sections.

(iv) **Emotional intelligence:** Concepts, and their utilities and application in administration and governance.

(v) Contributions of moral thinkers and philosophers from India and world.

(vi) **Public/civil service values and ethics in public administration:** Status and problems; ethical concerns and dilemmas in government and private institutions; laws, rules, regulations and conscience as sources of ethical guidance; accountability and ethical governance; strengthening of ethical and moral values in governance; ethical issues in international relations and funding; corporate governance.

(vii) **Probity in Governance:** Concept of public service; Philosophical basis of governance and probity; Information sharing and transparency in government, Right to Information, Codes of Ethics, Codes of Conduct, Citizen's Charters, Work culture, Quality of service delivery, Utilization of public funds, challenges of corruption.

(viii) Case Studies on above issues.

Paper-VI & Paper VII

Optional Subject Papers I & II: Candidate may choose any optional subject from amongst the List of Optional Subjects given in Para 2.

1. AGRICULTRE

Paper-I

Ecology and its relevance to man, natural resources, their sustainable management and conservation. Physical and social environment as factors of crop distribution and production. Agro ecology; cropping pattern as indicators of environments.

Environmental pollution and associated hazards to crops, animals and humans. Climate change—International conventions and global initiatives. Greenhouse effect and global warming. Advance tools for ecosystem analysis—Remote Sensing (RS) and Geographic Information Systems (GIS).

Cropping patterns in different agro-climatic zones of the country. Impact of high-yielding and short-duration varieties on shifts in cropping patterns. Concepts of various cropping, and farming systems. Organic and Precision farming. Package of practices for production of important cereals, pulses, oil seeds, fibres, sugar, commercial and fodder crops.

Important features, and scope of various types of forestry plantations such as social forestry, agro-forestry, and natural forests: Propagation of forest plants. Forest products. Agro-forestry and value addition. Conservation of forest flora and fauna.

Weeds, their characteristics, dissemination and association with various crops; their multiplications; cultural, biological, and chemical control of weeds.

Soil—physical, chemical and biological properties. Processes and factors of soil formation. Soils of India. Mineral and organic constituents of soils and their role in maintaining soil productivity. Essential plant nutrients and other beneficial elements in soils and plants. Principles of soil fertility, soil testing and fertiliser recommendations, integrated nutrient management Biofertilizers. Losses of nitrogen in soil, nitrogen-use efficiency in submerged rice soils, nitrogen fixation in soils. Efficient phosphorus and potassium use. Problem soils and their reclamation.

Soil factors affecting greenhouse gas emission.

Soil conservation, integrated watershed management. Soil erosion and its management. Dry land agriculture and its problems. Technology for stabilising agriculture production in rainfed areas.

Water-use efficiency in relation to crop production, criteria for scheduling irrigations, ways and means of reducing run-off losses of irrigation water. Rainwater harvesting. Drip and sprinkler irrigation. Drainage of water-logged soils, quality of irrigation water, effect of industrial effluents on soil and water pollution. Irrigation projects in India.

Farm management, scope, importance and characteristics, farm planning. Optimum resource use and budgeting. Economics of different types of farming systems. Marketing management strategies for development, market intelligence. Price fluctuations and their cost; role of co-operatives in agricultural economy; types and systems of farming and factors affecting them. Agricultural price policy. Crop Insurance.

Agricultural extension, its importance and role, methods of evaluation of extension programmes, socio-economic survey and status of big, small and marginal farmers and landless agricultural labourers; Training programmes for extension workers. Role of Krishi Vigyan Kendra's (KVK) in dissemination of Agricultural technologies. Non-Government Organisation (NGO) and self-help group approach for rural development.

Paper-II

Cell structure, function and cell cycle. Synthesis, structure and function of genetic material. Laws of heredity. Chromosome structure, chromosomal aberrations, linkage and cross-over, and their significance in recombination breeding. Polyploidy, euploids and aneuploids. Mutation—and their role in crop improvement. Heritability, sterility and incompatibility, classification and their application in crop improvement. Cytoplasmic inheritance, sex-linked, sex-influenced and sex-limited characters.

History of plant breeding. Modes of reproduction, selfing and crossing techniques. Origin, evolution and domestication of crop plants, center of origin, law of homologous series, crop genetic resources—conservation and utilization. Application of principles of plant breeding, improvement of crop plants. Molecular markers and their application in plant improvement. Pure-line selection, pedigree, mass and recurrent selections, combining ability, its significance in plant breeding. Heterosis and its exploitation. Somatic hybridization. Breeding for disease and pest resistance. Role of interspecific and intergeneric hybridization. Role of genetic engineering and biotechnology in crop improvement gernetically modified crop plants.

Seed production and processing technologies. Seed certification, Seed testing and storage. DNA finger printing and seed registration. Role of public and private sectors in seed production, and marketing. Intellectual Property Rights (IPR) issues, WTO issues and its impact on Agriculture.

Principles of Plant Physiology with reference to plant nutrition, absorption, translocation and metabolism of nutrients. Soil-water-plant relationship.

Enzymes and plant pigments; photosynthesis—modern concepts and factors affecting the process, aerobic and anaerobic respiration; C_3, C_4 and CAM mechanisms. Carbohydrate, protein and fat metabolism. Growth and development; photoperiodism and vernalization. Plant growth substances and their role in crop production. Physiology of seed development and germination; dormancy. Stress physiology—draught, salt and water stress.

Major fruits, plantation crops, vegetables, spices and flower crops. Package practices of major horticultural crops. Protected cultivation and high tech horticulture. Post-harvest technology and value addition of fruits and vegetables. Landscaping and commercial floriculture. Medicinal and aromatic plants. Role of fruits and vegetables in human nutrition.

Diagnosis of pests and diseases of field crops, vegetables, orchard and plantation crops and their economic importance. Classification of pests and diseases and their management. Intergrated pest and diseases management. Storage pests and their management. Biological control of pests and diseases. Epidemiology and forecasting of major crop pests and diseases. Plant quarantine measures. Pesticides, their formulation and modes of action.

Food production and consumption trends in India. Food security and growing population—vision 2020. Reasons for grain surplus. National and International food policies. Production, procurement, distribution constraints. Availability of foodgtrains, per capita expenditure on food. Trends in poverty, Public Distribution System and Below Poverty Line population, Targeted Public Distribution System (PDS), policy implementation in context to globalization. Processing constraints. Relation of food production to National Dietary Guidelines and food consumption pattern. Food based dietary approaches to eliminate hunger. Nutrient deficiency—Micronutrient deficiency: Protein Energy Malnutrition or Protein Calorie Malnutrition (PEM or PCM), Micronutrient deficiency and HRD in context of work capacity of women and children. Food grain productivity and food security.

2. ANIMAL HUSBANDRY AND VETERINARY SCIENCE

Paper-I

1. **Animal Nutrition**

1.1 Partitioning of food energy within the animal. Direct and indirect calorimetry.

Carbon—nitrogen balance and comparative slaughter methods. Systems for expressing energy value of foods in ruminants, pigs and poultry. Energy requirements for maintenance, growth, pregnancy, lactation, egg, wool, and meat production.

1.2 Latest advances in protein nutrition. Energy protein inter-relationships. Evaluation of protein quality. Use of NPN compounds in ruminant diets. Protein requirements for maintenance, growth, pregnancy, lactation, egg, wool and meat production.

1.3 Major and trace minerals—Their sources, physiological functions and deficiency symptoms.

Toxic minerals. Mineral interactions. Role of fatsoluble and water-soluble vitamins in the body, their sources and deficiency symptoms.

1.4 Feed additives—methane inhibitors, probiotics, enzymes, antibiotics, hormones, oligosaccharides, antioxidants, emulsifiers, mould inhibitors, buffers etc. Use and abuse of growth promoters like harmones and antibiotics—latest concepts.

1.5 Conservation of fodders. Storage of feeds and feed ingredients. Recent advances in feed technology and feed processing. Anti-nutritional and toxic factors present in livestock feeds. Feed analysis and quality control. Digestibility trials—direct, indirect and indicator methods. Predicting feed intake in grazing animals.

1.6 Advances in ruminant nutrition. Nutrient requirements. Balanced rations. Feeding of calves, pregnant, work animals and breeding bulls. Strategies for feeding milch animals during different stages of lactation cycle. Effect of feeding on milk composition. Feeding of goats for meat and milk production. Feeding of sheep for meat and wool production.

1.7 Swine Nutrition. Nutrient requirements. Creep, starter, grower and finisher rations. Feeding of pigs for lean meat production. Low cost rations for swine.

1.8 Poultry nutrition. Special features of poultry nutrition. Nutrient requirements for meat and egg production. Formulation of rations for different classes of layers and broilers.

2. **Animal Physiology**

2.1 Physiology of blood and its circulation, respiration; excretion. Endocrine glands in health and disease.

2.2 Blood constituents—Properties and functions—blood cell formation—Haemoglobin synthesis and chemistry—plasma proteins production, classification and properties, coagulation of blood; Haemorrhagic disorders—anti-coagulants—blood groups—Blood volume—Plasma expanders—Buffer systems in blood. Biochemical tests and their significance in disease diagnosis.

2.3 Circulation—Physiology of heart, cardiac cycle, heart sounds, heart beat, electrocardiograms. Work and efficiency of heart—effect of ions on heart function-metabolism of cardiac muscle, nervous and chemical regulation of heart, effect of temperature and stress on heart, blood pressure and hypertension, osmotic regulation, arterial pulse, vasomotor regulation of circulation, shock. Coronary and pulmonary circulation, Blood–Brain barrier Cerebrospinal fluid-circulation in birds.

2.4 Respiration—Mechanism of respiration, Transport and exchange of gases-neural control of respiration-Chemo-receptors-hypoxia-respiration in birds.

2.5 Excretion—Structure and function of kidney–formation of urine-methods of studying renal function–renal regulation of acid-base balance: physiological constituents of urine-renal failure-passive venous congestion-Urinary secretion in chicken-Sweat glands and their function. Bio-chemical test for urinary dysfunction.

2.6 Endocrine glands—Functional disorders—their symptoms and diagnosis. Synthesis of hormones, mechanism and control of secretion—hormonal receptors-classification and function.

2.7 Growth and Animal Production—Prenatal and postnatal growth, maturation, growth curves, measures of growth, factors affecting growth, conformation, body composition, meat quality.

2.8 Physiology of Milk Production, Reproduction and Digestion—Current status of hormonal control of mammary development, milk secretion and milk ejection. Male and Female reproductive organs, their components and functions. Digestive organs and their functions.

2.9 Environmental Physiology—Physiological relations and their regulation; mechanisms of adaptation, environmental factors and regulatory mechanisms involved in animal behaviour, climatology—various parameters and their importance. Animal ecology. Physiology of behaviour. Effect of stress on health and production.

3. **Animal Reproduction:** Semen quality—Preservation and Artificial Insemination—Components of semen, composition of spermatozoa, chemical and physical properties of ejaculated semen, factors affecting semen in vivo and in vitro. Factors affecting semen production and quality, preservation, composition of diluents, sperm concentration, transport of diluted semen. Deep freezing techniques in cows, sheep, goats, swine and poultry. Detection of oestrus and time of insemination for better conception. Anoestrus and repeat breeding.

4. **Livestock Production and Management**

   4.1 Commercial Dairy Farming—Comparison of dairy farming in India with advanced countries. Dairying under mixed farming and as specialized farming, economic dairy farming. Starting of a dairy farm, Capital and land requirement, organization of the dairy farm. Opportunities in dairy farming, factors determining the efficiency of dairy animal. Heard recording, budgeting cost of milk production, pricing policy; Personnel Management. Developing Practical and Economic rations for dairy cattle; supply of greens throughout the year, feed and fodder requirements of Dairy Farm. Feeding regimes for young stock and bulls, heifers and breeding animals; new trends in feeding young and adult stock; Feeding records.

   4.2 Commercial meat, egg and wool production—Development of practical and economic rations for sheep, goats, pigs, rabbits and poultry. Supply of greens, fodder, feeding regimes for young and mature stock. New trends in enhancing production and management. Capital and land requirements and socio-economic concept.

   4.3 Feeding and management of animals under drought, flood and other natural calamities.

5. **Genetics and Animal Breeding**

   5.1 History of animal genetics. Mitosis and Meiosis: Mendelian inheritance; deviations to Mendelian genetics; Expression of genes; Linkage and crossing over; Sex determination, sex influenced and sex limited characters; Blood groups and polymorphism; Chromosome aberrations; Cytoplasmic inheritance, Gene and its structure; DNA as a genetic material; Genetic code and protein synthesis; Recombinant DNA technology. Mutations, types of mutations, methods for detecting mutations and mutation rate, Transgenesis.

   5.2 Population Genetics applied to Animal Breeding—Quantitative vs. Qualitative traits; Hardy Weinberg Law; Population vs. Individual; Gene and genotypic frequency; Forces changing gene frequency; Random drift and small populations; Theory of path coefficient; Inbreeding, methods of estimating inbreeding coefficient, systems of inbreeding; Effective population size; Breeding value, estimation of breeding value, dominance and epistatic deviation; Partitioning of variation; Genotype X environment correlation and genotype X environment interaction; role of multiple measurements; Resemblance between relatives.

5.3 Breeding Systems—Breeds of livestsock and Poultry. Heritability, repeatability and genetic and phenotypic correlations, their methods of estimation and precision of estimates; Aids to selection and their relative merits; Individual, pedigree, family and within family selection; Pregnency testing; Methods of selection; Construction of selection indices and their uses; Comparative evaluation of genetic gains through various selection methods; Indirect selection and correlated response; Inbreeding, out breeding, upgrading, cross-breeding and synthesis of breeds; Crossing of inbred lines for commercial production; Selection for general and specific combining ability; Breeding for threshold characters. Sire index.

6. **Extension:** Basic philosophy, objectives, concept and principles of extension. Different methods adopted to educate farmers under rural conditions. Generation of technology, its transfer and feedback. Problems and constraints in transfer of technology. Animal husbandry programmes for rural development.

Paper-II

1. **Anatomy, Pharmacology and Hygiene**

1.1 **Histology and Histological Techniques:** Paraffin embedding technique of tissue processing and H.E. staining—Freezing microtomy—Microscopy Bright field microscope and electron microscope. Cytology-structure of cell organells and inclusions; cell division-cell types—Tissues and their classification-embryonic and adult tissues—Comparative histology of organs—Vascular, Nervous, digestive, respiratory, musculo-skeletal and urogenital systems—Endocrine glands—Integuments—sense organs.

1.2 **Embryology:** Embryology of vertebrates with special reference to aves and domestic mammals gametogenesis-fertilization-germ layers-foetal membranes and placentation-types of placenta in domestic mammals-Teratology-twins and twinning-organogenesis-germ layer derivatives-endodermal, mesodermal and ectodermal derivatives.

1.3 **Bovine Anatomy:** Regional Anatomy: Paranasal sinuses of OX— surface anatomy of salivary glands. Regional anatomy of infraorbital, maxillary, mandi-buloalveolar, mental and cornnal nerve block. Regional anatomy of paravertebral nerves, pudental nerve, median, ulnar and radial nervestibial, fibular and digital nerves—Cranial nerves-structures involved in epidural anaesthesia-superficial lymph nodes-surface anatomy of visceral organs of thoracic, abdominal and pelvic cavities-comparative-features of locomotor apparatus and their application in the biomechanics of mammalian body.

1.4 **Anatomy of Fowl:** Musculo-skeletal system-functional anatomy in relation to respiration and flying, digestion and egg production.

1.5 **Pharmacology and Therapeutics Drugs:** Cellular level of pharmacodynamics and pharmacokinetics. Drugs acting on fluids and electrolyte balance. Drugs acting on Autonomic nervous system. Modern concepts of anaesthesia and dissociative anaesthetics. Autocoids. Antimicrobials and principles of chemotherapy in microbial infections. Use of hormones in therapeutics—chemotherapy of parasitic infections. Drug and economic concerns in the Edible tissues of animals—chemotherapy of Neoplastic diseases. Toxicity due to "insecticides, plants, metals, non-metals, zootoxins and mycotoxins".

1.6 **Veterinary Hygiene with Reference to Water, Air and Habitation:** Assessment of pollution of water, air and soil—Importance of climate in animal health—effect of environment on animal function and performance relationship between industrialisation and animal agriculture—animal housing requirements for specific categories of domestic animals viz. pregnant cows and sows, milking cows, broiler birds—stress, strain and productivity in relation to animal habitation.

2. **Animal Diseases**

2.1 Etiology, epidemiology pathogenesis, symptoms, post-mortem lesions, diagnosis, and control of infectious diseases of cattle, sheep and goat, horses, pigs and poultry.

2.2 Etiology, epidemiology, symptoms, diagnosis, treatment of production diseases of cattle, horse, pig and poultry.

2.3 Deficiency diseases of domestic animals and birds.

2.4 Diagnosis and treatment of non-specific conditions like impaction, Bloat, Diarrhoea, Indigestion, dehydration, stroke, poisioning.

2.5 Diagnosis and treatment of neurological disorders.

2.6 Principles and methods of immunisation of animals against specific diseases—hard immunity—disease free zones—'zero' disease concept—chemoprophylaxis.

2.7 **Anaesthesia**—local, regional and general-prenesthetic medication. Symptoms and surgical interference in fractures and dislocation. Hernia, choking abomassal displacement—Caesarian operations. Rumenotomy—Castrations.

2.8 **Disease Investigation Techniques**—Materials for laboratory investigation—Establishment. Animal Health Centres—Disease free zone.

3. **Veterinary Public Health**

3.1 **Zoonoses**—Classification, definition, role of animals and birds in prevalence and transmission of zoonotic diseases—occupational zoonotic diseases.

3.2 **Epidemiology**—Principle, definition of epidemiological terms, application of epidemiological measures in the study of diseases and disease control. Epidemiological features of air, water and food borne infections. OIE regulation, WTO, sanitary and phytosanitary measures.

3.3 **Veterinary Jurisprudence**—Rules and Regulations for improvement of animal quality and prevention of animal diseases—State and Central Rules for prevention of animal and animal product borne diseases—S.P. C.A.—Veterolegal cases—Certificates—Materials and Methods of collection of samples for veterolegal investigation.

4. **Milk and Milk Products Technology**

4.1 **Market Milk**—Quality, testing and grading of raw milk. Processing, packaging, storing, distribution, marketing defects and their control. Preparation of the following milks: Pasteurized, standardized, toned, double toned, sterilized, homogenized, reconstituted, recombined and flavoured milks. Preparation of cultured milks, cultures and their management, yoghurt, Dahi, Lassi and Srikhand. Preparation of flavoured and sterilized milks. Legal standards. Sanitation requirement for clean and safe milk and for the milk plant equipment.

4.2 **Milk Products Technology**—Selection of raw materials, processing, storing, distributing and marketing milk products such as Cream, Butter, Ghee, Khoa, Channa, Cheese, condensed, evaporated, dried milk and baby food, ice cream and Kulfi; by-products, whey products, butter milk, lactose and casein. Testing, grading, judging milk products—BIS and Agmark specifications, legal standards, quality control nutritive properties. Packaging processing and operational control. Costing of dairy products.

5. **Meat Hygiene and Technology**

5.1 **Meat Hygiene**

5.1.1 Ante mortem care and management of food animals, stunning, slaughter and dressing operations; abattoir requirements and designs; Meat inspection procedures and judgement of carcass meat cuts—grading of carcass meat cuts—duties and functions of Veterinarians in wholesome meat production.

5.1.2 **Hygienic Methods of Handling Production of Meat**—Spoilage of meat and control measures—Post- slaughter physicochemical changes in meat and factors that influence them—Quality improvement methods—Adulteration of meat and detection—Regulatory provisions in Meat trade and Industry.

5.2 **Meat Technology**

5.2.1 **Physical and Chemical Characteristics of Meat**—Meat emulsions—Methods of preservation of meat—Curing, canning, irradiation, packaging of meat and meat products, processing and formulations.

5.3 **By-products**—Slaughter house by-products and their utilisation—Edible and inedible by products—Social and economic implications of proper utilisation of slaughter house by-products—Organ products for food and pharmaceuticals.

5.4 **Poultry Products Technology**—Chemical composition and nutritive value of poultry meat, pre-slaughter care and management. Slaughtering techniques, inspection, preservation of poultry meat and products. Legal and BIS standards.
Structure composition and nutritive value of eggs Microbial spoilage. Preservation and maintenance. Marketing of poultry meat, eggs and products.

5.5 **Rabbit/Fur Animal Farming**—Rabbit meat production. Disposal and utilization of fur and wool and recycling of waste by products. Grading of wool.

3. ANTHROPOLOGY

Paper-I

1.1 Meaning, Scope and Development of Anthropology.

1.2 Relationships with other disciplines: Social Sciences, behavioural Sciences, Life Sciences, Medical Sciences, Earth Sciences and Humanities.

1.3 Main branches of Anthropology, their scope and relevance:
   (a) Social-cultural Anthropology.
   (b) Biological Anthropology.
   (c) Archaeological Anthropology.
   (d) Linguistic Anthropology.

1.4 Human Evolution and Emergence of Man
   (a) Biological and Cultural factors in human evolution.
   (b) Theories of Organic Evolution (Pre-Darwinian, Darwinian and Post-Darwinian).
   (c) Synthetic theory of evolution; Brief outline of terms and concepts of evolutionary biology (Doll's rule, Cope's rule, Gause's rule, parallelism, convergence, adaptive radiation, and mosaic evolution).

1.5 Characteristics of Primates; Evolutionary Trend and Primate Taxonomy; Primate Adaptations; (Arboreal and Terrestrial) Primate Taxonomy; Primate Behaviour; Tertiary and Quaternary fossil primates; Living Major Primates; Comparative Anatomy of Man and Apes; Skeletal changes due to erect posture and its implications.

1.6 Phylogenetic status, characteristics and geographical distribution of the following:
   (a) Plio-preleistocene hominids in South and East Africa—Australopithecines.

(b) ***Homo erectus: Africa (Paranthropus),*** Europe ***(Homo erectus (heidelbergensis),*** Asia ***(Homo erectus javanicus, Homo erectus pekinensis.***

(c) Neanderthal man—La-chapelle-aux-saints (Classical type), Mt. Carmel (Progressive type).

(d) Rhodesian man.

(e) ***Homo sapiens***—Cromagnon, Grimaldi and Chancelede.

1.7 The biological basis of Life: The Cell, DNA structure and replication, Protein Synthesis, Gene, Mutation, Chromosomes, and Cell Division.

1.8 (a) Principles of Prehistoric Archaeology. Chronology: Relative and Absolute Dating methods.

(b) Cultural Evolution—Broad Outlines of Prehistoric cultures:

(i) Paleolithic (ii) Mesolithic
(iii) Neolithic (iv) Chalcolithic
(v) Copper-Bronze Age (vi) Iron Age

2.1 **The Nature of Culture:** The concept and Characteristics of culture and civilization; Ethnocentrism vis-a-vis cultural Relativism.

2.2 **The Nature of Society:** Concept of Society; Society and Culture; Social Institution; Social groups; and Social stratification.

2.3 **Marriage:** Definition and universality; Laws of marriage (endogamy, exogamy, hypergamy, hypogamy, incest taboo); Type of marriage (monogamy, polygamy, polyandry, group marriage). Functions of marriage; Marriage regulations (preferential, prescriptive and proscriptive); Marriage payments (bride wealth and dowry).

2.4 **Family:** Definition and universality; Family, household and domestic groups; functions of family; Types of family (from the perspectives of structure, blood relation, marriage, residence and succession); Impact of urbanization, industrialization and feminist movements on family.

2.5 **Kinship:** Consanguinity and Affinity; Principles and types of descent (Unilineal, Double, Bilateral Ambilineal); Forms of descent groups (lineage, clan, phratry, moiety and kindred); Kinship terminology (descriptive and classificatory); Descent, Filiation and Complimentary Filiation; Decent and Alliance.

3. **Economic Organization:** Meaning, scope and relevance of economic anthropology; Formalist and Substantivist debate; Principles governing production, distribution and exchange (reciprocity, redistribution and market), in communities, subsisting on hunting and gathering, fishing, swiddening, pastoralism, horticulture, and agriculture; globalization and indigenous economic systems.

4. **Political Organization and Social Control:** Band, tribe, chiefdom, kingdom and state; concepts of power, authority and legitimacy; social control, law and justice in simple Societies.

5. **Religion:** Anthropological approaches to the study of religion (evolutionary, psychological and functional); monotheism and polytheism; sacred and profane; myths and rituals; forms of religion in tribal and peasant Societies (animism, animatism, fetishism, naturism and totemism); religion, magic and science distinguished; magico-religious functionaries (priest, shaman, medicine man, sorcerer and witch).
6. **Anthropological Theories**
   (a) Classical evolutionism (Tylor, Morgan and Frazer)
   (b) Historical particularism (Boas) Diffusionism (British, German and American)
   (c) Functionalism (Malinowski); Structural—Functionlism (Radcliffe-Brown)
   (d) Structuralism (L'evi-Strauss and E. Leach)
   (e) Culture and personality (Benedict, Mead, Linton, Kardiner and Cora-du Bois)
   (f) Neo—evolutionism (Childe, White, Steward, Sahlins and Service)
   (g) Cultural materialism (Harris)
   (h) Symbolic and interpretive theories (Turner, Schneider and Geertz)
   (i) Cognitive theories (Tyler, Conklin)
   (j) Post-modernism in anthropology.
7. **Culture, Language and Communication:** Nature, origin and characteristics of language; verbal and non-verbal communication; social contex of language use.
8. **Research Methods in Anthropology**
   (a) Fieldwork tradition in anthropology
   (b) Distinction between technique, method and methodology
   (c) Tools of data collection: observation, interview, schedules, questionnaire, case study, genealogy, life-history, oral history, secondary sources of information, participatory methods.
   (d) Analysis, interpretation and presentation of data.
9. **Human Genetics**
   9.1 **Methods and Application** - Methods for study of genetic principles in man-family study (pedigree analysis, twin study, foster child, co-twin method, cytogenetic method, chromosomal and karyo-type analysis), biochemical methods, immunological methods, D.N.A. technology and recombinant technologies.
   9.2 **Mendelian Genetics in Man**-family study, single factor, multifactor, lethal, sub-lethal and polygenic inheritance in man.
   9.3 Concept of genetic polymorphism and selection, Mendelian population, Hardy-Weinberg law; causes and changes which bring down frequency-mutation, isolation, migration, selection, inbreeding and genetic drift. Consanguineous and non-consanguineous mating, genetic load, genetic effect of consanguineous and cousin marriages.

9.4 Chromosomes and chromosomal aberrations in man, methodology.

(a) Numerical and structural aberrations (disorders).

(b) Sex chromosomal aberration - Klinefelter (XXY), Turner (XO), Super female (XXX), intersex and other syndromic disorders.

(c) Autosomal aberrations - Down syndrome, Patau, Edward and Cri-du-chat syndromes.

(d) Genetic imprints in human disease, genetic screening, genetic counseling, human DNA profiling, gene mapping and genome study.

9.5 Race and racism, biological basis of morphological variation of non-metric and characters. Racial criteria, racial traits in relation to heredity and environment; biological basis of racial classification, racial differentiation and race crossing in man.

9.6 **Age, sex and population variation as genetic marker:** ABO, Rh blood groups, HLA Hp, transferring, Gm, blood enzymes. Physiological characteristics-Hb level, body fat, pulse rate, respiratory functions and sensory perceptions in different cultural and socio-ecomomic groups.

9.7 **Concepts and methods of Ecological Anthropology:** Bio-cultural Adaptations—Genetic and Non-genetic factors. Man's physiological responses to environmental stresses: hot desert, cold, high altitude climate.

9.8 **Epidemiological Anthropology:** Health and disease. Infectious and non-infectious diseases, Nutritional deficiency related diseases.

10. **Concept of Human Growth and Development:** Stages of growth—pre-natal, natal, infant, childhood, adolescence, maturity, senescence.

- Factors affecting growth and development genetic, environmental, biochemical, nutritional, cultural and socio-economic.
- Ageing and senescence. Theories and observations.
- Biological and chronological longevity. Human physique and somatotypes. Methodologies for growth studies.

11.1 Relevance of menarche, menopause and other bioevents to fertility. Fertility patterns and differentials.

11.2 Demographic theories—biological, social and cultural.

11.3 Biological and socio—ecological factors influencing fecundity, fertility, natality and mortality.

12. **Applications of Anthropology:** Anthropology of sports, Nutritional anthropology, Anthroplogy in designing of defence and other equipment, Forensic Anthroplogy, Methods and principles of personal identification and reconstruction, Applied human genetics—Paternity diagnosis, genetic counselling and eugenics, DNA technology in diseases and medicine, serogenetics and cytogenetics in reproductive biology.

Paper-II

1.1 **Evolution of the Indian Culture and Civilization**—Prehistoric (Palaeolithic, Mesolithic, Neolithic and Neolithic-Chalcolithic), Protohistoric (Indus Civilization). Pre-Harappan, Harappan and post-Harappan cultures. Contributions of the tribal cultures to Indian civilization.

1.2 **Palaeo**—Anthropological evidences from India with special reference to Siwaliks and Narmada basin (***Ramapithecus, Sivapithecus and Narmada Man***).

1.3 **Ethno-archaeology in India:** The concept of ethno-archaeology; Survivals and Parallels among the hunting, foraging, fishing, pastoral and peasant communities including arts and crafts producing communities.

2. **Demographic Profile of India**—Ethnic and linguistic elements in the Indian population and their distribution. Indian population—factors influencing its structure and growth.

3.1 The structure and nature of traditional Indian social system—Varnashram, Purushartha, Karma, Rina and Rebirth.

3.2 **Caste system in India**—Structure and characteristics Varna and caste, Theories of origin of caste system, Dominant caste, Caste mobility, Future of caste system, Jajmani system. Tribe-case continuum.

3.3 Sacred Complex and Nature-Man-Spirit Complex.

3.4 Impact of Buddhism, Jainism, Islam and Christianity of Indian society.

4. Emergence, growth and development in India—Contributions of the 18th, 19th and early 20th Century scholar-administrators. Contributions of Indian anthropologists to tribal and caste studies.

5.1 **Indian Village**—Significane of village study in India; Indian village as a social system; Traditional and changing patterns of settlement and inter-caste relations; Agrarian relations in Indian villages; Impact of globalization on Indian villages.

5.2 Linguistic and religious minorities and their social, political and economic status.

5.3 Indigenous and exogenous processes of socio-cultural change in Indian society: Sanskritization, Westernization, Modernization; Inter-play of little and great traditions; Panchayati Raj and social change; Media and Social change.

6.1 **Tribal Situation in India**—Bio-genetic variability, linguistic and socio-economic characteristics of the tribal populations and their distribution.

6.2 **Problems of the Tribal Communities**—Land alienation, poverty, indebtedness, low literacy, poor educational facilities, unemployment, under-employment, health and nutrition.

6.3 Developmental projects and their impact on tribal displacement and problems of rehabilitation. Development of forest policy and tribals. Impact of urbanisation and industrialization on tribal populations.

7.1 Problems of exploitation and deprivation of Scheduled Castes, Scheduled Tribes and Other Backward Classes. Constitutional safeguards for Scheduled Tribes and Scheduled Castes.

7.2 Social change and contemporary tribal societies: Impact of modern democratic institutions, development programmes and welfare measures on tribals and weaker sections.

7.3 The concept of ethnicity; Ethnic conflicts and political developments; Unrest among tribal communities; Regionalism and demand for autonomy; Pseudo-tribalism. Social change among the tribes during colonial and post-Independent India.

8.1 Impact of Hinduism, Buddhism, Christianity, Islam and other religions on tribal societies.

8.2 Tribe and nation state—a comparative study of tribal communities in India and other countries.

9.1 History of administration of tribal areas, tribal policies, plans, programmes of tribal development and their implementation. The concept of PTGs (Primitive Tribal Groups), their distribution, special programmes for their development. Role of N.G.O.s in tribal development.

9.2 Role of anthropology in tribal and rural development.

9.3 Contributions of anthropology to the understanding of regionalism, communalism and ethnic and political movements.

4. BOTANY

Paper-I

1. **Microbiology and Plant Pathology:** Structure and reproduction/ multiplication of viruses, viroids, bacteria, fungi and mycoplasma; Applications of microbiology in agriculture, industry, medicine and in control of soil and water pollution; Prion and Prion hypothesis.

   Important crop diseases caused by viruses, bacteria, mycoplasma, fungi and nematodes; Modes of infection and dissemination; Molecular basis of infection and disease resistance/defence; Physiology of parasitism and control measures. Fungal toxins. Modelling and disease forecasting; Plant quarantine.

2. **Cryptogams:** Algae, fungi, lichens, bryophytes, pteridophytes-structure and reproduction from evolutionary viewpoint; Distribution of Cryptogams in India and their ecological and economic importance.

3. **Phanerogams:** Gymnosperms: Concept of Progymnosperms. Classification and distribution of gymnosperms. Salient features of Cycadales, Ginkgoales, Coniferales and Gnetales, their structure and reproduction. General account of Cycadofilicales, Bennettitales and Cordiaitailes; Geological time scale; Type of fossils and their study techniques.

Angiosperms: Systematics, anatomy, embryology, palynology and phylogency. Taxonomic hierarchy; International Code of Botanical Nomenclature; Numerical taxomomy and chemotaxomomy; Evidence from anatomy, embryology and palynology.

Origin and evolution of angiosperms; Comparative account of various systems of classification of angiosperms; Study of angiospermic families—Mangnoliaceae, Ranunculaceae, Brassicaceae, Rosaceae, Fabaceae, Euphorbiaceae, Malvaceae, Dipterocarpaceae, Apiaceae, Asclepiadaceae, Verbenaceae, Solanaceae, Rubiaceae, Cucurbitaceae, Asteraceae, Poaceae, Arecaceae, Liliaceae, Musaceae and Orchidaceae.

Stomata and their types; Glandular and non-glandular trichomes; Unusual secondary growth; Anatomy of C_3 and C_4 plants; Xylem and phloem differentiation; Wood anatomy.

Development of male and female gametophytes, pollination, fertilization; Endosperm—its development and function. Patterns of embryo development; Polyembroyony, apomixes; Applications of palynology; Experimental embryology including pollen storage and test-tube fertilization.

4. **Plant Resource Development:** Domestication and introduction of plants; Origin of cultivated plants, Vavilov's centres of origin. Plants as sources for food, fodder, fibres, spices, beverages, edible oils, drugs, narcotics, insecticides, timber, gums, resins and dyes; latex, cellulose, starch and its products; Perfumery; Importance of Ethnobotany in Indian context; Energy plantations; Botanical Gardens and Herbaria.
5. **Morphogenesis:** Totipotency, polarity, symmetry and differentiation; Cell, tissue, organ and protoplast culture. Somatic hybrids and Cybrids; Micropropagation; Somaclonal variation and its applications; Pollen haploids, embryo rescue methods and their applications.

Paper-II

1. **Cell Biology:** Techniques of cell biology. Prokaryotic and eukaryotic cells—structural and ultrastructural details; Structure and function of extracellular matrix (cell wall) and membranes-cell adhesion, membrane transport and vesicular transport; Structure and function of cell organelles (chloroplasts, mitochondria, ER, dictyosomes ribosomes, endosomes, lysosomes, peroxisomes; Cytoskelaton and microtubules; Nucleus, nucleolus, nuclear pore complex; Chromatin and nucleosome; Cell signalling and cell receptors; Signal transduction Mitosis and meiosis; molecular basis of cell cycle. Numerical and structural variations in chromosomes and their significance; Chromatin organization and packaging of genome; Polytene chromosomes; B-chromosomes—structure, behaviour and significance.
2. **Genetics, Molecular Biology and Evolution:** Development of genetics, and gene versus allele concepts (Pseudoalleles); Quantitative genetics and multiple

factors; Incomplete dominance, polygenic inheritance, multiple alleles; Linkage and crossing over of gene mapping including molecular maps (idea of mapping, function); Sex chromosomes and sex-linked inheritance; sex determination and molecular basis of sex differentiation; Mutations (biochemical and molecular basis); Cytoplasmic inheritance and cytoplasmic genes (including genetics of male sterility).

Structure and synthesis of nucleic acids and proteins; Genetic code and regulation of gene expression; Gene silencing; Multigene families; Organic evolution-evidences, mechanism and theories.

Role of RNA in origin and evolution.

3. **Plant Breeding, Biotechnology and Biostatistics:** Methods of plant breeding—introduction, selection and hybridization (pedigree, backcross, mass selection, bulk method); Mutation, polyploidy, male sterility and heterosis breeding. Use of apomixes in plant breeding; DNA sequencing; Genetic engineering—methods of transfer of genes; Transgenic crops and biosafety aspects; Development and use of molecular markers in plant breeding; Tools and techniques—probe, southern blotting, DNA fingerprinting, PCR and FISH. Standard deviation and coefficient of variation (CV). Tests of significance (Z-test, t-test and chi-square tests). Probability and distributions (normal, binomial and Poisson). Correlation and regression.
4. **Physiology and Biochemistry:** Water relations, mineral nutrition and ion transport, mineral deficiencies. Photosynthesis—photochemical reactions, photophosphorylation and carbon fixation pathways; C_3, C_4 and CAM pathways; Mechanism of pholem transport, Respiration (anerobic and aerobic, including fermentation)—electron transport chain and oxidative phosphorylation; Photorespiration; Chemiosmotic theory and ATP synthesis; Lipid metabolism; Nitrogen fixation and nitrogen metabolism. Enzymes, coenzymes; Energy transfer and energy conservation. Importance of secondary metabolites. Pigments as photoreceptors (plastidial pigments and phytochrome). Plant movements; Photoperiodism and flowering, vernalization, senescence; Growth substances—their chemical nature, role and applications in agri-horticulture; growth indices, growth movements. Stress physiology (heat, water, salinity, metal); Fruit and seed physiology. Dormancy, storage and germination of seed. Fruit ripening—its molecular basis and manipulation.
5. **Ecology and Plant Geography:** Concept of ecosystem; Ecological factors. Concepts and dynamics of community; Plant succession. Concepts of biosphere; Ecosystems; Conservation; Pollution and its control (including phytoreme diation); Plant indicators; Environment (Protection) Act.

   Forest types of India—'Ecological and ecomomic importance of forests, afforestation, deforestation and social forestry; Endangered plants, endemism

IUCN categories, Red Data Books; Biodiversity and its conservation; Protected Area Network; Convention of Biological Diversity, Farmers' Rights; and Intellectual Property Rights; Concept of Sustainable Development; Biogeochemical cycles. Global warming and climatic change; Invasive species; Environmetal Impact Assessment; Phytogeographical regions of India.

5. CHEMISTRY

Paper-I

1. **Atomic Structure:** Heisenberg's uncertainty principle Schrodinger wave equation (time independent); Interpretation of wave function, particle in one-dimensional box, quantum numbers, hydrogen atom wave functions; Shapes of s, p and d orbitals.
2. **Chemical Bonding:** Ionic bond, characteristics of ionic compounds, lattice energy, Born-Haber cycle; covalent bond and its general characteristics, polarities of bonds in molecules and their dipole moments; Valence bond theory, concept of resonance and resonance energy; Molecular orbital theory (LCAO method); bonding H_2 +, H2 He_2 + to Ne_2, NO, CO, HF, CN^-, Comparison of valence bond and molecular orbital theories, bond order, bond strength and bond length.
3. **Solid State:** Crystal systems; Designation of crystal faces, lattice structures and unit cell; Bragg's law; X-ray diffraction by crystals; Close packing, radius ratio rules, calculation of some limiting radius ratio values; Structures of NaCl, ZnS, CsCl, CaF_2; Stoichiometric and nonstoichiometric defects, impurity defects, semi-conductors.
4. **The Gaseous State and Transport Phenomenon:** Equation of state for real gases, intermolecular interactions, and critical phenomena and liquefaction of gases; Maxwell's distribution of speeds, intermolecular collisions, collisions on the wall and effusion; Thermal conductivity and viscosity of ideal gases.
5. **Liquid State:** Kelvin equation; Surface tension and surface energy, wetting and contact angle, interfacial tension and capillary action.
6. **Thermodynamics:** Work, heat and internal energy; first law of thermodynamics. Second law of thermodynamics; entropy as a state function, entropy changes in various processes, entropy-reversibility and irreversibility, Free energy functions; Thermodynamic equation of state; Maxwell relations; Temperature, volume and pressure dependence of U, H, A, G, Cp and Cv, and ; J-T effect and inversion temperature; criteria for equilibrium, relation between equilibrium constant and thermodynamic quantities; Nernst heat theorem, introductory idea of third law of thermodynamics.
7. **Phase Equilibria and Solutions:** Clausius-Clapeyron equation; phase diagram for a pure substance; phase equilibria in binary systems, partially miscible liquids—upper and lower critical solution temperatures; partial molar

quantities, their significance and determination; excess thermodynamic functions and their determination.

8. **Electrochemistry:** Debye-Huckel theory of strong electrolytes and Debye-Huckel limiting Law for various equilibrium and transport properties.
   Galvanic cells, concentration cells; electrochemical series, measurement of e.m.f. of cells and its applications fuel cells and batteries.
   Processes at electrodes; double layer at the interface; rate of charge transfer, current density; overpotential; electroanalytical techniques: amperometry, ion selective electrodes and their use.
9. **Chemical Kinetics:** Differential and integral rate equations for zeroth, first, second and fractional order reactions; Rate equations involving reverse, parallel, consecutive and chain reactions; Branching chain and explosions; effect of temperature and pressure on rate constant. Study of fast reactions by stop-flow and relaxation methods. Collisions and transition state theories.
10. **Photochemistry:** Absorption of light; decay of excited state by different routes; photochemical reactions between hydrogen and halogens and their quantum yields.
11. **Surface Phenomena and Catalysis:** Adsorption from gases and solutions on solid adsorbents; Langmuir and B.E.T. adsorption isotherms; determination of surface area, characteristics and mechanism of reaction on heterogeneous catalysts.
12. **Bio-inorganic Chemistry:** Metal ions in biological systems and their role in ion-transport across the membranes (molecular mechanism), oxygen-uptake proteins, cytochromes and ferrodoxins.
13. **Coordination Chemistry:**
    (i) Bonding in transition of metal complexes. Valence bond theory, crystal field theory and its modifications; applications of theories in the explanation of magnetism and elctronic spectra of metal complexes.
    (ii) Isomerism in coordination compounds; IUPAC nomenclature of coordination compounds; stereochemistry of complexes with 4 and 6 coordination numbers; chelate effect and polynuclear complexes; trans effect and its theories; kinetics of substitution reactions in square-planar complexes; thermodynamic and kinetic stability of complexes.
    (iii) EAN rule, Synthesis structure and reactivity of metal carbonyls; carboxylate anions, carbonyl hydrides and metal nitrosyl compounds.
    (iv) Complexes with aromatic systems, synthesis, structure and bonding in metal olefin complexes, alkyne complexes and cyclopentadienyl complexes; coordinative unsaturation, oxidative addition reactions, insertion reactions, fluxional molecules and their characterization; Compounds with metal—metal bonds and metal atom clusters.

14. **Main Group Chemistry:** Boranes, borazines, phosphazenes and cyclic phosphazene, silicates and silicones, Interhalogen compounds; Sulphur—nitrogen compounds, noble gas compounds.
15. **General Chemistry of 'f ' Block Element:** Lanthanides and actinides: separation, oxidation states, magnetic and spectral properties; lanthanide contraction.

Paper-II

1. **Delocalised Covalent Bonding:** Aromaticity, anti-aromaticity; annulenes, azulenes, tropolones, fulvenes, sydnones.
2. (i) **Reaction mechanisms:** General methods (both kinetic and non-kinetic) of study of mechanisms or organic reactions: isotopies, mathod cross-over experiment, intermediate trapping, stereochemistry; energy of activation; thermodynamic control and kinetic control of reactions.

   (ii) **Reactive intermediates:** Generation, geometry, stability and reactions of carboniumions and carbanions, free radicals, carbenes, benzynes and nitrenes.

   (iii) **Substitution reactions:** S_N 1, S_N 2, and S_N i, mechanisms; neighbouring group participation; electrophilic and nucleophilic reactions of aromatic compounds including heterocyclic compounds—pyrrole, furan, thiophene and indole.

   (iv) **Elimination reactions:** E1, E2 and E1cb mechanisms; orientation in E2 reactions—Saytzeff and Hoffmann; pyrolytic *syn* elimination—acetate pyrolysis, Chugaev and Cope eliminations.

   (v) **Addition reactions:** Electrophilic addition to C=C and C C; nucleophilic addition to C=O, C N, conjugated olefins and carbonyls.

   (vi) **Reactions and Rearrangements**

   (a) Pinacol-pinacolone, Hoffmann, Beckmann, Baeyer-Villiger, Favorskii, Fries, Claisen, Cope, Stevens and Wagner—Meerwein rearrangements.

   (b) Aldol condensation, Claisen condensation, Dieckmann, Perkin, Knoevenagel, Witting, Clemmensen, Wolff-Kishner, Cannizzaro and von Richter reactions; Stobbe, benzoin and acyloin condensations; Fischer indole synthesis, Skraup synthesis, Bischler-Napieralski, Sandmeyer, Reimer-Tiemann and Reformatsky reactions.
3. **Pericyclic reactions:** Classification and examples; Woodward-Hoffmann rules—electrocyclic reactions, cycloaddition reactions [2+2 and 4+2] and sigmatropic shifts [1, 3; 3, 3 and 1, 5], FMO approach.
4. (i) **Preparation and Properties of Polymers:** Organic polymerspolyethylene, polystyrene, polyvinyl chloride, teflon, nylon, terylene, synthetic and natural rubber.

   (ii) **Biopolymers**: Structure of proteins, DNA and RNA.

5. **Synthetic Uses of Reagents:** OsO_4, HlO_4, CrO_3, $Pb(OAc)_4$, SeO_2, NBS, B_2H_6, Na-Liquid NH_3, $LiAIH_4$, $NaBH_4$, n-BuLi, MCPBA.
6. **Photochemistry:** Photochemical reactions of simple organic compounds, excited and ground states, singlet and triplet states, Norrish-Type I and Type II reactions.
7. **Spectroscopy:** Principle and applications in structure elucidation:
   (i) **Rotational:** Diatomic molecules; isotopic substitution and rotational constants.
   (ii) **Vibrational:** Diatomic molecules, linear triatomic molecules, specific frequencies of functional groups in polyatomic molecules.
   (iii) **Electronic:** Singlet and triplet states. ***n*** and transitions; application to conjugated double bonds and conjugated carbonyls Woodward-Fieser rules; Charge transfer spectra.
   (iv) **Nuclear Magnetic Resonance (^{1}HNMR):** Basic principle; chemical shift and spin-spin interaction and coupling constants.
   (v) **Mass Spectrometry:** Parent peak, base peak, metastable peak, McLafferty rearrangement.

6. CIVIL ENGINEERING

Paper-I

1. Engineering Mechanics, Strength of Materials and Structural Analysis.

1.1 **Engineering Mechanics:** Units and Dimensions, SI Units, Vectors, Concept of Force, Concept of particle and rigid body. Concurrent, Non-Concurrent and parallel forces in a plane, moment of force free body diagram, conditions of equilibrium, Principle of virtual work, equivalent force system.

First and Second Moment of area, Mass moment of Inertia. Static Friction.

Kinematics and Kinetics: Kinematics in cartesian co-ordinates, motion under uniform and non-uniform acceleration, motion under gravity. Kinetics of particle: Momentum and Energy principles, collision of elastic bodies, rotation of rigid bodies.

1.2 **Strength of Materials:** Simple Stress and Strain, Elastic constants, axially loaded compression members, Shear force and bending moment, theory of simple bending, Shear Stress distribution across cross sections, Beams of uniform strength.

Deflection of beams: Mecaulay's method, Mohr's Moment area method, Conjugate beam method, unit load method. Torsion of Shafts, Elastic stability of columns, Euler's, Rankine's and Secant formulae.

1.3 **Structural Analysis: Castiglianio's Theorems I and II,** unit load method, of consistent deformation applied to beams and pin jointed trusses. Slope-deflection, moment distribution.

Rolling Loads and Influences Lines: Influences lines for Shear Force and Bending moment at a section of a beam. Criteria for maximum shear force and bending moment in beams traversed by a system of moving loads. Influences lines for simply supported plane pin jointed trusses.

Arches: Three hinged, two hinged and fixed arches, rib shortening and temperature effects.

Matrix Mehods of Analysis: Force method and displacement method of analysis of indeterminate beams and rigid frames.

Plastic Analysis of Beams and Frames: Theory of plastic bending, plastic analysis, statical method, mechanism method.

Unsymmetrical bending: Moment of inertia, product of inertia, position of Neutral Axis and Principal axes, calculation of bending stresses.

2. **Design of Structures: Steel, Concrete and Masonry Structures.**

2.1 **Structural Steel Design: Structural Steel:** Factors of safety and load factors. Riveted, bolted and welded joints and connections. Design of tension and compression members, beams of built up section, riveted and welded plate girders, gantry girders, stancheons with battens and lacings.

2.2 **Design of Concrete and Masonry Structures:** Concept of mix design. Reinforced Concrete. Working Stress and Limit State method of design—Recommendations of I. S. codes. Design of one way and two way slabs, stair-case slabs, simple and continuous beams of rectangular, T and L sections. Compression members under direct load with or without eccentricity. Cantilever and Counter fort type retaining walls.

Water Tanks: Design requirements for Rectangular and circular tanks resting on ground. Prestressed Concrete: Methods and systems of prestressing, anchorages, Analysis and design of sections for flexure based on working stress, loss of prestress.

Design of brick masonry as per I. S. Codes

3. **Fluid Mechanics, Open Channel Flow and Hydraulic Machines**

3.1 **Fluid Mechanics:** Fluid properties and their role in fluid motion, fluid statics including forces acting on plane and curve surfaces.

Kinematics and Dynamics of Fluid flow: Velocity and accelerations, stream lines, equation of continuity, irrotational and rotational flow, velocity potential and stream functions.

Continuity, momentum, energy equation, Navier Stokes equation, Euler's equation of motion, application to fluid flow problems, pipe flow, sluice gates, weirs.

3.2 **Dimensional Analysis and Similitude:** Buckingham's Pi-theorem, dimensionless parameters.

3.3 **Laminar Flow:** Laminar flow between parallel, stationary and moving plates, flow through tube.

3.4 **Boundary Layer:** Laminar and turbulent boundary layer on a flat plate, laminar sub-layer, smooth and rough boundaries, drag and lift.

Turbulent Flow through Pipes: Characteristics of turbulent flow, velocity distribution and variation of pipe friction factor, hydraulic grade line and total energy line.

3.5 **Open Channel Flow:** Uniform and non-uniform flows, momentum and energy correction factors, specific energy and specific force, critical depth, rapidly varied flow, hydraulic jump, gradually varied flow, classification of surface profiles, control section, step method of integration of varied flow equation.

3.6 **Hydraulic Machines and Hydropower:** Hydraulic turbines, types classification, choice of turbines performance parameters, controls, characteristics, specific speed.
Principles of hydropower development.

4. **Geotechnical Engineering:** Soil Type and Structure—gradation and particle size distribution—consistency limits. Water in soil—capillary and structural—effective stress and pore water pressure—permeability concept—filed and laboratory determination of permeability—Seepage pressure—quick sand conditions—Shear strength determination—Mohr Coulomb concept.

Compaction of soil—Laboratory and filed test.

Compressibility and consolidation concept—consolidation theory—consolidation settlement analysis.

Earth pressure theory and analysis for retaining walls, Application for sheet piles and Braced excavation.

Bearing capacity of soil—approaches for analysis-Filed tests—settlement analysis—stability of slope of earth walk. Subsuface exploration of soils—methods

Foundation—Type and selection criteria for foundation of structures—Design criteria for foundation—Analysis of distribution of stress for footings and pile—pile group action—pile load test.

Ground improvement techniques.

Paper-II

1. **Construction Technology, Equipment, Planning and Management**

1.1 **Construction Technology: Engineering Materials:** Physical properties of construction materials with respect to their use in construction—Stones, Bricks and Tiles; Lime, Cement, different types of Mortars and Concrete.
Specific use of ferro cement, fibre reinforced C. C., High stength concrete.
Timber; Properties defects—common preservation treatments.
Use and selection of materials for specific use like Low Cost Housing, Mass Housing, High Rise Buildings.

1.2 **Construction:** Masonry principles using Brick, stone, Blocks—construction detailing and strength characteristics.
Types of plastering, pointing, flooring, roofing and construction features.
Common repairs in buildings.

Principle of functional planning of building for residents and specific use—Building code provisions.

Basic principles of detailed and approximate estimating—specification writing and rate analysis-principles of valuation of real property.

Machinery for earthwork, concreting and their specific uses—Factors affecting selection of equipments—operating cost of equipments.

1.3 **Construction Planning and Management:** Construction activity—schedules—organization for construction industry—Quality assurance principles.

Use Basic principle of network—analysis in form of CPM and PERT—their use in construction monitoring, Cost optimization and resource allocation.

Basic principles of Economic analysis and methods.

Project profitability—Basic principles of Boot approach to financial planning-simple toll fixation criterions.

2. **Surveying and Transportation Engineering**

2.1 **Surveying:** Common methods and instruments for distance and angle measurement for CE work—their use in plane table, traverse survey, levelling work, triangulation, contouring and topographical map.
Basic principles of photogrammetry and remote sensing.

2.2 **Railways Engineering:** Permanent way—components, types and their function-Functions and Design constituents of turn and crossing—Necessity of geometric design of track—Design of station and yards.

2.3 **Highway Engineering:** Principles of Highway alignments—classification and geometrical design elements and standards for Roads.

Pavement structure for flexible and rigid pavements—Design principles and methodology of pavements.

Typical construction methods and standards of materials for stabilized soil, WBM, Bituminous works and CC roads.

Surface and sub-surface drainge arrangements for roads—culvert structures. Pavement distresses and strengthening by overlays.

Traffic surveys and their application in traffic planning—Typical design features for channelized, intersection rotary etc.—signal designs—standard Traffic signs and markings.

3. Hydrology, Water Resources and Engineering

3.1 **Hydrology:** Hydrological cycle, precipitation, evaporation, transpiration, infiltration, overland flow, hydrograph, flood frequency analyses, flood routing through a reservoir, channel flow routing—Muskingam method.

3.2 **Ground Water Flow:** Specific yield, storage coefficient, coefficient of permeability, confined and unconfined aquifers, aquifers, aquitards, radial flow into a well under confined and unconfined conditions.

3.3 **Water Resources Engineering:** Ground and surface water resources, single and multipurpose projects, storage capacity of reservoirs, reservoir losses, reservoir sedimentation.

3.4 **Irrigation Engineering**

(i) **Water Requirements of Crops:** Consumptive use, duty and delta, irrigation methods and their efficiencies.

(ii) **Canals:** Distribution systems for cannal irrigation, canal capacity, canal losses, alignment of main and distributory canals, most efficient section, lined canals, their design, regime theory, critical shear stress, bed load.

(iii) **Water Logging:** causes and control, salinity.

(iv) **Canal Structures:** Design of head regulators, canal falls, aqueducts, metering flumes and canal outlets.

(v) **Diversion Head Work:** Principles and design of weirs on permeable and impermeable foundation, Khosla's theory, energy dissipation.

(vi) **Storage Works:** Types of dams, design, principles of rigid gravity stability analysis.

(vii) **Spillways:** Spillway types, energy dissipation.

(viii) **River Training:** Objectives of river training, methods of river training.

4. **Environmental Engineering**

4.1 **Water Supply:** Predicting demand for water, impurities of water and their significance, physical, chemical and bacteriological analysis, waterborne diseases, standards for potable water.

4.2 **Intake of Water: Water treatment**- principles of coagulation, flocculation and sedimentation; slow-, rapid-, pressure-, filters; chlorination, softening, removal of taste, odour and salinity.

4.3 **Sewerage Systems:** Domestic and industrial wastes, store sewage—separate and combined systems, flow through sewers, design of sewers.

4.4 **Sewage Characterisation:** BOD, COD, solids, dissolved oxygen, nitrogen and TOC. Standards of disposal in normal water course and on land.

4.5 **Sewage Treatment:** Working principles, units, chambers, sedimentation tank, trickling filters, oxidation ponds, activated sludge process, septic tank, disposal of sludge, recycling of waste water.

4.6 **Solid Waste:** Collection and disposal in rural and urban contexts, management of long-term ill-effects.

5. **Environmental Pollution:** Sustainable development. Radioactive wastes and disposal. Environmental impact assessment for thermal power plants, mines, river valley projects. Air pollution. Pollution control acts.

7. COMMERCE AND ACCOUNTANCY

Paper-I

Accounting, Finance, Taxation & Auditing

1. **Financing Accounting:** Accounting as a financial information system; Impact of behavioural sciences. Accounting Standards e.g., Accounting for Depreciation, Inventories, Research and Development Costs, Long-term Construction Contracts, Revenue Recognition, Fixed Assets, Contingencies, Foreign Exchange Transactions, Investments and Government Grants, Cash Flow Statement, Earnings per Share. Accounting for Share Capital Transactions including Bonus Shares, Right Shares. Emplyees Stock Option and Buy-Back of Securities.

   Preparation and Presentation of Company Final Accounts. Amalgamations, Absorption and Reconstruction of Companies.

2. **Cost Accounting:** Nature and functions of cost accounting. Installation of Cost Accounting System. Cost Concepts related to Income Measurement, Profit Planning, Cost Control and Decision Making. Methods of Costing: Job Costing, Process Costing, Activity Based Costing. Volume-cost-Profit Relationship as a tool of Profit Planning. Incremental Analysis/Differential Costing as a Tool of Pricing Decisions, Product Decisions, Make or Buy Decisions, Shut-Down Decisions etc. Techniques of Cost Control and Cost Reduction: Budgeting as a Tool of Planning and Control. Standard Costing and Variance Analysis. Responsibility Accounting and Divisional Performance Measurement.

3. **Taxation**

   Income Tax: Definitions. Basis of charge; Incomes which do not form part of total income. Simple problems of Computation of Income (of individuals only) under various heads, i.e., Salaries, Income from House Property, Profits and Gains from Business or Profession, Capital Gains, Income from other sources, Income of other Persons included in Assessee's Total Income.

   Set-off and Carry forward of Loss. Deductions from Gross Total Income.

   Salient Features/Provisions Related to VAT and Services Tax.

4. **Auditing**

   Company Audit: Audit related to Divisible Profits, Dividends, Special investigations, Tax audit. Audit of Banking, Insurance, Non-Profit Organization and Charitable Societies/Trusts/Organizations.

Financial Management, Financial Institutions and Markets

1. **Financial Management**

   Finance Function: Nature, Scope and Objectives of Financial Management: Risk and Return Relationship.

Tools of Financial Analysis: Ratio Analysis, Funds-Flow and Cash-Flow Statement.
Capital Budgeting Decisions: Process, Procedures and Appraisal Methods. Risk and Uncertainty Anlysis and Methods.
Cost of Capital: Concept, Computation of Specific Costs and Weighted Average Cost of Capital. CAPM as a Tool of Determining Cost of Equity Capital.
Financing Decisions: Theories of Capital Structure—Net Income (NI) Approach. Net Operating Income (NOI) Approach, MM Approach and Traditional Approach.
Designing of Capital structure: Types of Leverages (Operating, Financial and Combined), EBIT-EPS Analysis, and other Factors.
Dividend Decisions and Valuation of Firm: Walter's Model, MM Thesis, Gordan's Model Lintner's Model. Factors Affecting Dividend Policy.
Working Capital Management: Planning of Working Capital. Determinants of Working Capital. Components of Working Capital—Cash, Inventory and Receivables. Corporate Restructuring with focus on Mergers and Acquisitions (Financial aspect only).

2. **Financial Markets and Institutions**
Indian Financial System: An Overview
Money Markets: Participants, Structure and Instruments. Commercial Banks. Reforms in Banking Sector. Monetary and Credit Policy of RBI. RBI as a Regulator.
Capital Market: Primary and Secondary Market. Financial Market Instruments and Innovative Debt Instruments; SEBI as a Regulator.
Financial Services: Mutual Funds, Venture Capital, Credit Rating Agencies, Insurance and IRDA.

Paper-II

Organisation Theory and Behaviours, Human Resource Management and Industrial Relations

Organisation Theory and Behaviour

1. **Organisation Theory:** Nature and Concept of Organisation; External Environment of Organisation—Technological, Social, Political, Ecomomical and Legal; Organizational Goals Primary and Secondary Goals, Single and Multiple Goals; Management by Objectives.
Evolution of Organisation Theory: Classical Neo-classical and system approach. Modern Concepts of Organisation Theory: Organisational Design, Organisational Structure and Organisational Culture.
Organisational Design: Basic Challenges; Differentiation and Intergration Process; Centralization and Decentralization Process; Standardization/ Formalization and Mutual Adjustment. Coordinating Formal and Informal Organizations. Mechanistic and Organic Structures.

Designing Organizational Structures: Authority and Control; Line and Staff Functions, Specialization and Coordination. Types of Organization Structure—Functional. Matrix Structure, Project Structure. Nature and Basis of Power, Sources of Power, Power Structure and Politics. Impact of Information Technology on Organizational Design and Structure. Managing Organizational Culture.

2. **Organisation Behaviour:** Meaning and Concept; Individual in organization; Personality, Theories, and Determinants; Pereception Meaning and Process.

   Motivation: Concepts, Theories and Applications. Leadership—Theories and Styles. Quality of Work Life (QWL): Meaning and its impact on Performance, Ways of its Enhancement. Quality Circles (QC)—Meaning and their Importance. Management of Conflicts in Organizations. Transactional Analysis, Organizational Effectiveness, Management of Change.

Human Resources Management and Industrial Relations

1. **Human Resources Management (HRM):** Meaning Nature and Scope of HRM, Human Resource Planning, Job Analysis, Job Description, Job Specification, Recruitment Process, Selection Process, Orientational and Placement, Training and Development Process, Performance Appraisal and 360° Feed Back, Salary and Wage Administration, Job Evaluation, Employee Welfare, Promotions, Transfers and Separations.
2. **Industrial Relations (IR):** Meaning, Nature, Importance and Scope of IR, Formation of Trade Union, Trade Union Legislation, Trade Union Movement in India. Recognition of Trade Unions, Problems of Trade Unions in India. Impact of Liberalization on Trade Union Movement.

   Nature of Industrial Disputes: Strikes and Lockouts, Causes of Disputes, Prevention and Settlement of Disputes.

   Worker's Participation in Management: Philosophy, Rationale, Present Day Status and Future Prospects. Adjudication and Collective Bargaining. Industrial Relations in Public Enterprises Absenteeism and Labour Turnover in Indian Industries and their Causes and Remedies. ILO and its Functions.

8. ECONOMICS

Paper-I

1. **Advanced Micro Economics:**
   (a) Marshallian and Varrasiam Approaches to Price determination.
   (b) Alternative Distribution Theories; Ricardo, Kaldor, Kaleeki.
   (c) **Markets Structure:** Monopolistic Competition, Duopoly, Oligopoly.
   (d) **Modern Welfare Criteria:** Pareto Hicks and Scitovsky, Arrow's Impossibility Theorem, A. K. Sen's Social Welfare Function.

2. **Advance Macro Economics:** Approaches to Employment Income and Interest Rate determination: Classical, Keynes (IS)-LM) curve, Neo-classical synthesis and New classical, Theories of Interest Rate determination and Interest Rate Structure.
3. **Money-Banking and Finance**
   (a) **Demand for and Supply of Money:** Money Multiplier Quantity Theory of Money (Fisher, Pique and Friedman) and Keyne's Theory on Demand for Money, Goals and Instruments of Monetary Management in Closed and Open Economies. Relation between the Central Bank and the Treasury. Proposal for ceiling on growth rate of money.
   (b) **Public Finance and Its Role in Market Economy:** In stabilisation of supply, allocative, of resources and in distribution and development. Sources of Government revenue, forms of Taxes and Subsidies, their incidence and effects. Limits to taxation, loans, crowding-out effects and limits to borrowings. Public expenditure and its effects.
4. International Economics
   (a) Old and New theories of International Trade.
      (i) Comparative advantage.
      (ii) Terms of Trade and Offer Curve.
      (iii) Product Cycle and Strategic Trade Theories.
      (iv) Trade as an engine of growth and theories of underdevelopment in an open economy.
   (b) Forms of Protection: Tariff and quota.
   (c) Balance of Payments Adjustment: Alternative Approaches.
      (i) Price versus income, income adjustments under fixed exchange rates.
      (ii) Theories of Policy Mix.
      (iii) Exchange rate adjustments under capital mobility.
      (iv) Floating Rates and their Implications for Developing Countries: Currency Boards.
      (v) Trade Policy and Developing Countries.
      (vi) BOP, adjustments and Policy Coordination in open economy macro model.
      (vii) Speculative attacks.
      (viii) Trade Blocks and Monetary Unions.
      (ix) WTO: TRIMS, TRIPS, Domestic Measures, Different Rounds of WTO talks.
5. **Growth and Development**
   (a) (i) Theories of growth: Harrod's model;
      (ii) Lewis model of development with surplus labour.
      (iii) Balanced Unbalanced Growth.
      (iv) Human Capitals and Economic Growth.
      (v) Research and Development and Economic Growth.

(b) Process of Economic Development of less developed countries; Myrdal and Kuzments on economic development and structural change; Role of Agriculture in Economic Development of less developed countries.

(c) Economic Development and International Trade and Investment, Role of Multinationals.

(d) Planning and Economic Development; changing role of Markets and Planning, Private-Public Partnership.

(e) Welfare indicators and measures of growth—Human Development Indices. The basic needs approach.

(f) Development and Environmental Sustainability—Renewable and Non-renewable Resources, Environmental Degradation, Intergenerational equity development.

Paper-II

Indian Economics in Post-Independence Era

Land System and its changes, commercialization of agriculture Drain theory, Laissez faire theory and critique.

Manufacture and Transport: Jute, Cotton, Railways, Money and Credit.

Indian Economy after Independence

A. The Pre-Liberalization Era

(i) Contribution of Vakil, Gadgil and V.K.R.V. Rao.

(ii) Agricultrure: Land Reforms and land tenure system, Green Revolution and capital formation in agriculture.

(iii) Industry Trends in composition and growth, Role of public and private sector, small scale and cottage industries.

(iv) National and Per capita income: Patterns, trends, aggregate and sectoral composition and changes therein.

(v) Broad factors determining National Income and distribution, Measures of poverty, Trends in poverty and inequality.

B. The Post-Liberalization Era

(i) New Economic Reform and Agriculture: Agriculture and WTO, Food processing, subsidies, Agricultural prices and public distribution system, Impact of public expenditure on agricultural growth.

(ii) New Economic Policy and Industry: Strategy of industrialization, Privatization, Disinvestments, Role of foreign direct investment and multinationals.

(iii) New Economic Policy and Trade: Intellectual property rights: Implications of TRIPS, TRIMS, GATS and new EXIM policy.

(iv) New Exchange Rate Regime: Partial and full convertibility, Capital account convertibility.

(v) New Economic Policy and Public Finance: Fiscal Responsibility Act, Twelfth Finance Commission and Fiscal Federalism and Fiscal Consolidation.

(vi) New Economic Policy and Monetary System. Role of RBI under the new regime.

(vii) Planning: From central Planning to indivative planning, Relation between planning and markets for growth and decentralized planning: 73rd and 74th Constitutional amendments.

(viii) New Economic Policy and Employment: Employment and poverty, Rural wages, Employment Generation, Poverty alleviation schemes, New Rural, Employment Guarantee Scheme.

9. ELECTRICAL ENGINEERING

Paper-I

1. **Circuits—Theory:** Circuit components; network graphs; KCL, KVL; Circuit analysis methods: nodal analysis, mesh analysis; basic network theorems and applications; transient analysis: RL, RC and RLC circuits; sinusoidal steady state analysis; resonant circuits; coupled circuits; balanced 3-phase circuits. Two-port networks.
2. **Signals and Systems:** Representation of continuous-time and discrete-time signals and systems; LTI systems; convolution; impulse response; time-domain analysis of LTI systems based on convolution and differential/difference equations. Fourier transform, Laplace transform, Z-transform, Transfer function. Sampling and recovery of signals DFT, FFT Processing of analog signals through discrete-time systems.
3. **E.M. Theory**: Maxwell's equations, wave propagation in bounded media. Boundary conditions, reflection and refraction of plane waves. Transmission lines: travelling and standing waves, impedance matching, Smith chart.
4. **Analog Electronics:** Characteristics and equivalent circuits (large and small-signal) of Diode, BJT, JFET and MOSFET. Diode circuits: Clipping, clamping, rectifier. Biasing and bias stability. FET amplifiers. Current mirror; Amplifiers: single and multi-stage, differential, operational feedback and power. Analysis of amplifiers; frequency-response of amplifiers. OPAMP circuits. Filters; sinusoidal oscillators: criterion for oscillation; single-transistor and OPAMP configurations. Function generators and wave-shaping circuits. Linear and switching power supplies.
5. **Digital Electronics:** Boolean algebra; minimisation of Boolean functions; logic gates; digital IC families (DTL, TTL, ECL, MOS, CMOS). Combinational circuits: arithmetic circuits, code converters, multiplexers and decoders. Sequential circuits: latches and flip-flops, counters and shift-registers.

Comparators, timers, multivibrators. Sample and hold circuits, ADCs and DACs. Semiconductor memories. Logic implementation using programmable devices (ROM, PLA, FPGA).

6. **Energy Conversion:** Principles of electromechanical energy conversion: Torque and emf in rotating machines. DC machines: characteristics and performance analysis; starting and speed control of motors. Transformers: principles of operation and analysis; regulation, efficiency; 3-phase transformers. 3-phase induction machines and synchronous machines: characteristics and performance analysis; speed control.
7. **Power Electronics and Electric Drives:** Semi-conductor power devices: diode, transistor, thyristor, triac, GTO and MOSFET-static characteristics and principles of operation; triggering circuits; phase control rectifiers; bridge converters: fully-controlled and half-controlled; principles of thyristor choppers and inverters; DC-DC converters; Switch mode inverter; basic concepts of speed control of dc and ac motor drives applications of variable-speed drives.
8. **Analog Communication:** Random variables: continuous, discrete; probability, probability functions. Statistical averages; probability models; Random signals and noise; white noise, noise equivalent bandwidth; signal transmission with noise; signal to noise ratio. Linear CW modulation; Amplitude modulation; DSB, DSB-SC and SSB. Modulators and Demodulators; Phase and Frequency modulation; PM & FM signals; narrows band FM; generation & detection of FM and PM, Deemphasis, Preemphasis. CW modulation system; Superhetrodyne receivers, AM receivers, communication receivers, FM receivers, phase locked loop, SSB receiver Signal to noise ratio calculation or AM and FM receivers.

Paper-II

1. **Control Systems:** Elements of control systems; block-diagram representations; open-loop & closed-loop systems; principles and applications of feed-back. Control system components. LTI systems: time-domain and transform-domain analysis. Stability: Routh Hurwitz criterion, root-loci, Bode-plots and polor plots, Nyquist's criterion; Design of lead-lad compensators. Proportional, PI, PID controllers. State-variable representation and analysis of control systems.
2. **Microprocessors and Microcomputers:** PC organisation; CPU, instruction set, register settiming diagram, programming, interrupts, memory interfacing, I/O interfacing, programmable peripheral devices.
3. **Measurement and Instrumentation:** Error analysis; measurement of current voltage, power, energy, power-factor, resistance, inductance, capacitance and frequency; bridge measurements. Signal conditioning circuit; Electronic measuring instruments: multimeter, CRO, digital voltmeter, frequency counter, Q-meter, spectrum-analyser, distoration-meter. Transducers: thermocouple, thermistor, LVDT, strain-guage, piezo-electric crystal.

4. **Power Systems: Analysis and Control:** Steady-state performance of overhead transmission lines and cables; principles of active and reactive power transfer and distribution; per-unit quantities; bus admittance and impedance matrices; load flow; voltage control and power factor correction; economic operation; symmetrical components, analysis of symmetrical and unsymmetrical faults. Concepts of system stability: swing curves and equal area criterion. Static VAR system. Basic concepts of HVDC transmission.
5. **Power System Protection:** Principles of overcurrent, differential and distance protection. Concept of solid state relays. Circuit brakers. Computer aided protection, introduction; line, bus, generator, transformer protection; numeric relays and application of DSP to protection.
6. **Digital Communication:** Pulse code modulation (PCM), defferential pulse code modulation (DPCM), delta modulation (DM), Digital modulation and demodulation schemes: amplitude, phase and frequency keying schemes (ASK, PSK, FSK). Error control coding: error detection and correction, linear block codes, convolation codes. Information measure and source coding. Data networks, 7-layer architecture.

10. GEOGRAPHY

Paper-I: Principles of Geography

Physical Geography

1. **Geomorphology:** Factors controlling landform development; endogenetic and exogenetic forces; Origin and evolution of the Earth's crusts; Fundamentals of geomagnetism; Physical conditions of the earth's interior; Geosynclines; Continental drift; Isostasy; Plate tectonics; Recent views on mountain building; Volcanicity; Earthquakes and Tsunamis; Concepts of geomorphic cycles and Land scape development; Denudation chronology; Channel morphology; Erosion surfaces; Slope development; Applied Geomorphology; Geomorphology, economic geology and environment.
2. **Climatology:** Temperature and pressure belts of the world; Heat budget of the Earth; Atmospheric circulation; Atmospheric stability and instability. Planetary and local winds; Monsoons and jet streams; Air masses and fronto; Temperate and tropical cyclones; Types and distribution of precipitation; Weather and Climate; Koppen's Thornthwaite's and Trewar Tha's classification of world climate; Hydrological cycle; Global climatic change, and role and response of man in climatic changes Applied climatology and Urban climate.
3. **Oceanography:** Bottom topography of the Atlantic, Indian and Pacific Oceans; Temperature and salinity of the oceans; Heat and salt budgets, Ocean deposits; Waves, currents and tides; Marine resources; biotic, mineral and energy resources; Coral reefs coral bleaching; Sea-level changes; Law of the sea and marine pollution.

4. **Biogeography:** Genesis of soils; Classification and distribution of soils; Soil profile; Soil erosion, Degradation and conservation; Factors influencing world distribution of plants and animals; Problems of deforestation and conservation measures; Social forestry, agro-forestry; Wild life; Major gene pool centres.
5. **Environmental Geography:** Principle ecology; Human ecological adaptations; Influence of man on ecology and environment; Global and regional ecological changes and imbalances; Ecosystem their management and conservation; Environmental degradation, management and conservation; Biodiversity and sustainable development; Environmental policy; Environmental hazards and remedial measures; Environmental education and legislation.

Human Geography

1. **Perspectives in Human Geography:** Areal differentiation; Regional synthesis; Dichotomy and dualism; Environmentalism; Quantitative revolution and locational analysis; Radical, behavioural, human and welfare approaches; Languages, religions and secularisation; Cultural regions of the world; Human development index.
2. **Economic Geography:** World economic development: measurement and problems; World resources and their distribution; Energy crisis; the limits to growth; World agriculture: typology of agricultural regions; Agricultural inputs and productivity; Food and nutritions problems; Food security; famine: causes, effects and remedies; World industries: location patterns and problems; Patterns of world trade.
3. **Population and Settlement Geography:** Growth and distribution of world population; Demographic attributes; Causes and consequences of migration; Concepts of over-under-and optimum population; Population theories, world population problems and policies, Social well-being and quality of life; Population as social capital. Types and patterns of rural settlements; Environmental issues in rural settlements; Hierarchy of urban settlements; Urban morphology; Concept of primate city and rank-size rule; Functional classification of towns; Sphere of urban influence; Rural-urban fringe; Satellite towns; Problems and remedies of urbanization; Sustainable development of cities.
4. **Regional Planning:** Concept of a region; Types of regions and methods of regionalisation; Growth centres and growth poles; Regional imbalances; Regional development strategies; Environmental issues in regional planning; Planning for sustainable development.
5. **Models, Theories and Laws in Human Geography:** System analysis in Human geography; Malthusian, Marxian and demographic transition models; Central Place theories of Christaller and Losch; Perroux and Boudeville; Von Thunen's model of agricultural location; Weber's model of industrial location; Ostov's model of stages of growth. Heart-land and Rimland theories; Laws of international boundaries and frontiers.

Paper-II: Geography of India

1. **Physical Setting:** Space relationship of India with neighbouring countries; Structure and relief; Drainage system and watersheds; Physiographic regions; Mechanism of Indian monsoons and rainfall patterns; Tropical cyclones and western disturbances; Floods and droughts; Climatic regions; Natural vegetation, Soil types and their distributions.
2. **Resources:** Land, surface and ground water, energy, minerals, biotic and marine resources, Forest and wild life resources and their conservation; Energy crisis.
3. **Agriculture:** Infrastructure: irrigation, seeds, fertilizers, power; Institutional factors; land holdings, land tenure and land reforms; Cropping pattern, agricultural productivity, agricultural intensity, crop combination, land capability; Agro and social-forestry; Green revolution and its socio-economic and ecological implications; Significance of dry farming; Livestock resources and white revolution; Aqua-culture; Sericulture, Agriculture and poultry; Agricultural regionalisation; Agro-climatic zones; Agro-ecological regions.
4. **Industry:** Evolution of industries; Locational factors of cotton, jute, textile, iron and steel, aluminium, fertiliser, paper, chemical and pharmaceutical, automobile, cottage and ago-based industries; Industrial houses and complexes including public sector underkings; Industrial regionalisation; New industrial policy; Multinationals and liberalisation; Special Economic Zones; Tourism including ecotourism.
5. **Transport, Communication and Trade:** Road, railway, waterway, airway and pipeline networks and their complementary roles in regional development; Growing importance of ports on national and foreign trade; Trade balance; Trade Policy; Export processing zones; Developments in communication and information technology and their impacts on economy and society; Indian space programme.
6. **Cultural Setting:** Historical Perspective of Indian Society; Racial linguistic and ethnic diversities; religious minorities; Major tribes, tribal areas and their problems; Cultural regions; Growth, distribution and density of population; Demographic attributes: sex-ratio, age structure, literacy rate, work-force, dependency ratio, longevity; migration (inter-regional, interaregional and international) and associated problems; Population problems and policies; Health indicators.
7. **Settlements:** Types, patterns and morphology of rural settlements; Urban developments; Morphology of Indian cities; Functional classification of Indian cities; Conurbations and metropolitan regions; Urban sprawl; Slums and asssociated problems; Town planning; Problems of urbanisation and remedies.
8. **Regional Development and Planning:** Experience of regional planning in India; Five Year Plans; Integrated rural development programmes; Panchayati

Raj and decentralised planning; Command area development; Watershed management; Planning for backward area, desert, drought-prone, hill tribal area development; Multi-level planning; Regional planning and development of island territories.

9. **Political Aspects:** Geographical basis of Indian federalism; State reorganisation; Emergence of new states; Regional consciousness and inter-state issues; International boundary of India and related issues; Cross-border terrorism; India's role in world affairs; Geopolitics of South Asia and Indian Ocean realm.
10. **Contemporary Issues:** Ecological issues: Environmental hazards: landslides, Earthquakes, Tsunamis, floods and droughts, epidemics; Issues related to environmental pollution; Changes in patterns of land use; Principles of environmental impact assessment and environmental management; Population explosion and food security; Environmental degradation; Deforestation, desertification and soil erosion; Problems of agrarian and industrial unrest; Regional disparities in economic development; Concept of sustainable growth and development; Environmental awareness; Linkage of rivers; Globalisation and Indian economy.

    Note: Candidates will be required to answer one compulsory map question pertinent to subjects covered by this paper.

11. GEOLOGY

Paper-I

1. **General Geology:** The Solar System, meteorites, origin and interior of the Earth and age of Earth; Volcanoes—causes and products, Volcanic belts. Earthquakes—causes, effects, seismic of zone of India; Island arcs, trenches and mid-ocean ridges; Continental drift; Seafloor spreading, plate tectonics. Isostasy.
2. **Geomorphology and Remote Sensing:** Basic concepts of geomorphology. Weathering and soil formations; Landforms, slopes and drainage. Geomorphic cycles and their interpretation. Morphology and its relation to structures and lithology; Coastal geomorphology; Applications of geomorphology in mineral prospecting, civil engineering; hydrology and environmental studies; Geomorphology of Indian sub-continent.

    Aerial photographs and their interpretation—merits and limitations; The Electromagnetic spectrum. Orbiting Satellites and Sensor Systems. Indian Remote Sensing Satellites. Satellite data products; Applications of remote sensing in geology; The Geographic Information System (GIS) and Global Positioning System (GPS)—its applications.
3. **Structural Geology:** Principles of geologic mapping and map reading, projection diagrams, Stress and strain ellipsoid and stress-strain relationships

of elastic, plastic and viscous materials; Strain markers in deformed rocks. Behaviour of minerals and rocks under deformation conditions. Folds and faults classification and mechanics; Structural analysis of folds, foliations, lineations, joints and faults, unconformities; Time-relationship between crystallization and deformation.

4. **Paleontology:** Species—definition and nomenclature; Megafossils and Microfossils. Modes of preservation of fossils; Different kinds of microfossils; Application of microfossils in correlation, petroleum exploration, paleoclimatic and paleoceanographic studies; Evolutionary trend in Hominidae, Equidae and Proboscidae. Siwalik fauna. Gondwana flora and fauna and its importance; Index fossils and their significance.
5. **Indian Stratigraphy:** Classification of stratigraphic sequences: lithostratigraphic, biostratigraphic, chrono-stratigraphic and magnetostratigraphic and their interrelationships; Distribution and classification of Precambrian rocks of India; Study of stratigraphic distribution and lithology of Phanerozoic rocks of India with reference to fauna, flora and economic importance. Major boundary problems—Cambrian/Precambrian, Permian/Triassic, Cretaceous/Tertiary and Pliocene/Pleistocene; Study of climatic conditions, paleogeography and igneous activity in the Indian sub-continent in the geological past. Tectonic framework of India. Evolution of the Himalayas.
6. **Hydrogeology and Engineering Geology:** Hydrologic cycle and genetic classification of water; Movement of subsurface water; Springs; Porosity, permeability, hydraulic conductivity, transmissivity and storage coefficient, classification of aquifers; Water-bearing characteristics of rocks; Groundwater chemistry. Salt water intrusion. Types of wells. Drainage basin morphometry; Exploration for groundwater; Groundwater recharge; Problems and management of groundwater; Rainwater harvesting; Engineering properties of rocks; Geological investigations for dams, tunnels highways, railway and bridges; Rock as construction material; Landslides causes, prevention and rehabilitation; Earthquake-resistant structures.

Paper-II

1. **Mineralogy:** Classification of crystals into systems and classes of symmetry; International system of crystallographic notation; Use of projection diagrams to represent crystal symmetry; Elements of X-ray crystallography. Physical and chemical characters of rock forming silicate mineral groups; Structural classification of silicates; Common minerals of igneous and metamorphic rocks; Minerals of the carbonate, phosphate, sulphide and halide groups; Clay minerals. Optical properties of common rock forming minerals; Pleochroism, extinction angle, double refraction, birefringence, twinning and dispersion in minerals.

2. **Igneous and Metamorphic Petrology:** Generation and crystallisation of magmas. Crystallisation of albite—anorthite, diopside—anorthite and diopside—wollastonite—silica systems. Bowen's Reaction Principle; Magmatic differentiation and assimilation. Petrogenetic significance of the textures and structures of igneous rocks. Petrography and petrogenesis of granite, syenite, diorite, basic and ultrabasic groups, charnockite, anorthosite and alkaline rocks. Carbonatites. Deccan volcanic province.

   Types and agents of metamorphism. Metamorphic grades and zones; Phase rule. Facies of regional and contact metamorphism; ACF and AKF diagrams; Textures and structures of metamorphic rocks. Metamorphism of arenaceous, argillaceous and basic rocks; Minerals assemblages. Retrograde metamorphism; Metasomatism and granitisation, migmatites. Granulite terrains of India.

3. **Sedimenary Petrology:** Sedimentas and Sedimentary rocks: Processes of formation; digenesis and lithification; Clastic and non-clastic rocks-their classification, petrography and depositional environment; Sedimentary facies and provenance. Sedimentary structures and their significance. Heavy minerals and their significance. Sedimentary basins of India.

4. **Economic Geology:** Ore, ore mineral and gangue, tenor of ore. Classification of ore deposits; Processes of formation of mineral deposits; Controls of ore localisation; Ore texures and structures; Metallogenic epochs and provinces; Geology of the important Indian deposits of aluminium, chromium, copper, gold, iron, lead, zinc, manganese, titanium, uranium and thorium and industrial minerals; Deposits of coal and petroleum in India, National Mineral Policy; Conservation and utilization of mineral resources. Marine mineral resources and Law of Sea.

5. **Mining Geology:** Methods of prospecting—geological, geophysical, geochemical and geobotanical; Techniques of sampling. Estimation of reserves of ore; Methods of exploration and mining-metallic ores, industrial minerals, marine mineral resources and building stones. Mineral beneficiation and ore dressing.

6. **Geochemistry and Environmental Geology:** Cosmic abundance of elements. Composition of the planets and meteorites. Structure and composition of Earth and distribution of elements. Trace elements. Elements of crystal chemistry-types of chemical bonds, coordination number. Isomorphism and polymorphism. Elementary thermodynamics.

   Natural hazards—floods, mass wasting, costal hazards, earthquakes and volcanic activity and mitigation; Environmental impact of urbanization, mining, industrial and radioactive waste disposal, use of fertilizers, dumping of mine waste and fly-ash. Pollution of ground and surface water, marine pollution. Environment protection—legislative measures in India; Sea level changes: causes and impact.

12. HISTORY

Paper-I

1. **Sources**
   Archaeological Sources: Exploration, excavation, epigraphy, numismatics, monuments.
   Literary Sources: Indigenous: Primary and secondary; poetry, scientific literature, literature, literature in regional languages, religious literature.
   Foreign Account: Greek, Chinese and Arab writers.
2. **Pre-history and Proto-history:** Geographical factors; hunting and gathering (paleolithic and mesolithic); Beginning of agriculture (neolithic and chalcolithic).
3. **Indus Valley Civilization**: Origin, date, extent, characteristics-decline, survival and significance, art and architecture.
4. **Megalithic Cultures:** Distribution of pastoral and farming cultures outside the Indus, Development of community life, Settlements, Development of agriculture, Crafts, Pottery, and Iron industry.
5. **Aryans and Vedic Period:** Expansions of Aryans in India: Vedic Period: Religious and philosophic literature; Transformation from Rig Vedic period to the later Vedic period; Political, social and economical life; Significance of the Vedic Age; Evolution of Monarchy and Varna system.
6. **Period of Mahajanapadas:** Formation of States (Mahajanapada): Republics and monarchies; Rise of urban centres; Trade routes; Economic growth; Introduction of coinage; Spread of Jainism and Buddism; Rise of Magadha and Nandas. Iranian and Mecedonian invasions and their impact.
7. **Mauryan Empire:** Foundation of the Mauryan Empire, Chandragupta, Kautilya and Arthashastra; Ashoka; Concept of Dharma; Edicts; Polity, Administration, Economy; Art, architecture and sculpture; External contacts; Religion; Spread of religion; Literature. Disintegration of the empire; sungas and Kanvas.
8. **Post-Mauryan Period (Indo-Greeks, Sakas, Kushanas, Western Kshatrapas):** Contact with outside world; growth of urban centres, economy, coinage, development of religions, Mahayana, social conditions, art, architecture, culture, literature and science.
9. **Early State and Society in Eastern India, Deccan and South India**: Kharavela, The Satavahanas, Tamil States of the Sangam Age; Administration, Economy, land grants, coinage, trade guilds and urban centres; Buddhist centres; Sangam literature and culture; Art and architecture.
10. **Guptas, Vakatakas and Vardhanas:** Polity and administration, Economic conditions, Coinage of the Guptas, Land grants, Decline of urban centres, Indian feudalism, Caste system, Position of women, Education and educational institutions; Nalanda, Vikramshila and Vallabhi, Literature, scientific literature, art and architecture.

11. **Regional States during Gupta Era:** The Kadambas, Pallavas, Chalukyas of Badami; Polity and Administration, Trade guilds, Literature; growth of Vaishnava and Saiva religions. Tamil Bhakit movement, Shankaracharya; Vedanta; Institutions of temple and temple architecture; Palas, Senas, Rashtrakutas, Paramaras, Polity and administration; Cultural aspects. Arab conquest of Sind; Alberuni, The Chaluky as of Kalyana, Cholas, Hoysalas, Pandyas; Polity and Administration; Local Government; Growth of art and architecture, religious sects, Institution of temple and Mathas, Agraharas, education and literature, economy and society.
12. **Themes in Early Indian Cultural History:** Languages and texts, major stages in the evolution of art and architecture, major philosophical thinkers and schools, ideas in Science and Mathematics.
13. Early Medieval India, 750-1200
    - Polity: Major political developments in Northern India and the peninsula, origin and the rise of Rajputs.
    - The Cholas: administration, village economy and society "Indian Feudalism".
    - Agrarian economy and urban settlements.
    - Trade and commerce.
    - Society: The status of the Brahman and the new social order.
    - Condition of women.
    - Indian science and technology.
14. **Cultural Traditions in India, 750-1200: Philosophy:** Skankaracharya and Vedanta, Ramanuja and Vishishtadvaita, Madhva and Brahma-Mimansa.
    Religion: Forms and features of religion, Tamil devotional cult, growth of Bhakti, Islam and its arrival in India, Sufism.
    Literature: Literature in Sanskrit, growth of Tamil literature, literature in the newly developing languages, Kalhan's Rajtarangini, Alberuni's India.
    Art and Architecture: Temple architecture, sculpture, painting.
15. **The Thirteenth Century:** Establishment of the Delhi Sultanate: The Ghurian invasions factors behind Ghurian success.
    - Economic, Social and cultural consequences.
    - Foundation of Delhi Sultanate and early Turkish Sultans.
    - Consolidation: The rule of Iltutmish and Balban.
16. **The Fourteenth Century:**
    - "The Khalji Revolution".
    - Alauddin Khalji: Conquests and territorial expansion, agrarian and economic measure.
    - Muhammad Tughluq: Major projects, agrarian measures, bureaucracy of Muhammad Tughluq.
    - Firuz Tugluq: Agrarian measures, achievements in civil engineering and public works, decline of the Sultanate, foreign contacts and Ibn Battuta's account.

17. **Society, Culture and Economy in the Thirteenth and Fourteenth Centuries**
    - Society: Composition of rural society, ruling classes, town dwellers, women, religious classes, caste and slavery under the Sultanate, Bhakti movement, Sufi movement.
    - Culture: Persian literature, literature in the regional languages of North India, literaute in the languages of South India, Sultanate architecture and new structural forms, painting, evolution of a composite culture.
    - Economy: Agricultural Production, rise of urban economy and non-agricultural production, trade and commerce.
18. **The Fifteenth and Early Sixteenth Century-Political Developments and Economy**
    - Rise of Provincial Dynasties: Bengal, Kashmir (Zainul Abedin), Gujarat.
    - Malwa, Bahmanids.
    - The Vijayanagara Empire.
    - Lodis.
    - Mughal Empire, first phase: Babur, Humayun.
    - The Sur Empire: Sher Shah's administration.
    - Portuguese colonial enterprise, Bhakti and Sufi Movements.
19. **The Fifteenth and Early Sixteenth Century—Society and culture**
    - Regional cultures specificities.
    - Literary traditions.
    - Provincial architectural.
    - Society, culture, literature and the arts in Vijayanagara Empire.
20. **Akbar**
    - Conquests and consolidation of empire.
    - Establishment of ***jagir*** and ***mansab*** systems.
    - Rajput policy.
    - Evolution of religious and social outlook. Theory of ***Sulh-i-kul*** and religious policy.
    - Court patronage of art and technology.
21. **Mughal Empire in the Seventeenth Century**
    - Major administrative policies of Jahangir, Shahjahan and Aurangzeb.
    - The Empire and the Zamindars.
    - Religious policies of Jahangir, Shahjahan and Aurangzeb.
    - Nature of the Mughal State.
    - Late Seventeenth Century crisis and the revolts.
    - The Ahom kingdom.
    - Shivaji and the early Maratha Kingdom.
22. **Economy and society, in the 16th and 17th Centuries**
    - Population Agricultural and craft production.
    - Towns, commerce with Europe through Dutch, English and French companies: a trade revolution.

- Indian mercantile classes. Banking, insurance and credit systems.
- Conditions of peasants, Condition of Women.
- Evolution of the Sikh community and the Khalsa Panth.

23. **Culture during Mughal Empire**
    - Persian histories and other literature.
    - Hindi and religious literatures.
    - Mughal architecture.
    - Mughal painting.
    - Provincial architecture and painting.
    - Classical music.
    - Science and technology.
24. **The Eighteenth Century**
    - Factors for the decline of the Mughal Empire.
    - The regional principalities: Nizam's Deccan, Bengal, Awadh.
    - Maratha ascendancy under the Peshwas.
    - The Maratha fiscal and financial system.
    - Emergence of Afghan power Battle of Panipat, 1761.
    - State of, political, cultural and economic, on eve of the British conquest.

Paper-II

1. **European Penetration into India:** The Early European Settlements; The Portuguese and the Dutch; The English and the French East India Companies; Their struggle for supremacy; Carnatic Wars; Bengal-The conflict between the English and the Nawabs of Bengal; Siraj and the English; The Battle of Plassey; Significance of Plassey.
2. **British Expansion in India:** Bengal-Mir Jafar and Mir Kasim; The Battle of Buxar; Mysore; The Marathas; The three Anglo-Maratha Wars; The Punjab.
3. **Early Structure of the British Raj:** The Early administrative structure; From diarchy to direct contol; The Regulating Act (1773); The Pitt's India Act (1784); The Charter Act (1833); The Voice of free trade and the changing character of British colonial rule; The English utilitarian and India.
4. **Economic Impact of British Colonial Rule**
   (a) Land revenue settlements in British India; The Permanent Settlement; Ryotwari Settlement; Mahalwari Settlement; Economic impact of the revenue arrangements; Commercialization of agriculture; Rise of landless agrarian labourers; Impoverishment of the rural society.
   (b) Dislocation of traditional trade and commerce; De-industrialisation; Decline of traditional crafts; Drain of wealth; Economic transformation of India; Railroad and communication network including telegraph and postal services; Famine and poverty in the rural interior; European business enterprise and its limitations.

5. **Social and Cultural Developments:** The state of indigenous education, its dislocation; Orientalist-Anglicist controversy, The introduction of western education in India; The rise of press, literature and public opinion; The rise of modern vernacular literature; Progress of Science; Christian missionary activities in India.
6. **Social and Religious Reform Movements in Bengal and Other Areas:** Ram Mohan Roy, The Brahmo Movement; Devendranath Tagore; Iswarchandra Vidyasagar; The Young Bengal Movement; Dayanada Saraswati; The social reform movements in India including Sati, widow remarriage, child marriage etc.; The contribution of Indian renaissance to the growth of modern India; Islamic revivalism-the Feraizi and Wahabi Movements.
7. **Indian Response to British Rule:** Peasant movement and tribal uprisings in the 18th and 19th centuries including the Rangpur Dhing (1783), the Kol Rebellion (1832), the Mopla Rebellion in Malabar (1841-1920), the Santal Hul (1855), Indigo Rebellion (1859-60), Deccan Uprising (1875) and the Munda Ulgulan (1899-1900); The Great Revolt of 1857—Origin, character, casuses of failure, the consequences; The shift in the character of peasant uprisings in the post-1857 period; the peasant movements of the 1920s and 1930s.
8. **Factors leading to the birth of Indian Nationalism:** Politics of Association; The Foundation of the Indian National Congress; The Safety-valve thesis relating to the birth of the Congress; Programme and objectives of Early Congress; the social composition of early Congress leadership; the Moderates and Extremists; The Partition of Bengal (1905); The Swadeshi Movement in Bengal; the economic and political aspects of Swadeshi Movement; The beginning of revolutionary extremism in India.
9. **Rise of Gandhi:** Character of Gandhian nationalism; Gandhi's popular appeal; Rowlatt Satyagraha; the Khilafat Movement; the Non-cooperation Movement; National politics from the end of the Non-cooperation movement to the beginning of the Civil Disobedience Movement; the two phases of the Civil Disobedience Movement; Simon Commission; The Nehru Report; the Round Table Conferences; Nationalism and the Peasant Movements; Nationalism and Working class movements; Women and Indian youth and students in Indian politics (1885-1947); the election of 1937 and the formation of ministries; Cripps Mission; the Quit India Movement; the Wavell Plan; The Cabinet Mission.
10. Constitutional Developments in the Colonial India between 1858 and 1935.
11. **Other strands in the National Movement:** The Revolutionaries: Bengal, the Punjab, Maharashtra, U.P. the Madras Presidency, Outside India.
    The Left: The Left within the Congress: Jawaharlal Nehru, Subhas Chandra Bose, the Congress Socialist Party; the Communist Party of India, other left parties.

12. **Politics of Separatism:** The Muslim League; the Hindu Mahasabha; Communalism and the politics of partition; Transfer of power; Independence.
13. **Consolidation as a Nation**: Nehru's Foreign Policy; India and her neighbours (1947-1964); The linguistic reorganisation of States (1935-1947); Regionalism and regional inequality; Integration of Princely States; Princes in electoral politics; the Question of National Language.
14. **Caste and Ethnicity after 1947**: Backward Castes and Tribes in post-colonial electoral politics; Dalit movements.
15. **Economic Development and Political Change**: Land reforms; the politics of planning and rural reconstruction; Ecology and environmental policy in post-colonial India; Progress of Science.
16. **Enlightenment and Modern ideas**
    - (i) Major Ideas of Enlightenment: Kant, Rousseau.
    - (ii) Spread of Enlightenment in the colonies.
    - (iii) Rise of socialist ideas (up to Marx); spread of Marxian Socialism.
17. **Origins of Modern Politics**
    - (i) European States System.
    - (ii) American Revolution and the Constitution.
    - (iii) French Revolution and Aftermath, 1789-1815.
    - (iv) American Civil War with reference to Abraham Lincoln and the abolition of slavery.
    - (v) British Democratic politics, 1815-1850: Parliamentary Reformers, Free Traders, Chartists.
18. **Industrialization**
    - (i) English Industrial Revolution: Causes and Impact on Society.
    - (ii) Industrialization in other countries: USA, Germany, Russia, Japan.
    - (iii) Industrialization and Globalization.
19. **Nation-State System**
    - (i) Rise of Nationalism in 19th century.
    - (ii) Nationalism: State-building in Germany and Italy.
    - (iii) Disintegration of Empires in the face of the emergence of nationalities across the World.
20. **Imperialism and Colonialism**
    - (i) South and South-East Asia.
    - (ii) Latin America and South Africa.
    - (iii) Australia.
    - (iv) Imperialism and free trade: Rise of neo-imperialism.
21. **Revolution and Counter-Revolution**
    - (i) 19th Century European revolutions.
    - (ii) The Russian Revolution of 1917-1921.
    - (iii) Fascist Counter-Revolution, Italy and Germany.
    - (iv) The Chinese Revolution of 1949.

22. **World Wars**
    (i) 1st and 2nd World Wars as Total Wars: Societal implications.
    (ii) World War I: Causes and Consequences.
    (iii) World War II: Causes and Consequences.
23. **The World after World War II**
    (i) Emergence of Two power blocs.
    (ii) Emergence of Third World and non-alignment.
    (iii) UNO and the global disputes.
24. **Liberation from Colonial Rule**
    (i) Latin America-Bolivar.
    (ii) Arab World-Egypt.
    (iii) Africa-Apartheid to Democracy.
    (iv) South-East Asia-Vietnam.
25. **Decolonization and Underdevelopment**
    (i) Factors constraining Development; Latin America, Africa.
26. **Unification of Europe**
    (i) Post War Foundations; NATO and European Community.
    (ii) Consolidation and Expansion of European Community
    (iii) European Union.
27. **Disintegration of Soviet Union and the Rise of the Unipolar World**
    (i) Factors leading to the collapse of Soviet Communism and Soviet Union, 1985-1991.
    (ii) Political Changes in East Europe 1989-2001.
    (iii) End of the Cold War and US Ascendancy in the World as the lone superpower.

13. LAW

Paper-I

Constitutional and Administrative Law

1. **Constitution and Constitutionalism:** The distinctive features of the Constitution.
2. Fundamental Rights—Public interest litigation; Legal Aid; Legal services authority.
3. Relationship between Fundamental rights, Directive principles and Fundamental duties.
4. Constitutional Position of the President and relation with the Council of Ministers.
5. Governor and his powers.
6. Supreme Court and the High Courts:
    (a) Appointments and transfer.
    (b) Powers, functions and jurisdiction.

7. **Centre, States and Local Bodies:**
   (a) Distribution of legislative powers between the Union and the States.
   (b) Local Bodies.
   (c) Administrative relationship among Union, State and Local Bodies.
   (d) Eminent domain-State property-common property-community property.
8. Legislative powers, privileges and immunities.
9. Services under the Union and the States
   (a) Recruitment and conditions of services; Constitutional safeguards; Administrative tribunals.
   (b) Union Public Service Commission and State Public Service Commissions—Power andfunctions.
   (c) Election Commission—Power and functions.
10. Emergency provisions.
11. Amendment of the Constitution.
12. Principle of Natural Justice—Emerging trends and judicial approach.
13. Delegated legislation and its constitutionality.
14. Separation of powers and constitutional governance.
15. Judicial review of administrative action.
16. Ombudsman: Lokayukta, Lokpal etc.

International Law

1. Nature and Definition of International Law.
2. Relationship between International Law and Municipal Law.
3. State Recognition and State Succession.
4. **Law of the Sea:** Inland Waters,Territorial Sea, Contiguous Zone, Continental Shelf, Exclusive Economic Zone and High Seas.
5. **Individuals:** Nationality, statelessness; Human Rights and procedures available for their enforcement.
6. Territorial jurisdiction of States, Extradition and Asylum.
7. **Treaties:** Formation, application, termination and reservation.
8. **United Nations:** Its principal organs, powers and functions and reform.
9. Peaceful settlement of disputes—different modes.
10. Lawful recourse to force: aggressions, self-defence, intervention.
11. Fundamental principles of international humanitarian law—International conventions and contemporary developments.
12. Legality of the use of nuclear weapons; ban on testing of nuclear weapons; Nuclear non- proliferation treaty, CTST.
13. International Terrorism, State sponsored terrorism, Hijacking, International Criminal Court.
14. New International Economic Order and Monetary Law: WTO, TRIPS, GATT, IMF, World Bank.
15. Protection and Improvement of the Human Environment: International Efforts.

Paper-II

Law of Crimes

1. General principles of Criminal liability: mens rea and actus reus, mens rea in statutory offences.
2. Kinds of punishment and emerging trends as to abolition of capital punishment.
3. Preparations and criminal attempt.
4. General exceptions.
5. Joint and constructive liability.
6. Abetment.
7. Criminal conspiracy.
8. Offences against the State.
9. Offences against public tranquility.
10. Offences against human body.
11. Offences against property.
12. Offences against women.
13. Defamation.
14. Prevention of Corruption Act, 1988.
15. Protection of Civil Rights Act, 1955 and subsequent legislative developments.
16. Plea bargaining.

Law of Torts

1. Nature and definition.
2. Liability based upon fault and strict liability; Absolute liability.
3. Vicarious liability including State Liability.
4. General defences.
5. Joint tort fessors.
6. Remedies.
7. Negligence.
8. Defamation.
9. Nuisance.
10. Conspiracy.
11. False imprisonment.
12. Malicious prosecution.
13. Consumer Protection Act, 1986.

Law of Contracts and Mercantile Law

1. Nature and formation of contract/E-contract.
2. Factors vitiating free consent.
3. Void, voidable, illegal and unenforceable agreements.
4. Performance and discharge of contracts.
5. Quasi-contracts.
6. Consequences of breach of contract.
7. Contract of indemnity, guarantee and insurance.

8. Contract of agency.
9. Sale of goods and hire purchase.
10. Formation and dissolution of partnership.
11. Negotiable Instruments Act, 1881.
12. Arbitration and Conciliation Act, 1996.
13. Standard form contracts.

Contemporary Legal Developments

1. Public Interest Litigation.
2. Intellectual property rights—Concept, types/prospects.
3. Information Technology Law including Cyber Laws—Concept, purpose/prospects.
4. Competition Law—Concept, purpose/prospects.
5. Alternate Dispute Resolution—Concept, types/prospects.
6. Major statutes concerning environmental law.
7. Right to Information Act.
8. Trial by media.

LITERATURE OF THE FOLLOWING LANGUAGES

NOTE (i): A candidate may be required to answer some or all the Questions in the language concerned.

NOTE (ii): In regard to the languages included in the Eighth Schedule to Constitution, the scripts will be the same as indicated in Section II (B) of Appendix I relating to the Main Examination.

NOTE (iii): Candidates should note that the questions not required to be answered in a specific language will have to be answered in the language medium indicated by them for answering papers on Essay, General Studies and Optional Subjects.

14. ASSAMESE

Paper-I

[Answers must be written in Assamese]

Section A

Language

(a) History of the origin and development of the Assamese Language —its position among the Indo-Aryan language—periods in its history.

(b) Development of Assamese prose.

(c) Vowels and consonants of the Assamese Language—Rules of phonetic changes with stress on Assamese coming down from Old Indo-Aryan.

(d) Assamese vocabulary—and its sources.

(e) Morphology of the language—conjugation—enclitic definitives and pleonastic suffixes. (f) Dilectical divergences—the Standard colloquial and the Kamrupi dialect in particular. (g) Assamese script—its evolution through the ages till 19th century A.D.

Section B

Literary Criticism and Literary History

(a) Principles of literary criticism up to New criticism.
(b) Different literary genres.
(c) Development of literary forms in Assamese.
(d) Development of literary criticism in Assamese.
(e) Periods of the literary history of Assam from the earliest beginnings, i.e. from the period of the charyyageeta with their socio-cultural background: the proto Assamese Pre-Sankaradeva—Sankaradeva—Post-Sankaradeva—Modern period (from the coming of the Britishers)—Post-Independence period. Special emphasis is to be given on the Vaisnavite period, the gonaki and the post-independence periods.

Paper-II

This paper will require first-hand reading of the texts prescribed and will be designed to test the candidate's critical ability.

[**Answers must be written in Assamese**]

Section A

Râmâyana (Ayodhyâ Kânda — by Madhava Kandali only)
Pârijât-Harana — by Sankaradeva.
Râsakrîdâ — by Sankaradeva (From Kirtana Ghosa)
Bârgeet — by Madhavadeva.
Râjasûya — by Madhavadeva.
Kathâ-Bhâgavata(Books I and II) — by Baikurthanath Bhattacharyya.
Gurucarit-Kathâ (Sankaradeva's Part only) — ed. by Maheswar Neog.

Section B

Râmâyana (Ayodhyâ Kânda — by Madhava Kandali only)
Mor Jeevan Soñwaran — by Lakshminath Bezbaroa. Kripâbar
BorbaruârKakatar Topola — by Lakshminath Bezbaroa.
Pratimâ — by Chandra KumarAgarwalla.
Gâonburhâ — by Padmanath GohainBarua. Manomatî
— by Rajanikanta Bordoloi. Purani Asamîyâ Sâhitya — by Banikanta Kakati.
Kârengar
Ligirî — by Jyotiprasad Agarwalla
Jeevanar Bâtat — by Bina Barva(BirinchiKumar Barua)
Mrityunjoy — by Birendrakumar Bhattacharyya
Samrât — by Navakanta Barua

15. BENGALI

Paper-1

History of Language and Literature. [Answers must be written in Bengali]

Section A: Topics from the History of Bangla language

1. The chronological track from Proto Indo-European to Bangla (Family tree with branches and approximate dates).
2. Historical stages of Bangla (Old, Middle, New) and their linguistic features.
3. Dialects of Bangla and their distinguishing characteristics.
4. Elements of Bangla Vocabulary.
5. Forms of Bangla Literary Prose—Sadhu and Chalit.
6. Processes of language change relevant for Bangla:
   Apinihiti (Anaptyxis), Abhishruti (umlaut), Murdhanyibhavan (cerebralization), Nasikyibhavan (Nasalization), Samibhavan (Assimilation), Sadrishya (Analogy), Svaragama (Vowel insertion) —Adi Svaragama, Madhya Svaragama or Svarabhakti, Antya Svaragama, Svarasangati (Vowel harmony), y—shruti and w—shruti.
7. Problems of standardization and reform of alphabet and spelling, and those of transliteration and Romanization.
8. Phonology, Morphology and Syntax of Modern Bangla.
   (Sounds of Modern Bangla, Conjuncts; word formations, compounds; basic sentence patterns.)

Section B: Topics from the History of Bangla Literature

1. Periodization of Bangla Literature: Old Bangla and Middle Bangla.
2. Points of difference between modern and pre-modern Bangla Literature.
3. Roots and reasons behind the emergence of modernity in Bangla Literature.
4. Evolution of various Middle Bangla forms ; Mangal Kavyas, Vaishnava lyrics, Adapted narratives (Ramayana, Mahabharata, Bhagavata) and religious biographies.
5. Secular forms in middle Bangla literature.
6. Narrative and lyric trends in the nineteenth century Bangla poetry.
7. Development of prose.
8. Bangla dramatic literature (nineteenth century, Tagore, Post-1944 Bangla drama).
9. Tagore and post-Tagoreans.
10. Fiction, major authors:
    Bankimchandra, Tagore, Saratchandra, Bibhutibhusan, Tarasankar, Manik).
11. Women and Bangla literature: creators and created.

Paper-II

Prescribed texts for close study [Answers must be written in Bengali]

Section A

1. **Vaishnava Padavali** (Calcutta University)
   Poems of Vidyapati, Chandidas, Jnanadas, Govindadas and Balaramdas.
2. **Chandimangal** Kalketu episode by Mukunda (Sahitya Akademi).
3. **Chaitanya Charitamrita,** Madhya Lila. by Krishnadas Kaviraj (Sahitya Akademi).
4. **Meghnadbadh Kavya** by Madhusudan Dutta.
5. **Kapalkundala** by Bankimchandra Chatterjee.
6. **Samya** and **Bangadesher Krishak** by Bankimchandra Chatterjee.
7. **Sonar Tari** by Rabindranath Tagore.
8. **Chhinnapatravali** by Rabindranath Tagore.

Section B

9. **Raktakarabi** by Rabindranath Tagore.
10. **Nabajatak** by Rabindranath Tagore.
11. **Grihadaha** by Saratchandra Chatterjee.
12. **Prabandha Samgraha,** Vol. 1, by Pramatha Choudhuri.
13. **Aranyak** by Bibhutibhusan Banerjee.
14. **Short stories** by Manik Bandyopadhyay: Atashi Mami, Pragaitihasik, Holud-Pora, Sarisrip, Haraner Natjamai, Chhoto-Bokulpurer Jatri, Kustharogir Bou, Jakey Ghush Ditey Hoy.
15. **Shrestha Kavita** by Jibanananda Das.
16. **Jagori** by Satinath Bhaduri.
17. **Ebam Indrajit** by Badal Sircar.

16. BODO

Paper-I

History of Bodo Language and Literature [Answers Must be Written in Bodo]

Section A

History of Bodo Language

1. Homeland, language family, its present status and its mutual contact with Assamese.
2. (a) phonemes: Vowel and Consonant Phonemes. (b) Tones.
3. Morphology: Gender, Case and Case endings, Plural suffix, Definitives, Verbal suffix.
4. Vocabulary and its sources.
5. Syntax: Types of sentences, Word Order.
6. History of scripts used in writing Bodo Language since inception.

Section B

History of Bodo Literature

1. General introduction of Bodo folk Literature.
2. Contribution of the Missionaries.
3. Periodization of Bodo Literature.
4. Critical analysis of different genre (Poetry, Novel, Short Story and Drama).
5. Translation Literature.

Paper-II

The paper will require first-hand reading of the texts prescribed and will be designed to test the critical ability of the candidates. (Answers must be written in Bodo)

Section A

(a) Khonthai-Methai
(Edited by Madaram Brahma & Rupnath Brahma)
(b) Hathorkhi-Hala
(Edited by Pramod Chandra Brahma)
(c) Boroni Gudi Sibsa Arw Aroz: Madaram Brahma
(d) Raja Nilambar: Dwarendra Nath Basumatary
(e) Bibar (prose section): (Edited by Satish Chandra Basumatary).

Section B

(a) Bibi Bithai (Aida Nwi): Bihuram Boro
(b) Radab: Samar Brahma Chaudhury
(c) Okhrang Gongse Nangou: Brajendra Kumar Brahma
(d) Baisagu Arw Harimu: Laksheswar Brahma
(e) Gwdan Boro: Manoranjan Lahary
(f) Jujaini Or: Chittaranjan Muchahary
(g) Mwihoor: Dharanidhar Wary
(h) Hor Badi Khwmsi: Kamal Kumar Brahma
(i) Jaolia Dewan: Mangal Singh Hozowary
(j) Hagra Guduni Mwi: Nilkamal Brahma

17. DOGRI

Paper-I

History of Dogri Language and Literature (Answers Must be Written in Dogri)

Section A

History of Dogri Language

1. Dogri language: Origin and development through different stages.
2. Linguistic boundaries of Dogri and its dialects.
3. Characteristic features of Dogri Language.
4. Structure of Dogri Langauge:

(a) Sound Structure: Segmental,
Vowels and Consonants
Non-segmental: Length, Stress, Nasalization, Tone and Junture

(b) Morphology of Dogri:
  (i) Inflection Categories: Gender, Number, Case, Person, Tense and Voice.
  (ii) Word Formation; use of prefixes, infixes and suffixes.
  (iii) Vocabulary: tatsam, tadbhav, foreign and regional.

(c) Sentence Structure; Major Sentence-types and their constituents, agreement and concord in Dogri syntax.

5. Dogri Language and Scripts: Dogre/Dogra Akkhar, Devanagari and Persia.

Section B

History of Dogri Language

1. A brief account of Pre-independence Dogri Literature: Poetry & Prose.
2. Development of modern Dogri Poetry and main trends in Dogri Poetry.
3. Development of Dogri short-story, main trends and prominent short-story writers.
4. Development of Dogri Novel, main trends and contribution of Dogri Novelists.
5. Development of Dogri Drama and contribution of prominent playwrights.
6. Development of Dogri Prose; Essays, Memoirs and travelogues.
7. An introduction to Dogri Folk Literature—Folk songs, Folk tales 7 Ballads.

Paper-II

Textual criticism of dogri Literature (Answers must be written in dogri)

Section A

Poetry

1. Azadi Paihle Di Dogri Kavita
   The following poets:
   Devi Ditta, Lakkhu, Ganga Ram, Ramdhan, Hardutt, Pahari Gandhi Baba Kanshi Ram & Permanand Almast
2. Modern Dogri Poetry Azadi Bad Di Dogri Kavita The following poets:
   Kishan Smailpuri, Tara Smailpuri, Mohan Lal Sapolia, Yash Sharma, K.S. Madhukar, Padma Sachdev, Jitendra Udhampuri, Charan Singh and Prakash Premi
3. Sheeraza Dogri Number 102, Ghazal Ank
   The following poets:
   Ram Lal Sharma, Ved Pal Deep, N.D. Jamwal, Shiv Ram Deep, Ashwini Magotra and Virendra Kesar

4. Sheeraza Dogri Number 147, Ghazal Ank
   The following poets:
   R.N. Shastri, Jitendra Udhampuri, Champa Sharma and Darshan Darshi.
5. Ramayan (Epic) by Shambhu Nath Sharma (up to Ayodhya Kand)
6. Veer Gulab (Khand Kavya) by Dinoo Bhai Pant.

Section B

Prose

1. Ajakani Dogri Kahani
   The following Short Story Writers:
   Madan Mohan Sharma, Narendra Khajuri and B.P. Sathe
2. Ajakani Dogri Kahani Part-II
   The following Short Story Writers:
   Ved Rahi, Narsingh Dev Jamwal, Om Goswami, Chahttrapal, Lalit Magotra, Chaman Arora and Ratan Kesar.
3. Khatha Kunj Bhag II
   The following Story Writers:
   Om Vidyarthi, Champa Sharma and Krishan Sharma.
4. Meel Patthar (collection of short stories) by Bandhu Sharma.
5. Kaiddi (Novel) by Desh Bandhu Dogra Nutan.
6. Nanga Rukkh (Novel) by O.P. Sharma Sarathi.
7. Nayaan (Drama) by Mohan Singh.
8. Satrang (A collection of one act plays).
   The following play wrights:
   Vishwa Nath Khajuria, Ram Nath Shastri, Jitendra Sharma, Lalit Magotra and Madan Mohan Sharma.
9. Dogri Lalit Nibandh
   The following authors:
   Vishwa Nath Khajuria, Narayan Mishra, Balkrishan Shastri, Shiv Nath, Shyam Lal Sharma, Lakshmi Narayan, D.C. Prashant, Ved Ghai, Kunwar Viyogi.

18. ENGLISH

The syllabus consists of two papers, designed to test a first-hand and critical reading of texts prescribed from the following periods in English Literature: Paper-1: 1600-1900 and Paper 2: 1900–1990.

There will be two compulsory questions in each paper:

(a) A short-notes question related to the topics for general study, and
(b) A critical analysis of UNSEEN passages both in prose and verse.

Paper-I

(Answers must be written in English)

Texts for detailed study are listed below. Candidates will also be required to show adequate knowledge of the following topics and movements:

The Renaissance; Elizabethan and Jacobean Drama; Metaphysical Poetry; The Epic and the

Mock-epic; Neo-classicism; Satire; The Romantic Movement; The Rise of the Novel; The Victorian Age.

Section A

1. William Shakespeare: King Lear and The Tempest.
2. John Donne. The following poems:
   - Canonization;
   - Death be not proud;
   - The Good Morrow;
   - On his Mistress going to bed;
   - The Relic;
3. John Milton: Paradise Lost, I, II, IV, IX.
4. Alexander Pope. The Rape of the Lock.
5. William Wordsworth. The following poems:
   - Ode on Intimations of Immortality.
   - Tintern Abbey.
   - Three years she grew.
   - She dwelt among untrodden ways.
   - Michael.
   - Resolution and Independence.
   - The World is too much with us.
   - Milton, thou shouldst be living at this hour.
   - Upon Westminster Bridge.
6. Alfred Tennyson: In Memoriam.
7. Henrik Ibsen: A Doll's House.

Section B

1. Jonathan Swift, Gulliver's Travels.
2. Jane Austen. Pride and Prejudice.
3. Henry Fielding. Tom Jones.
4. Charles Dickens. Hard Times.
5. George Eliot. The Mill on the Floss.
6. Thomas Hardy. Tess of the d'Urbervilles.
7. Mark Twain. The Adventures of Huckleberry Finn.

Paper-II

(Answers must be written in English)

Texts for detailed study are listed below. Candidates will also be required to show adequate knowledge of the following topics and movements:

Modernism; Poets of the Thirties; The stream-of-consciousness Novel; Absurd Drama; Colonialism and Post-Colonialism; Indian Writing in English; Marxist, Psychoanalytical and Feminist approaches to literature; Post-Modernism.

Section A

1. William Butler Yeats. The following poems:
   - Easter 1916.
   - The Second Coming.
   - A Prayer for my daughter.
   - Sailing to Byzantium.
   - The Tower.
   - Among School Children.
   - Leda and the Swan.
   - Meru.
   - Lapis Lazuli.
   - The Second Coming.
   - Byzantium.
2. T.S. Eliot. The following poems:
   - The Love Song of J. Alfred Prufrock.
   - Journey of the Magi.
   - Burnt Norton.
3. W.H. Auden. The following poems:
   - Partition
   - Musee des Beaux Arts
   - In Memory of W.B. Yeats
   - Lay your sleeping head, my love
   - The Unknown Citizen
   - Consider
   - Mundus Et Infans
   - The Shield of Achilles
   - September 1, 1939
   - Petition
4. John Osborne: Look Back in Anger.
5. Samuel Beckett. Waiting for Godot.

6. Philip Larkin. The following poems:
    - Next
    - Please
    - Deceptions
    - Afternoons
    - Days
    - Mr. Bleaney
7. A.K. Ramanujan. The following poems:
    - Looking for a Cousin on a Swing
    - A River
    - Of Mothers, among other Things
    - Love Poem for a Wife 1
    - Small-Scale Reflections on a Great House
    - Obituary

    (All these poems are available in the anthology Ten Twentieth Century Indian Poets, edited by R. Parthasarthy, published by Oxford University Press, New Delhi).

Section B

1. Joseph Conrad. Lord Jim.
2. James Joyce. Portrait of the Artist as a Young Man.
3. D.H. Lawrence. Sons and Lovers.
4. E.M. Forster. A Passage to India.
5. Virginia Woolf. Mrs. Dalloway.
6. Raja Rao. Kanthapura.
7. V.S. Naipaul. A House for Mr. Biswas.

19. GUJARATI

Paper-I

(Answers must be written in Gujarati)

Section A

Gujarati Language: Form and History

1. History of Gujarati Language with special reference to New Indo-Aryan i.e. last one thousand years.
2. Significant features of the Gujarati language: phonology, morphology and syntax.
3. Major dialects: Surti, pattani, charotari and Saurashtri.

History of Gujarati literature

Medieval

4. Jaina tradition
5. Bhakti tradition: Sagun and Nirgun (Jnanmargi)
6. Non-sectarian tradition (Laukik parampara)

Modern

7. Sudharak yug
8. Pandit yug
9. Gandhi yug
10. Anu-Gandhi yug
11. Adhunik yug

Section B

Literary Forms: (Salient features, history and development of the following literary forms)

(a) **Medieval**

1. Narratives: Rasa, Akhyan and Padyavarta
2. Lyrical: Pada

(b) **Folk**

3. Bhavai

(c) **Modern**

4. Fiction: Novel and Short Story
5. Drama
6. Literary Essay
7. Lyrical Poetry

(d) **Criticism**

8. History of theoretical Gujarati criticism
9. Recent research in folk tradition.

Paper-II

(Answers must be written in Gujarati)

The paper will require first-hand reading of the texts prescribed and will be designed to test the critical ability of the candidate.

Section A

1. **Medieval**

(i) Vasantvilas phagu—AJNATKRUT
(ii) Kadambari—BHALAN
(iii) Sudamacharitra—PREMANAND
(iv) Chandrachandravatini varta—SHAMAL
(v) Akhegeeta—AKHO

2. **Sudharakyug & Pandityug**
   - (vi) Mari Hakikat—NARMADASHA
   - (vii) Farbasveerah—DALPATRAM
   - (viii) Saraswatichandra-Part 1—GOVARDHANRAM TRIPATHI
   - (ix) Purvalap—'KANT' (MANISHANKAR RATNAJI BHATT)
   - (x) Raino Parvat—RAMANBHAI NEELKANTH

Section B

1. **Gandhiyug & Anu Gandhiyug**
   - (i) Hind Swaraj—MOHANDAS KARAMCHAND GANDHI
   - (ii) Patanni Prabhuta—KANHAIYALAL MUNSHI
   - (iii) Kavyani Shakti—RAMNARAYAN VISHWANATH PATHAK
   - (iv) Saurashtrani Rasdhar-Part 1—ZAVERCHAND MEGHANI
   - (v) Manvini Bhavai—PANNALAL PATEL
   - (vi) Dhvani—RAJENDRA SHAH
2. **Adhunik Yug**
   - (vii) Saptapadi—UMASHANKAR JOSHI
   - (viii) Janantike—SURESH JOSHI
   - (ix) Ashwatthama—SITANSHU YASHASCHANDRA.

20. HINDI

Paper-I

(Answers must be written in Hindi) Section A

1. **History of Hindi Language and Nagari Lipi**
   - I. Grammatical and applied forms of Apbhransh, Awahatta & Arambhik Hindi.
   - II. Development of Braj and Awadhi as Literary language during medieval period.
   - III. Early form of Khari-boli in Siddha-Nath Sahitya, Khusero, Sant Sahitaya, Rahim etc. and Dakhni Hindi.
   - IV. Development of Khari-boli and Nagari Lipi during 19th Century.
   - V. Standardisation of Hindi Bhasha & Nagari Lipi.
   - VI. Development of Hindi as a National Language during freedom movement.
   - VII. The development of Hindi as a National Language of Union of India.
   - VIII. Scientific & Technical Development of Hindi Language.
   - IX. Prominent dialects of Hindi and their inter-relationship.
   - X. Salient features of Nagari Lipi and the efforts for its reform & Standard form of Hindi.
   - XI. Grammatical structure of Standard Hindi.

Section B

2. **History of Hindi Literature**
   I. The relevance and importance of Hindi literature and tradition of writing History of Hindi Literature.
   II. Literary trends of the following four periods of history of Hindi Literature.
   A: Adikal—Sidh, Nath and Raso Sahitya.
   Prominent poets—Chandvardai, Khusaro, Hemchandra, Vidyapati.
   B: Bhaktikal—Sant Kavyadhara, Sufi Kavyadhara, Krishna Bhaktidhara and Ram Bhaktidhara.
   Prominent Poets—Kabir, Jayasi, Sur & Tulsi.
   C: Ritikal—Ritikavya, Ritibaddhkavya & Riti Mukta Kavya. Prominent Poets—Keshav, Bihari, Padmakar and Ghananand.
   D: Adhunik Kal—
   a. Renaissance, the development of Prose, Bharatendu Mandal.
   b. Prominent Writers—Bharatendu, Bal Krishna Bhatt & Pratap Narain Mishra.
   c. Prominent trends of modern Hindi Poetry: Chhayavad, Pragativad, Prayogvad, Nai
   Kavita, Navgeet and Contemporary poetry and Janvadi Kavita.
   Prominent Poets—Maithili Sharan Gupta, Prasad, Nirala, Mahadevi, Dinkar, Agyeya, Muktibodh, Nagarjun.
3. Katha Sahitya
   A: Upanyas & Realism
   B: The origin and development of Hindi Novels.
   C: ProminentNovelists—Premchand, Jain-endra, Yashpal, Renu and Bhism Sahani.
   D: The origin and development of Hindi short story.
   E: Prominent Short Story Writers—Premchand, Prasad, Agyeya, Mohan Rakesh & Krishna Sobti.
4. Drama & Theatre
   A: The Origin & Development of Hindi Drama.
   B: Prominent Dramatists—Bharatendu, Prasad, Jagdish Chandra Mathur, Ram Kumar Verma, Mohan Rakesh.
   C: The development of Hindi Theatre.
5. Criticism
   A: The origin and development of Hindi criticism: Saiddhantik, Vyavharik, Pragativadi. Manovishleshanvadi & Nai Alochana.
   B: Prominent critics—Ramchandra Shukla, Hajari Prasad Dwivedi, Ram Vilas Sharma & Nagendra.
6. The other form of Hindi prose—Lalit Nibandh,Rekhachitra, Sansmaran, Yatra-vrittant.

Paper-II

(Answers must be written in Hindi)

The paper will require first-hand reading of the prescribed texts and will test the critical ability of the candidates.

Section A

1.	Kabir	:	Kabir Granthawali, Ed. Shyam Sundar Das (First hundred Sakhis)
2.	Soordas	:	Bhramar Geetsar, Ed. Ramchandra Shukla (First hundred Padas)
3.	Tulsidas	:	Ramcharit Manas (Sundar Kand) Kavitawali (Uttarkand)
4.	Jayasi	:	Padmawat Ed. Shyam Sundar Das (Sinhal Dwip Khand & Nagmativiyog Khand)
5.	Bihari	:	Bihari Ratnakar Ed. Jagnnath Prasad Ratnakar (First 100 Dohas)
6.	Maithili Sharan Gupta	:	Bharat Bharati
7.	Prasad	:	Kamayani (Chinta and Shraddha Sarg)
8.	Nirala	:	Rag-Virag, Ed. Ram Vilas Sharma (Ram Ki Shakti Pooja & Kukurmutta)
9.	Dinkar	:	Kurukshetra
10.	Agyeya	:	Angan Ke Par Dwar (Asadhya Veena)
11.	Muktiboth	:	Brahm Rakhashas
12.	Nagarjun	:	Badal Ko Ghirte Dekha Hai, Akal Ke Bad, Harijan Gatha.

Section B

1.	Bharatendu	:	Bharat Durdasha
2.	Mohan Rakesh	:	Ashadh Ka Ek Din
3.	Ramchandra	:	Chintamani (Part I) (KavitaKya Shukla Hai, ShraddhaAurBhakti)
4.	Dr. Satyendra	:	Nibandh Nilaya—Bal Krishna Bhatt, Premchand, Gulab Rai, Hajari Prasad Dwivedi, Ram Vilas Sharma, Agyeya, Kuber Nath Rai.
5.	Premchand Godan, Premchand ki Sarvashreshtha Kahaniyan, Ed. Amrit Rai/ Manjusha—Prem Chand ki Sarvashreshtha Kahaniyan. Ed. Amrit Rai.		
6.	Prasad	:	Skandgupta
7.	Yashpal	:	Divya
8.	Phaniswar Nath Renu	:	Maila Anchal
9.	Mannu Bhandari	:	Mahabhoj
10.	Rajendra Yadav	:	Ek Dunia Samanantar (All Stories)

21. KANNADA

Paper-I

(Answers must be written in Kannada)

Section A

A. **History of Kannada Language:** What is Language? General characteristics of Language. Dravidian Family of Languages and its specific features. Antiquity of Kannada Language. Different phases of its Development.
Dialects of Kannada Language: Regional and Social. Various aspects of developments of Kannada Language: phonological and Semantic changes. Language borrowing.

B. **History of Kannada Literature:** Ancient Kannada literature: Influence and Trends; Poets for study: Specified poets from Pampa to Ratnakara Varni are to be studied in the light of contents; Form and expression: Pampa, Janna, Nagachandra.
Medieval Kannada literature: Influence and Trends. Vachana Literature: Basavanna, Akka Mahadevi. Medieval Poets: Harihara, Raghavanka, Kumara-Vyasa. Dasa literature: Purandara and Kanaka. Sangataya: Ratnakarvarni

C. **Modern Kannada Literature:** Influence, trends and ideologies, Navodaya, Pragatishila, Navya, Dalita and Bandaya.

Section B

A. **Poetics and Literary Criticism:** Definition and concepts of poetry; Word, Meaning, Alankara, Reeti, Rasa, Dhwani, Auchitya.
Interpretations of Rasa Sutra. Modern Trends of literary criticism: Formalist, Historical, Marxist, Feminist, Post-colonial criticism.

B. **Cultural History of Karnataka:** Contribution of Dynasties to the culture of Karnataka: Chalukyas of Badami and Kalyani, Rashtrakutas, Hoysalas, Vijayanagara rulers, in literary context.
Major religions of Karnataka and their cultural contribution.
Arts of Karnataka; Sculpture, Architecture, Painting, Music, Dance—in the literary context. Unification of Karnataka and its impact of Kannada literature.

Paper-II

(Answers must be written in Kannada)

The Paper will require first-hand reading of the Texts prescribed and will be designed to test the critical ability of the candidates.

Section A

A. **Old Kannada Literature**

1. Vikramaarjuna Vijaya of Pampa (Cantos 12 & 13), (Mysore University Pub.)
2. Vaddaraadhane (Sukumaraswamyia Kathe, Vidyutchorana Kathe)

B. **Medieval Kannada Literature**

1. Vachana, Kammata, Ed. K. Marulasiddappa K.R. Nagaraj (Bangalore University Pub.)
2. Janapriya Kanakasamputa, Ed. D. Javare Gowda (Kannada and Culture Directorate, Bangalore)
3. Nambiyannana Ragale, Ed., T.N. Sreekantaiah (Ta. Vem. Smaraka Grantha Male, Mysore)
4. Kumaravyasa Bharata: Karna Parva (Mysore University)
5. Bharatesha Vaibhava Sangraha Ed Ta. Su. Shama Rao (Mysore University)

Section- B

A. **Modern Kannada Literature**

1. Poetry : Hosagannada Kavite, Ed. G.H. Nayak (Kannada Saahitya Parishattu, Bangalore)
2. Novel : Bettada Jeeva—Shivarama Karanta Madhavi—Anupama NiranjanaOdalaala-Deva-nuru Mahadeva
3. Short Story : Kannada Sanna Kathegalu, Ed. G.H. Nayak (Sahitya Academy, New Delhi)
4. Drama : Shudra Tapaswi—Kuvempu. Tughalak—Girish Karnad.
5. Vichara Sahitya : Devaru—A.N. Moorty Rao (Pub: D.V.K.Moorty, Mysore.)

B. Folk Literature

1. Janapada Swaroopa—Dr. H.M. Nayak. (Ta. Vem. Smaraka Grantha Male, Mysore.)
2. Janpada Geetaanjali—Ed. D. Javare Gowda.(Pub: Sahitya Academy, New Delhi).
3. Kannada Janapada Kathegalu—Ed. J.S. Paramashiviaah (Mysore University).
4. Beedi Makkalu Beledo—Ed. Kalegowda Nagavara (Pub: Bangalore University).
5. Savirada Ogatugalu—Ed. S.G. Imrapura.

22. KASHMIRI

Paper-I

(Answers must be written in Kashmiri)

Section A

1. Genealogical relationship of the Kashmiri language: various theories.
2. Areas of occurence and dialects (geographical/social)
3. Phonology and grammar:

(i) Vowel and consonant system;
(ii) Nouns and pronouns with various case inflections;
(iii) Verbs: various types and tenses.

4. Syntactic structure:
   (i) Simple, active and declarative statements;
   (ii) Coordination;
   (iii) Relativisation.

Section B

1. Kashmiri literature in the 14th century (Socio-cultural and intellectual background with special reference to ***Lal Dyad*** and ***Sheikhul Alam***).
2. Nineteenth century Kashmiri literature (development of various genres: ***vatsun; ghazal and mathnavi***).
3. Kashmiri literature in the first half of the twentieth century (with special reference to Mahjoor and Azad; various literary influences).
4. Modern Kashmiri literature (with special reference to the development of the short story, drama, novel and nazm).

Paper-II

(Answers must be written in Kashmiri)

Section A

1. Intensive study of Kashmiri poetry up to the nineteenth century:
   (i) Lal Dyad,
   (ii) Sheikhul Aalam
   (iii) Habba Khatoon
2. Kashmiri poetry: 19th Century
   (i) Mahmood Gami ***(Vatsans)***
   (ii) Maqbool shah ***(Gulrez)***
   (iii) Rasool Mir ***(Ghazals)***
   (iv) Abdul Ahad Nadim ***(N'at)***
   (v) Krishanjoo Razdan ***(Shiv Lagun)***
   (vi) Sufi Poets (Test in ***Sanglaab***, published by the Deptt. of Kashmiri, University of Kashmir)
3. Twentieth Century Kashmiri poetry (text in ***Azich Kashir Shairi,*** published by the Deptt. of Kashmiri, University of Kashmir).
4. Literary criticism and research work: development and various trends.

Section B

1. **An analytical study of the short story in Kashmiri**
   (i) ***Afsana Majmu'a,*** published by the Deptt. of Kashmiri, University of Kashmir.
   (ii) ***Kashur Afsana Az,*** published by the Sahitya Akademi.

(iii) *Hamasar Kashur Afsana,* published by the Sahitya Akademi.
The following short story writers only: Akhtar Mohi-ud Din, Kamil, Hari Krishan Kaul, Hraday Kaul Bharti, Bansi Nirdosh, Gulshan Majid.

2. **Novel in Kashmiri**
   (i) ***Mujrim by*** G. N. Gowhar
   (ii) ***Marun***—Ivan Ilyichun, (Kashmiri version of Tolstoy's) The Death of Ivan Ilyich (published by Kashmiri Deptt.)
3. **Drama in Kashmiri**
   (i) ***Natuk Kariv Band by*** Hari Krishan Kaul
   (ii) Qk Angy Natuk, ed. Motilal Keemu, published by the Sahitya Akademi.
   (iii) ***Razi Oedipus,*** tr. Naji Munawar, published by the Sahitya Akademi.
4. **Kashmiri Folk Literature**
   (i) ***Kashur Luki Theatre*** by Mohammad Subhan Bhagat, published by the Deptt. of Kashmiri, University of Kashmir.
   (ii) ***Kashiry Luki Beeth*** (all volumes) published by the J&K Cultural Academy.

23. KONKANI

Paper-I

(Answers must be written in Konkani)

Section A

History of the Konkani Language

(i) Origin and development of the language and influences on it.
(ii) Major variants of Konkani and their linguistic features.
(iii) Grammatical and lexicographic work in Konkani, including a study of cases, adverbs, indeclinables and voices.
(iv) Old Standard Konkani, New Standard and Standardisation problems.

Section B

History of Konkani Literature

Candidates would be expected to be well-acquainted with Konkani literature and its social and cultural background and consider the problems and issues arising out of them.

(i) History of Konkani literature from its probable source to the present times, with emphasis on its major works, writers and movements.
(ii) Social and cultural background of the making of Konkani literature from time to time.
(iii) Indian and Western influences on Konkani literature, from the earliest to modern times.
(iv) Modern literary trends in the various genres and regions including a study of Konkani folklore.

Paper-II

(Answers must be written in Konkani)

Textual Criticism of Konkani Literature

The paper will be designed to test the candidate's critical and analytical abilities. Candidates would be expected to be well-acquainted with Konkani Literature and required to have first-hand reading of the following texts.

Section A: Prose

1. (a) Konkani Mansagangotri (excluding poetry) ed. by Prof: Olivinho Gomes.
   (b) Old Konkani language and literature—the Portuguese Role
2. (a) Otmo Denvcharak—a novel by A. V. da Cruz.
   (b) Vadoll ani Varem—a novel by Antonio Pereira.
   (c) Devache Kurpen—a novel by V.J.P. Saldanha.
3. (a) Vajralikhani—Shenoy goem-bab-An anthology-ed. by Shantaram Varde Valavalikar.
   (b) Konkani Lalit Niband—Essays-ed. by Shyam Verenkar.
   (c) Teen Dasakam—An anthology—ed. by Chandrakant Keni.
4. (a) Demand—Drama-by Pundalik Naik.
   (b) Kadambini: A Miscellany of Modern Prose—ed. by Prof. O.J.F. Gomes and Smt. P.S. Tadkodkar.
   (c) Ratha Tujeo Ghudieo—by Smt. Jayanti Naik.

Section B: Poetry

1. (a) Ev ani Mori — Poetry by Eduardo Bruno de Souza.
   (b) Abravanchem Yadnyadan—by Luis Mascarenhas.
2. (a) Godde Ramayan—ed. by R.K. Rao.
   (b) Ratnahar I and II—collection of poems—ed. R. V. Pandit.
3. (a) Zayo Zuyo—poems- Manohar L. Sardessai.
   (b) Kanadi Mati Konkani Kavi—Anthology of Poems—ed. Pratap Naik.
4. (a) Adrushatache Kalle—Poems by Pandurang Bhangui.
   (b) Yaman—Poems by Madhav Borkar.

24. MAITHILI

Paper-I

History of Maithili Language and its Literature

(Answers must be written in Maithili)

PART A

History of Maithili Language

1. Place of Maithili in Indo-European Language family.
2. Origin and development of Maithili language. (Sanskrit, Prakrit, Avhatt, Maithili)

3. Periodic division of Maithili Language. (Beginning, Middle era, Modern era).
4. Maithili and its different dialects.
5. Relationship between Maithili and other Eastern languages (Bengali, Asamese, Oriya)
6. Origin and Development of Tirhuta Script.
7. Pronouns and Verbs in Maithili Language.

PART B

History of Maithili Literature

1. Background of Maithili Literature (Religious, Economic, Social, Cultural).
2. Periodic division of Maithili literature.
3. Pre-Vidyapati Literature.
4. Vidyapati and his tradition.
5. Medieval Maithili Drama (Kirtaniya Natak, Ankia Nat, Maithili dramas written in Nepal).
6. Maithili Folk Literature (Folk Tales, Folk Drama, Folk Stories, Folk Songs).
7. Development of different literary forms in modern era:
   (a) Prabandh-kavya (b) Muktak-kavya
   (c) Novel (d) Short Story
   (e) Drama (f) Essay
   (g) Criticism (h) Memoirs
   (i) Translation
8. Development of Maithili Magazines and Journals.

Paper-II

(Answers must be written in Maithili)

The paper will require first-hand reading of the prescribed texts and will test the critical ability of the candidates.

PART A

Poetry

1. Vidyapati Geet-Shati—Publisher: Sahitya Akademi, New Delhi (Lyrics— 1 to 50)
2. Govind Das Bhajanavali—Publisher: Maithili Acadamy, Patna (Lyrics— 1 to 25)
3. Krishnajanm—Manbodh
4. Mithilabhasha Ramayana—Chanda Jha (only Sunder-Kand)
5. Rameshwar Charit Mithila Ramayan—Lal Das (only Bal-kand)
6. Keechak-Vadh—Tantra Nath Jha.
7. Datta-Vati—Surendra Jah 'Suman' (only 1st and 2nd Cantos).
8. Chitra-Yatri
9. Samakaleen Maithili Kavita—Publisher: Sahitaya Akademi, New Delhi.

PART B

10. Varna Ratnakar—Jyotirishwar (only 2nd Kallol)
11. Khattar Kakak Tarang—Hari Mohan Jha
12. Lorik—Vijaya Manipadma
13. Prithvi Putra—Lalit
14. Bhaphait Chahak Jinagi—Sudhanshu 'Shekhar' Choudhary
15. Kriti Rajkamlak—Publisher: Maithili Acadamy, Patna (First Ten Stories only)
16. Katha–Sangrah–Publisher: Maithili Acadamy, Patna.

25. MALAYALAM

Paper-I

(Answers must be written in Malayalam)

Section A

1. **Early phase of Malayalam Language**
   - 1.1 Various theories: Origin from proto Dravidian, Tamil, Sanskrit.
   - 1.2 Relation between Tamil and Malayalam: Six nayas of A. R. Rajarajavarma.
   - 1.3 Pattu School—Definition, Ramacharitam, later pattu works—Niranam works and Krishnagatha.
2. **Linguistic features of**
   - 2.1 Manipravalam—definition. Language of early manipravala works—Champu, Sandesakavya, Chandrotsava, minor works. Later manipravala works—medieval Champu and Attakkatha.
   - 2.2 Folklore—Southern and Northern ballads, Mappila songs.
   - 2.3 Early Malayalam Prose—Bhashakautaliyam, Brahmandapuranam, Attaprakaram, Kramadipika and Nambiantamil.
3. **Standardisation of Malayalam**
   - 3.1 Peculiarities of the language of Pana, Kilippattu and Tullal.
   - 3.2 Contributions of indigenous and European missionaries to Malayalam.
   - 3.3 Characteristics of contemporary Malayalam; Malayalam as administrative language.

     Language of scientific and technical literature—media language.

Section B

Literary History

4. **Ancient and Medieval Literature**
   - 4.1 Pattu—Ramacharitam, Niranam Works and Krishnagatha.
   - 4.2 Manipravalam—early and medieval manipravala works including attakkatha and champu.
   - 4.3 Folk Literature.
   - 4.4 Kilippattu, Tullal and Mahakavya.

5. **Modern Literature—Poetry**
   5.1 Venmani poets and contemporaries.
   5.2 The advent of Romanticism—Poetry of Kavitraya i.e., Asan, Ulloor and Vallathol.
   5.3 Poetry after Kavitraya.
   5.4 Modernism in Malayalam Poetry.
6. **Modern Literature—Prose**
   6.1 Drama.
   6.2 Novel.
   6.3 Short story.
   6.4 Biography, travelogue, essay and criticism.

Paper-II

(Answers must be written in Malayalam)

This paper will require first hand reading of the texts prescribed and is designed to test the candidate's critical ability.

Section A

Unit 1

1.1 Ramacharitam—Patalam.
1.2 Kannassaramayanam—Balakandam first 25 stanzas.
1.3 Unnunilisandesam—Purvabhagam 25 slokas including Prastavana.
1.4 Mahabharatham Kilippattu—Bhishmaparvam.

Unit 2

2.1 Kumaran Asan—Chintavisthayaya Sita.
2.2 Vailoppilli—Kutiyozhikkal.
2.3 G. Sankara Kurup—Perunthachan.
2.4 N. V. Krishna Variar—Tivandiyile pattu.

Unit 3

3.1 O. N. V.—Bhumikkoru Charamagitam.
3.2 Ayyappa Panicker—Kurukshetram.
3.3 Akkittam—Pandatha Messanthi.
3.4 Attur Ravivarma—Megharupan.

Section B

Unit 4

4.1 O. Chanthu Menon—Indulekha.
4.2 Thakazhy—Chemmin.
4.3 O. V. Vijayan—Khasakkinte Ithihasam.

Unit 5

5.1 M. T. Vasudevan Nair—Vanaprastham (Collection).
5.2 N. S. Madhavan—Higvitta (Collection).
5.3 C. J. Thomas—1128-il Crime 27.

Unit 6

6.1 Kuttikrishna Marar—Bharataparyatanam.
6.2 M. K. Sanu—Nakshatrangalute Snehabhajanam.
6.3 V. T. Bhatttathirippad—Kannirum Kinavum.

26. MANIPURI

Paper-I

(Answers must be written in Manipuri)

Section A

Language

(a) General characteristics of Manipuri Language and history of its development; its importance and status among the Tibeto-Burman Languages of North-East India; recent development in the study of Manipuri Language; evolution and study of old Manipuri script.

(b) Significant features of Manipuri Language:
  (i) Phonology: Phoneme-vowels, consonants juncture, tone, consonant cluster and its occurrence, syllable-its structure, pattern and types.
  (ii) Morphology: Word-class, root and its types; affix and its types; grammatical categories-gender, number, person, case, tense and aspects, process of compounding (samas and sandhi).
  (iii) Syntax: Word order; types of sentences, phrase and clause structures.

Section B

(a) **Literary History of Manipuri:** Early period (up to 17th Century)–Social and cultural background; Themes, diction and style of the works. Medieval period (18th and 19th Century)-Social, religious and political background; Themes, diction and style of the works. Modern period-Growth of major literary forms; change of Themes, diction and style.

(b) **Manipuri Folk Literature:** Legend, Folktale, Folksong, Ballad, Proverb and Riddle.

(c) **Aspects of Manipuri Culture:** Pre-Hindu Manipuri Faith; Advent of Hinduism and the process of syncreticism; Performing arts-Lai Haraoba, Maha Ras; Indegenous games-Sagol Kangjei, Khong Kangjei, Kang.

Paper-II

(Answers must be written in Manipuri)

This paper will require first hand reading of the texts prescribed and will be designed to test candidate's critical ability to assess them.

Section A

Old and Medieval Manipuri Literature

(a) **Old Manipuri Literature**

1. O. Bhogeswar Singh (Ed.): Numit Kappa
2. M. Gourachandra Singh (Ed.): Thawanthaba Hiran
3. N. Khelchandra Singh (Ed.): Naothingkhong Phambal Kaba
4. M. Chandra Singh (Ed.): Panthoibi Khonggul

(b) **Medieval Manipuri Literature**

1. M. Chandra Singh (Ed.): Samsok Ngamba
2. R.K. Snahal Singh (Ed.): Ramayana Adi Kanda
3. N. Khelchandra Singh (Ed.): Dhananjoy Laibu Ningba
4. O. Bhogeswar Singh (Ed.): Chandrakirti Jila Changba

Section B

Modern Manipuri Literature

Poetry and Epic

(I) **Poetry**

(a) **Manipuri Sheireng (Pub) Manipuri Sahitya Parishad, 1998 (Ed.)**

Kh. Chaoba Singh : Pi Thadoi, Lamgi Chekla Amada, Loktak
Dr. L. Kamal Singh : Nirjanata, Nirab Rajani
A. Minaketan Singh : Kamalda, Nonggumlalkkhoda.
L. Samarendra Singh : Ingagi Nong, Mamang Leikai Thambal Satle
E. Nilakanta Singh : Manipur, Lamangnaba
Shri Biren : Tangkhul Hui
Th. Ibopishak : Anouba Thunglaba Jiba.

(b) **Kanchi Sheireng. (Pub) Manipur University 1998 (Ed.)**

Dr. L. Kamal Singh : Biswa-Prem
Shri Biren : Chaphadraba Laigi Yen
Th. Ibopishak : Norok Patal Prithivi

(II) **Epic**

1. A. Dorendrajit Singh : Kansa Bodha
2. H. Anganghal Singh : Khamba-Thoibi Sheireng (San-Senba, Lei Langba,Shamu Khonggi Bichar)

(III) **Drama**

1. S. Lalit Singh : Areppa Marup
2. G.C. Tongbra : Matric Pass
3. A. Samarendra : Judge Saheb ki Imung

Novel, Short-story and Prose

(I) **Novel**

1. Dr. L. Kamal Singh : Madhabi
2. H. Anganghal Singh : Jahera
3. H. Guno Singh : Laman
4. Pacha Meetei : Imphal Amasung, Magi Ishing, Nungsitki Phibam

(II) Short-story

(a) **Kanchi Warimacha (Pub) Manipur University 1997(Ed.)**

R.K. Shitaljit Singh : Kamala Kamala
M.K. Binodini : Eigi Thahoudraba Heitup Lalu
Kh. Prakash : Wanom Shareng

(b) **Parishadki Khangatlaba Warimacha (Pub) Manipuri Sahitya Parishad 1994 (Ed.)**

S. Nilbir Shastri : Loukhatpa
R.K. Elangba : Karinunggi

(c) **Anouba Manipuri Warimacha (Pub) The Cultural Forum Manipur 1992 (Ed.)**

N. Kunjamohon Singh : Ijat Tanba
E. Dinamani : Nongthak Khongnang

(III) Prose

(a) **Warenggi Saklon [Due Part] (Pub) The Cultural Forum Manipur 1992 (Ed.)**

Kh. Chaoba Singh : Khamba-Thoibigi WariAmasung Mahakavya

(b) **Kanchi Wareng (Pub) Manipur University, 1998 (Ed.)**

B. Manisana Shastri : Phajaba
Ch. Manihar Singh : Lai-Haraoba

(c) **Apunba Wareng (Pub) Manipur University, 1986 (Ed.)**

Ch. Pishak Singh : Samaj Amasung Sanskriti
M.K. Binodini : Thoibidu Warouhouida
Eric Newton : Kalagi Mahousa (translated by I.R. Babu)

(d) **Manipuri Wareng (Pub) The Cultural Forum Manipur 1999 (Ed.)**

S. Krishnamohan Singh : Lan

27. MARATHI

Paper-I

(Answers must be written in Marathi)

Section A

Language and Folk-lore

(a) Nature and Functions of Language (with reference to Marathi)

Language as a signifying system: Langue and Parole; Basic functions; Poetic Language; Standard Language and dialect; Language variations according to social parameters.

Linguistic features of Marathi in thirteenth century and seventeenth century.

(b) Dialects of Marathi; Ahirani; Varhadi; Dangi.

(c) Marathi Grammar; Parts of Speech; Case-system; Prayog-vichar (Voice).

(d) Nature and kinds of Folk-lore (with special reference to Marathi) Lok-Geet, Lok Katha, Lok Natya.

Section B

(History of Literature and Literary Criticism)

(a) History of Marathi Literature

1. From beginning to 1818 AD, with special reference to the following: The Mahanubhava writers, the Varkari poets, the Pandit poets, the Shahirs, Bakhar Literature.
2. From 1850 to 1990, with special reference to developments in the following major forms: Poetry, Fiction (Novel and Short Story), Drama; and major literary currents and movements, Romantic, Realist, Modernist, Dalit, Gramin, Feminist.

(b) Literary Criticism

1. Nature and function of Literature;
2. Evaluation of Literature;
3. Nature, Objectives and Methods of Criticism;
4. Literature, Culture and Society.

Paper-II

(Answer must be written in Marathi)

Textual study of prescribed literary works.

The paper will require first-hand reading of the texts prescribed and will be designed to test the candidate's critical ability.

Section A

Prose

1. 'Smritisthala'
2. Mahatma Jotiba Phule:
   "Shetkaryacha Asud'
   'Sarvajanik Satyadharma'
3. S.V. Ketkar: 'Brahmankanya'
4. P.K. Atre
   'Sashtang Namaskar'
5. Sharchchandra Muktibodh
   'Jana Hey Volatu Jethe'
6. Uddhav Shelke
   'Shilan'
7. Baburao Bagul
   'Jevha Mi Jaat Chorli Hoti'

8. Gouri Deshpande
   'Ekek Paan Galavaya'
9. P.I. Sonkamble
   'Athavaninche Pakshi'

Section-B

(Poetry)

1. 'Namadevanchi Abhangawani'
   Ed: Inamdar, Relekar, Mirajkar Modern Book Depot, Pune
2. 'Painjan'
   Ed: M.N. Adwant Sahitya Prasar Kendra, Nagpur
3. 'Damayanti-Swayamvar' By Raghunath Pandit
4. 'Balakvinchi Kavita' By Balkavi
5. 'Vishakha'
   By Kusumagraj
6. 'Maridgandh'
   By Vinda Karandikar
7. 'Jahirnama'
   By Narayan Surve
8. 'Sandhyakalchya Kavita' By Grace
9. 'Ya Sattet Jeev Ramat Nahi' By Namdev Dhasal

28. NEPALI

Paper-I

(Answers must be written in Nepali)

Section A

1. History of the origin and development of Nepali as one of the new Indo Aryan Languages.
2. Fundamentals of Nepali Grammar and phonology:
   (i) Nominal forms and categories: Gender, Number, Case, Adjectives, Pronouns, Avyayas
   (ii) Verbal forms and categories: Tense, Aspects, Voice, Roots and Fixes
   (iii) Nepali Swara and Vyanjana;
3. Major Dialects of Nepali
4. Standardisation and Modernisation of Nepali with special reference to language movements (viz. Halanta Bahiskar, Jharrovad etc.)
5. Teaching of Nepali language in India—Its history and development with special reference to its socio- cultural aspects.

Section B

1. History of Nepali literature with special reference to its development in India.
2. Fundamental concepts and theories of Literature: Kavya/Sahitya, Kavya Prayojan, Literary genres, Shabda Shakti, Rasa, Alankara, Tragedy, Comedy, Aesthetics, Stylistics.
3. Major literary trends and movements: Swachchhandatavad, Yatharthavad, Astitwavad, Ayamik Movement Contemporary Nepali writings, Postmodernism.
4. Nepali folklores (the following folk-form only): Sawai, Jhyaurey, Selo, Sangini, Lahari.

Paper-II

(Answers must be written in Nepali)

This paper will require first hand reading of the texts prescribed below and questions will be designed to test the candidate's critical acumen.

Section A		
1.	Santa Jnandil Das	Udaya Lahari
2.	Lekhnath Poudyal	Tarun Tapasi(Vishrams III, V, VI, XII, XV, XVIII only)
3.	Agam Sing Giri	Jaleko Pratibimba Royeko Pratidhwani (The following Poems only-Prasawako Chichyahatsanga Byunjheko Ek Raat, Chhorolai, Jaleko Pratibimba: Royeko Pratidhwani, Hamro Akashmani Pani Hunchha Ujyalo, Tihar).
4.	Haribhakta Katuwal	Yo Zinadagi Khai Ke Zindagi: (The following poems only-Jeevan: Ek Dristi, Yo Zindagi Khai Ke Zindagi, Akashka Tara Ke Tara, Hamilai Nirdho Nasamjha, Khai Manyata Yahan Atmahutiko Balidan Ko).
5.	Balkrishna Sama	Prahlad.
6.	Manbahadur Mukhia	Andhyaroma Banchneharu (The following One-Act only-Andhyaroma Banchneharu' 'Suskera')
Section B		
1.	Indra Sundas	Sahara.
2.	Lilbahadur Chhetri	Brahmaputra ko Chheuchhau
3.	Rupnarayan Sinha	Katha Navaratna (The following stories only—Biteka Kura, Jimmewari Kasko, Dhanamatiko Cinema—Swapna, Vidhwasta Jeevan).

4.	Indrabahadur Rai	Vipana Katipaya (The following stories only—Raatbhari Huri Chalyo, Jayamaya Aphumatra Lekhapani Aipugi, Bhagi, Ghosh Babu, Chhutuaiyo).
5.	Sanu Lama	Katha Sampaad (The following stories only—Swasni Manchhey, Khani Tarma Ekdin, Phurbale Gaun Chhadyo, Asinapo Manchhey).
6.	Laxmi Prasad	Laxmi Nibandha DevkotaSangraha (The following essays only—Sri Ganeshaya Namha, Nepali Sahityako Itihasma Sarvashrestha Purus, Kalpana, Kala Ra Jeevan, Gadha Buddhiman ki Guru?)
7.	Ramkrishna Sharma	Das Gorkha (The following essays only—Kavi, Samaj Ra Sahitya, Sahityama Sapekshata, Sahityik Ruchiko Praudhata, Nepali Sahityako Pragati).

29. ODIA

Paper-I

(Answers must be written in Odia)

Section A

History of Odia Language

(i) Origin and development of Odia Language: Influence of Austric, Dravidian, Perso— Arabic and English on Odia Language.
(ii) Phonetics and Phonemics: Vowels, Consonants Principles of changes in Odia sounds.
(iii) Morphology: Morphemes (free, bound compound and complex), derivational and inflectional affixes, case inflection, conjugation of verb.
(iv) Syntax: Kinds of sentences and their trans-formation, structure of sentences.
(v) Semantics: Different types of change in meaning. Euphemism.
(vi) Common errors in spellings, grammatical uses and construction of sentences.
(vii) Regional variations in Odia Language (Western, Southern and Northern Odia) and Dialects (Bhatri and Desia).

Section B

History of Odia Literature

(i) Historical backgrounds (social, cultural and political) of Odia Literature of different periods.
(ii) Ancient epics, ornate kavyas and padavalis.
(iii) Typical structural forms of Odia Literature (Koili, Chautisa, Poi, Chaupadi, Champu).
(iv) Modern trends in poetry, drama short story, novel essay and literary criticism.

Paper-II

(Answers must be written in Odia)

Critical Study of texts: The paper will require first hand reading of the text and test the critical ability of the candidate.

Section A

Poetry (Ancient)

1. Sāralā Dās—Shanti Parva from Mahābhārata.
2. Jaganāth Dās—Bhāgabata, XI Skadhā—Jadu Avadhuta Sambāda.

(Medieval)

3. Dinakrushna Dās—Raskallola—(Chhāndas—16 & 34)
4. Upendra Bhanja—Lāvanyabati (Chhāndas—1 & 2).

(Modern)

5. Rādhānath Rāy—Chandrabhāgā.
6. Māyādhar Mänasinha—Jeevan—Chitā.
7. Sātchidananda Routray—Kabitā—1962.
8. Ramākānta Ratha—Saptama Ritu.

Section B

Drama

9. Manoranjan Dās—Kätha-Ghoda.
10. Bijay Mishra—Tata Niranjanä.

Novel

11. Fakir Mohan Senāpati—Chhamāna Āthaguntha.
12. Gopināth Mohānty—Dānāpani.

Short Story

13. Surendra Mohānty—Marālara Mrityu.
14. Manoj Dās—Laxmira Abhisāra.

Essay

15. Chittaranjan Dās—Tranga O Tadit (First Five essays).
16. Chandra Sekhar Rath—Mun Satyadharmā Kahuchhi (First five essays).

30. PUNJABI

Paper-I

(Answers must be written in Punjabi in Gurumukhi script)

Section A

(a) Origin of Punjabi Language; different stages of development and recent development in Punjabi Language; characteristics of Punjabi phonology and the study of its tones; classification of vowels and consonants.

(b) Punjabi morphology; the number-gender system (animate and inanimate), prefixes, affixes and different categories of Post positions; Punjabi word formation; **Tatsam. Tad Bhav**. forms; Sentence structure, the notion of subject and object in Punjabi; Noun and verb phrases.

(c) Language and dialect: the notions of dialect and idiolect: major dialects of Punjabi: Pothohari, Majhi, Doabi, Malwai, Paudhi; the validity of speech variation on the basis of social stratification, the distinctive features of various dialects with special reference to tones Language and script; origin and development of Gurumukhi; Suitability of Gurumukhi for Punjabi.

(d) Classical background: Nath Jogi Sahit.

Medieval Literature: Gurmat, Suti, Kissa and Var: janamsakhis.

Section B

(a) Modern trends Mystic, romantic, progressive and neomystic (Vir Singh, Puran Singh, Mohan Singh, Amrita Pritam, Bawa Balwant, Pritam Singh Safeer, J. S. Neki). Experimentalist (Jasbir Singh Ahluwalia, Ravinder Ravi, Ajaib Kamal). Aesthetes (Harbhajan Singh, Tara Singh). Neo-progressive (Pash, Jagtar, Patar).

(b) Folk Literature Folk songs, Folk tales, Riddles, Proverbs.

Epic : (Vir Singh, Avtar Singh Azad, Mohan Singh).

Lyric : (Gurus, Sufis and Modern Lyricists-Mohan Singh, Amrita Pritam, Shiv Kumar, Harbhajan Singh).

(c) Drama : (I.C. Nanda, Harcharan Singh, Balwant Gargi, S.S. Sekhon, Charan Das Sidhu).

Novel : (Vir Singh, Nanak Singh, Jaswant Singh Kanwal, K.S. Duggal, Sukhbir, Gurdial Singh, Dalip Kaur Tiwana, Swaran Chandan).

Short Story : (Sujan Singh, K. S. Virk, Prem Parkash, Waryam Sandhu).

(d) Socio-cultural : Sanskrit, Persian and Western.

Literary influences: Essay (Puran Singh, Teja Singh, Gurbaksh Singh).

Literary Criticism (S.S. Sekhon, Attar Singh, Kishan Singh, Harbhajan Singh, Najam Hussain Sayyad).

Paper-II

Answers must be written in Punjabi in Gurumukhi script

This paper will require first-hand reading of the texts prescribed and will be designed to test the candidate's critical ability.

Section A

(a) Sheikh Farid : The complete Bani as includedin the Adi Granth.

(b) Guru Nanak : Japu Ji. Baramah. Asa di Var.

(c) Bulleh Shah : Kafian

(d) Waris Shah : Heer

Section B

(a) Shah Mohammad : Jangnama (Jang Singhante Firangian)
Dhani Ram Chatrik Chandan Vari (Poet): Sufi Khana Nawan Jahan

(b) Nanak Singh : Chitta Lahu (Novelist)
Pavittar Papi : Ek Mian Do Talwaran

(b) Gurbaksh Singh : Zindagi-di-Ras (Essayist)

(c) Nawan Shivala : Merian Abhul Yadaan.
Balraj Sahni : Mera Roosi Safarnama
(Travelogue). : Mera Pakistani Safarnama

(d) Balwant Gargi : Loha Kutt (Dramatist)
Dhuni-di-Agg : Sultan Razia
Sant Singh Sekhon : Sahityarth(Critic)
Parsidh Punjabi Kavi : Punjabi Kav Shiromani.

31. SANSKRIT

Paper-I

There will be three questions as indicated in the Question Paper which must be answered in Sanskrit. The Remaining questions must be answered either in Sanskrit or in the medium of examination opted by the candidate.

Section A

1. Significant features of the grammar, with particular stress on Sanjna, Sandhi, Karaka, Samasa, Kartari and Karmani vacyas (voice usages) (to be answered in Sanskrit).
2. (a) Main characteristics of Vedic Sanskrit language
   (b) Prominent feature of classical Sanskrit language
   (c) Contribution of Sanskrit to linguistic studies
3. General Knowledge of:
   (a) Literary history of Sanskrit
   (b) Principal trends of literary criticism
   (c) Ramayana
   (d) Mahabharata
   (e) The origin and development of literary geners of:
   Mahakavya
   Rupaka (drama)
   Katha
   Akhyayika Campu Khandakavya
   Muktaka Kavya.

Section B

4. Essential of Indian Culture with stress on:
   - (a) Purusārthas
   - (b) Samskāras
   - (c) Varnāsramavyavasthā
   - (d) Arts and fine arts
   - (e) Technical Sciences.
5. Trends of Indian Philosophy
   - (a) Mïmansā
   - (b) Vedānta
   - (c) Nyaya
   - (d) Vaisesika
   - (e) Sānkhya
   - (f) Yoga
   - (g) Bauddha
   - (h) Jaina
   - (i) Carvāka
6. Short Essay (in Sanskrit)
7. Unseen passage with the questions (to be answered in Sanskrit).

Paper-II

Question from Group 4 is to be answered in Sanskrit only. Questions from Groups 1, 2 and 3 are to be answered either in Sanskrit or in the medium opted by the candidate.

Section A

General study of the following groups:

Group 1
- (a) Raghuvamsam—Kalidasa
- (b) Kumarasambhavam—Kalidasa
- (c) Kiratarjuniyam—Bharavi
- (d) Sisupalavadham—Magha
- (e) Naisadhiyacaritam—Sriharsa
- (f) Kadambari—Banabhatta
- (g) Dasakumaracaritam—Dandin
- (h) Sivarajyodayam—S.B. Varnekar

Group 2
- (a) Isāvāsyopanisad
- (b) Bhagavadgitā
- (c) Sundarakanda of Valmiki's Ramayana
- (d) Arthasastra of Kautilya

Group 3
- (a) Svapanavasavadattam—Bhasa
- (b) Abhijnanasakuntalam—Kalidasa
- (c) Mricchakatikam—Sudraka
- (d) Mudraraksasam—Visakhadatta
- (e) Uttararamacaritam—Bhavbhuti
- (f) Ratnavali—Sriharshavardhana
- (g) Venisamharam—Bhattanarayana

Group 4 Short notes in Sanskrit on the following:—
- (a) Meghadutam—Kalidasa
- (b) Nitisatakam—Bhartrhari

(c) Pancatantra—
(d) Rajatarangini—Kalhana
(e) Harsacaritam—Banabhatta
(f) Amarukasatakam—Amaruka
(g) Gitagovindam—Jayadeva.

Section B

This section will require first hand reading of the following selected texts:— (Questions from Groups 1 & 2 are to be answered in Sanskrit only) Questions from Groups 3 and 4 are to be answered either in Sanskrit or in the Medium opted by the candidate.

Group 1 (a) Raghuvamsam—Canto I, Verses 1 to 10
(b) Kumarasambhavam—Canto I, Verses 1 to 10
(c) Kiratarjuniyaue—Canto I, Verses 1 to 10

Group 2 (a) Isavasyopanisad—Verses—1, 2, 4, 6, 7, 15 and 18
(b) Bhagavatgita II Chapter Verses 13 to 25
(c) Sundarakandam of Valmiki Canto15, Verses 15 to 30 (Geeta Press Edition)

Group 3 (a) Meghadutam—Verses 1 to 10
(b) Nitisatakam—Verses 1 to 10 (Edited by D.D. Kosambi Bharatiya Vidya Bhavan Publication)
(c) Kadambari—Sukanasopadesa (only)

Group 4 (a) Svapnavasavadattam Act VI
(b) Abhijnansakuntalam Act IV Verses 15 to 30 (M.R. Kale Edition)
(c) Uttararamacaritam Act I Verses 31 to 47 (M.R. Kale Edition).

32. SANTHALI

Paper-I

(Answers must be written in Santhali)

Section A

Part-I

History of Santhali Language

1. Main Austric Language family, population and distribution.
2. Grammatical structure of Santhali Language.
3. Important character of Santhali Language: Phonology, Morphology, Syntax, Semantics, Translation, Lexicography.
4. Impact of other languages of Santhali.
5. Standardization of Santhali Language.

Part-II

History of Santhali Literature

1. Literary trend of the following four periods of history of Santhali Literature.
   (a) Ancient Literature before 1854.
   (b) Missionary period Literature between 1855 to 1889 AD.

(c) Medieval period: Literature between 1890 to 1946 AD.
(d) Modern period: Literature from 1947 AD to till date.

2. Writing tradition in History of Santhali literature.

Section B

Literary forms—Main characteristics, history and development of following literary forms.

Part-I

Folk Literature in Santhali: folk song, folk tale, phrase, idioms puzzles, and Kudum.

Part-II

Modern literature in Santhali

1. Development of poetry and prominent poets.
2. Development of prose and prominent writers.
   (i) Novels and prominent Novelists.
   (ii) Stories and prominent story writers.
   (iii) Drama and Prominent Dramatist.
   (iv) Criticism and prominent critics.
   (v) Essay, sketches, memoirs, travelogues and prominent writers.

Santhali writers

Shyam Sundar Hembram, Pandit Raghunath Murmu, Barha Beshra, Sadhu Ramchand Murmu, Narayan Soren 'Toresutam', Sarda Prasad Kisku, Raghunath Tudu, Kalipada Soren, Sakla Soren, Digamber Hansda, Aditya Mitra 'Santhali', Babulal Murmu 'Adivasi', Jadumani Beshra, Arjun Hembram, Krishna Chandra Tudu, Rupchand Hansda, Kalendra Nath Mandi, Mahadev, Hansda, Gour Chandra Murmu, Thakur Prasad Murmu, Hara Prasad Murmu, Uday Nath Majhi, Parimal Hembram, Dhirendra Nath Baske, Shyam Charan Hembram, Damayanti Beshra, T.K. Rapaj, Boyha Biswanath Tudu.

Part-III

Cultural Heritage of Santhali tradition, customs, festival and rituals (birth, marriage and death).

Paper-II

(Answers must be written in Santhali)

Section A

This paper will require in-depth reading of the following texts and the questions will be designed to test the candidates' critical ability.

Ancient Literature

Prose

(a) Kherwal Bonso Dhorom Puthi—Majhi Ramdas Tudu "Rasika".
(b) Mare Hapramko Reyak Katha—L.O. Scrafsrud.

(c) Jomsim Binti Lita—Mangal Chandra Turkulumang Soren.
(d) Marang Buru Binti—Kanailal Tudu.

Poetry

(a) Karam Sereng—Nunku Soren.
(b) Devi Dasain Sereng—Manindra Hansda.
(c) Horh Sereng—W.G. Archer.
(d) Baha Sereng—Balaram Tudu.
(e) Dong Sereng—Padmashri Bhagwat Murmu 'Thakur'.
(f) Hor Sereng—Raghunath Murmu.
(g) Soros Sereng—Babulal Murmu "Adivasi".
(h) More Sin More Ndia—Rup Chand Hansda.
(i) Judasi Madwa Latar—Tez Narayan Murmu.

Section B

Modern Literature

Part-I

Poetry

(a) Onorhen Baha Dhalwak—Paul Jujhar Soren.
(b) Asar Binti—Narayan Soren "Tore Sutam".
(c) Chand Mala—Gora Chand Tudu.
(d) Onto Baha Mala—Aditya Mitra "Santhali".
(e) Tiryo Tetang—Hari Har Hansda.
(f) Sisirjon Rar—Thakur Prasad Murmu.

Part-II

Novels

(a) Harmawak Ato—R.Karstiars (Translator—R.K. Kisku Rapaz).
(b) Manu Mati—Chandra Mohan Hansda.
(c) Ato Orak—Doman Hansdak.
(d) Ojoy Gada Dhiph re—Nathenial Murmu.

Part-III

Stories

(a) Jiyon Gada—Rup Chand Hansda and Jadumani Beshra.
(b) Mayajaal—Doman Sahu 'Samir' and Padmashri Bhagwat Murmu 'Thakur'.

Part-IV

Drama

(a) Kherwar Bir—Pandit Raghunath Murmu.
(b) Juri Khatir—Dr. K.C. Tudu.
(c) Birsa Bir—Ravi Lal Tudu.

Part-V

Biography

Santal Ko Ren Mayam Gohako—Dr. Biswanath Hansda.

33. SINDHI

Paper-I

Answers must be written in Sindhi (Arabic or Devanagari Script)

Section A

1. (a) Origin and evolution of Sindhi language—views of different scholars.
   (b) Significant linguistic features of Sindhi language, including those pertaining to its phonology, morphology and syntax.
   (c) Major dialects of the Sindhi language.
   (d) Sindhi vocabulary—stages of its growth, including those in the pre-partition and post-partition periods.
   (e) Historical study of various Writing Systems (Scripts) of Sindhi.
   (f) Changesin the structure of Sindhi language in India, after partition, due to influence of other languages and social conditions.

Section B

2. Sindhi literature through the ages in context of socio-cultural conditions in the respective periods:
   (a) Early medieval literature upto 1350 A.D. including folk literature.
   (b) Late medieval period from 1350 A.D. to 1850 A.D.
   (c) Renaissance period from 1850 A.D. to 1947 A.D.
   (d) Modern period from 1947 and onwards.
   (Literary genres in Modern Sindhi literature andexperiments in poetry, drama, novel, short story, essay, literary criticism, biography, autobiography, memoirs and travelogues.)

Paper -II

Answer must be written in Sindhi (Arabic or Devanagari script)

This paper will require the first-hand reading of the texts prescribed and will be designed to test the candidate's critical ability.

Section A

References to context and critical appreciation of the texts included in this section.

1. **Poetry**
   (a) "Shah Jo Choond Shair": ed. H.I. Sadarangani, Published by Sahitya Akademi (First 100 pages).
   (b) "Sachal Jo Choond Kalam": ed. Kalyan B. Advani Published by Sahitya Akademi (Kafis only).
   (c) "Sami-a-ja Choond Sloka": ed. B.H. Nagrani Published by Sahitya Akademi (First 100 pages).

(d) "Shair-e-Bewas": by Kishinchand Bewas("Saamoondi Sipoon" portion only).
(e) "Roshan Chhanvro": Narayan Shyam.
(f) "Virhange Khapoi je Sindhi Shair jee Choond": ed. H.I. Sadarangani, published by Sahitya Akademi.

2. Drama

(g) "Behtareen Sindhi Natak" (One-act Plays): Edited by M. Kamal Published by Gujarat Sindhi Academy.
(h) "Kako Kaloomal" (Full-length Play): by Madan Jumani.

Section B

References to context and critical appreciation of the texts included in this section.

(a) 'Pakheeara Valar Khan Vichhrya' (Novel): by Gobind Malhi.
(b) 'Sat Deenhan' (Novel): by Krishin Khatwani.
(c) 'Choond Sindhi Kahanyoon' (Short Stories) Vol. III.: Edited by Prem Prakash, published by Sahitya Akademi.
(d) 'Bandhan' (Short Stories): Sundari Uttamchandani.
(e) 'Behtareen Sindhi Mazmoon' (Essays): Edited by Hiro Thakur, published by Gujarat Sindhi Academi.
(f) 'Sindhi Tanqeed' (Criticism): Edited by Harish Vaswani: Published by Sahitya Akademi.
(g) 'Mumhinjee Hayati-a-ja Sona Ropa varqa' (Autobiography): by Popati Hiranandani.
(h) "Dr. Choithram Gidwani" (Biography): by Vishnu Sharma.

34. TAMIL

Paper-I

Answers must be written in Tamil

Section A

Part-I

History of Tamil Language

Major Indian Language Families: The place of Tamil among Indian Languages in general and Dravidian in particular—Enumeration and Distribution of Dravidian languages.

The language of Sangam Literature: The language of medieval Tamil- Pallava Period only—Historical study of Nouns, Verbs, Adjectives, Adverbs—Tense markers and case markers in Tamil.

Borrowing of words from other languages into Tamil: Regional and social dialects—difference between literary and spoken Tamil.

Part-II

History of Tamil Literature

Tolkappiyam-Sangam Literature: The division of Akam and Puram—The secular characteristics of Sangam Literature—The development of Ethical literature—Silappadikaram and Manimekalai.

Part-III

Devotional Literature (Alwars and Nayanamars)

The bridal mysticism in Alwar hymns—Minor literary forms (Tutu, Ula, Parani, Kuravanji). Social factors for the development of Modern Tamil Literature; Novel, Short Story and New Poetry—The impact of various political ideologies on modern writings.

Section B

Part-I

Recent trends in Tamil Studies

Approaches to criticism: Social, psychological, historical and moralistic—the use of criticism—the various techniques in literature; Ullurai, Iraicchi, Thonmam (Myth) Otturuvagam (allegory), Angadam (Satire), Meyappadu, Padimam (image), Kuriyeedu (Symbol), Irunmai (Ambiguity)—The concept of comparative literature-the principle of comparative literature.

Part-II

Folk literature in Tamil

Ballads, Songs, proverbs and riddles—Sociological study of Tamil folklore. Uses of translation—Translation of Tamil works into other languages-Development of journalism in Tamil.

Part-III

Cultural Heritage of the Tamils

Concept of Love and War—Concept of Aram-the ethical codes adopted by the ancient Tamils in their warfare-customs beliefs, rituals, modes of worship in the five Thinais.

The Cultural changes as revealed in post sangam literature—cultural fusion in the medieval period (Janism and Buddhism). The development of arts and architecture through the ages (Pallavas, later Cholas, and Nayaks). The impact of various political, social, religious and cultural movements on Tamil Society. The role of mass media in the cultural change of contemporary

Tamil society.

Paper-II

Answers must be written in Tamil

The paper will require first-hand reading of the text prescribed and will be designed to test the critical ability of the candidate.

Section A

Part-I

Ancient Literature

1. Kuruntokai (1–25 poems)
2. Purananuru (182–200 poems)
3. Tirukkural Porutpal: Arasiyalum Amaichiyalum (from Iraimatchi to Avaianjamai).

Part-II

Epic Literature

1. Silappadikaram: Madhurai Kandam only.
2. Kambaramayanam: Kumbakarunan Vadhai Padalam.

Part-III

Devotional Literature

1. Tiruvasagam: Neetthal Vinnappam
2. Tiruppavai: (Full Text).

Modern Literature

Part-I

Poetry

1. Bharathiar: Kannan Pattu

Section B

2. Bharathidasan: Kudumba Vilakku
3. Naa. Kamarasan: Karappu Malarkal

Prose

1. Mu. Varadharajanar: Aramum Arasiyalum
2. C. N. Annadurai: Ye! Thazhntha Tamilagame.

Part-II

Novel, Short Story and Drama

1. Akilon ; Chittairappavai
2. Jayakanthan: Gurupeedam
3. Cho: Yaurkkum Vetkamillai

Part-III

Folk Literature

1. Muthuppattan kathai Edited by Na. Vanamamalai, (Publication: Madurai Kamaraj University).
2. Malaiyaruvi, Edited by Ki. Va Jagannathan (Publication: Saraswathi Mahal, Thanjavur).

35. TELUGU

Paper-I

Answer must be written in Telugu

Section A

Language

1. Place of Telugu among Dravidian languages and its antiquity—Etymological History of Telugu, Tenugu and Andhra.
2. Major linguistic changes in phonological, morphological, grammatical and syntactical levels, from Proto-Dravidian to old Telugu and from old Telugu to Modern Telugu.
3. Evolution of spoken Telugu when compared to classical Telugu-Formal and functional view of Telugu language.
4. Influence of other languages and its impact on Telugu.
5. Modernization of Telugu language:
   (a) Linguistic and literary movements and their role in modernization of Telugu.
   (b) Role of media in modernization of Telugu (News-papers, Radio, TV etc.)
   (c) Problems of terminology and mechanisms in coining new terms in Telugu in various discourses including scientific and technical.
6. Dialects of Telugu—Regional and social variations and problems of Standardization.
7. Syntax—Major divisions of Telugu sentences—simple, complex and compound sentences—Noun and verb predications—Processes of nominalization and relativization—Direct and indirect reporting-conversion processes.
8. Translation—Problems of translation, cultural, social and idiomatic—Methods of translation—Approaches to translation—Literary and other kinds of translation—Various uses of translation.
   1. Literature in Pre-Nannaya Period—Marga and Desi poetry.
   2. Nannaya Period—Historical and literary background of Andhra Mahabharata.
   3. Saiva poets and their contribution—Dwipada, Sataka, Ragada, Udaharana.
   4. Tikkana and his place in Telugu literature.
   5. Errana and his literary works—Nachana Somana and his new approach to poetry.
   6. Srinatha and Potana—Their works and contribution.
   7. Bhakti poets in Telugu literature—Tallapaka Annamayya, ramadasu, tyagayya.
   8. Evolution of prabandhas—Kavya and prabandha.
   9. Southern school of Telugu literature-raghunatha Nayaka, chemakura vankatakavi and women poets-Literary forms like yakshagana, prose and padakavita.

10. Modern Telugu Literature and literary forms—Novel, Short Story, Drama, Playlet and poetic forms.
11. Literary Movements: Reformation, Nationalism, Neo-classisicism, Romanticism and Progressive, Revolutionary movements.
12. Digambarakavulu, feminist and dalit Literature.
13. Main divisions of folk literature—Performing folk arts.

Paper-II

Answer must be written in Telugu

This paper will require first hand reading of the prescribed texts and will be designed to test the candidate's critical ability, which will be in relation to the following approaches:

(i) Aesthetic approach—Rassa, Dhawani, Vakroti and Auchitya—Formal and Structural-Imagery and Symbolism.

(ii) Sociological, Historical, Ideological, Psychological approaches.

Section A

1. Nannaya-Dushyanta Chritra (Adiparva 4th Canto verses 5—109).
2. Tikkana-Sri Krishna Rayabaramu (Udyoga parva-3rd Canto verses 1—144).
3. Srinath-Guna Nidhi Katha (Kasikhandam, 4th Canto, verses 76—133).
4. Pingali Surana-sugatri Salinulakatha (Kalapurno-dayamu 4 Canto verses, 60—142).
5. Molla-Ramayanamu (Balakanda including avatarika).
6. Kasula Purushothama Kavi—Andhra Nayaka Satakamu.

Section B

7. Gurajada Appa Rao—Animutyalu (Short stories).
8. Viswanatha Satyanarayana—Andhra prasasti.
9. Devulapalli Krishna Sastry—Krishnapaksham (excluding Uravsi and Pravasam).
10. Sri Sri-Maha prastanam.
11. Jashuva-Gabbilam (Part I).
12. C. Narayana Reddy—Karpuravasanta rayalu.
13. Kanuparti Varalakshmamma—Sarada lekhalu (Part I).
14. Atreya—N.G.O.
15. Racha Konda Viswanatha Sastry—Alpajaeevi.

36. URDU

Paper-I

Answer must be written in Urdu

Section A

Development of Urdu Language

(a) Development of Indo-Aryan
  (i) Old Indo-Aryan
  (ii) Middle Indo-Aryan
  (iii) New Indo-Aryan.

(b) Western Hindi and its dialects Brij Bhasha Khadi Boli, Haryanavi, Kannauji, Bundeli—Theories about the origin of Urdu language.

(c) Dakhani Urdu—origin and development, its significant linguistic features. (d) Social and Cultural roots of Urdu language— and its distinctive features. Script, Phonology, Morphology, Vocabulary.

Section B

(a) Genres and their development:
  (i) Poetry: Ghazal, Masnavi, Qasida, Marsia, Rubai Jadid Nazm.
  (ii) Prose: Novel, Short Story, Dastan, Drama, Inshaiya, Khutoot, Biography.

(b) Significant feaures of:
  (i) Deccani, Delhi and Lucknow schools,
  (ii) Sir Syed movement, Romantic movement, Progressive movement, Modernism.

(c) Literary Criticism and its development with reference to Hali, Shibli, Kaleemuddin Ahmad, Ehtisham Hussain, Ale-Ahmad Suroor.

(d) Essay writing (covering literary and imaginativetopics).

Paper-II

Answer must be written in Urdu

This paper will require first hand reading of the texts prescribed and will be designed to test the candidate's critical ability.

Section-A		
1.	Mir Amman	Bagho-Babar
2.	Ghalib	Intikhab-e-Khutoot-e Ghalib
3.	Mohd. Husain Azad	Nairang-e-Khayal
4.	Prem Chand	Godan
5.	Rajendra Singh Bedi	Apne Dukh Mujhe Dedo
6.	Abul Kalam Azad	Ghubar-e-Khatir

Section-B		
1.	Mir	Intikhab-e-Kalam-e-Mir (Ed. Abdul Haq.)
2.	Mir Hasan	Sahrul Bayan
3.	Ghalib	Diwan-e-Ghalib
4.	Iqbal	Bal-e-Jibrail
5.	Firaq	Gul-e-Naghma
6.	Faiz	Dast-e-Saba
7.	Akhtruliman	Bint-e-Lamhat

37. MANAGEMENT

The candidate should make a study of the concept of development of Management as s cience and art drawing upon the contributions of leading thinkers of management and apply the concepts to the real life of government and business decision-making keeping in view the changes in the strategic and operative environment.

Paper-I

1. **Managerial Function and Process:** Concept and foundations of management, Evolution of Management Thoughts; Managerial Functions—Planning, Organizing, Controlling; Decision-making; Role of Manager, Managerial skills; Entrepreneurship; Management of innovation; Managing in a global environment, Flexible Systems Management; Social responsibility and managerial ethics; Process and customer orientation; Managerial processes on direct and indirect value chain.
2. **Organisational Behaviour and Design** Conceptual model of organization behaviour; The individual processes—personality, values and attitude, perception, motivation, learning and reinforcement, work stress and stress management; The dynamics of Organization behaviour—power and politics, conflict and negotiation, leadership process and styles, communication; The Organizational Processes—decision-making, job design; Classical, Neoclassical and Contingency approaches to organizational design; Organizational theory and design—Organizational culture, managing cultural diversity, learning Organization; Organizational change and development; Knowledge Based Enterprise—systems and processes; Networked and virtual organizations.
3. **Human Resource Management:** HR challenges; HRM functions; The future challenges of HRM; Strategic Management of human resources; Human resource planning; Job analysis; Job evaluation, Recruitment and selection; Training and development; Promotion and transfer; Performance management; Compensation management and bnenefits; Employee morale and productivity; Management of Organizational climate and Industrial relations; Human resources accounting and audit; Human resource information system; International human resource management.

4. **Accounting for Managers:** Financial accounting—concept, importance and scope, generally accepted accounting principles, preparation of financial statements with special reference to analysis of a balance sheet and measurment of business income, inventory valuation and depreciation, financial statement analysis, fund flow analysis, the statement of cash flows; Management accounting concept, need, imporance and scope; Cost accounting—records and processes, cost ledger and control accounts, reconciliation and integration bwtween financial and cost accounts; Overhead cost and control, Job and process costing, Budget and budgetary control, Performance budgeting, Zero-base budgeting, relevant costing and costing for decision-making, standard costing and variance analysis, marginal costing and absorption costing.
5. **Financial Management:** Goal of Finance Function. Concepts of value and return. Valuation of bonds and Shares; Management of working capital: Estimation and Financing; Management of cash, receivables, inventory and current liabilities; Cost of capital ; Capital budgeting; Financial and operating leverage; Design of capital structure: theories and practices; Shareholder value creation: dividend policy, corporate financial policy and strategy, management of corporate distress and restructuring strategy; Capital and money markets: institutions and instruments; Leasing hire purchase and venture capital; Regulation of capital market; Risk and return: portfolio theory; CAPM; APT; Financial derivatives: option, futures, swap; Recent reforms in financial sector.
6. **Marketing Management:** Concept, evolution and scope; Marketing strategy formulation and components of marketing plan; Segmenting and targeting the market; Positioning and differentiating the market offering; Analyzing competition; Analyzing consumer markets; Industrial buyer behaviour; Market research; Product strategy; Pricing strategies; Designing and managing Marketing channels; Integrated marketing communications; Building customer staisfaction, Value and retention; Services and non-profit marketing; Ethics in marketing; Consumer protection; Internet marketing; Retail management; Customer relationship management; Concept of holistic marketing.

Paper-II

1. **Quantitative Techniques in Decision-making:** Descriptive statistics—tabular, graphical and numerical methods, introduction to probability, discrete and continuous probability distributions, inferential statistics-sampling distributions, central limit theorem, hypothesis testing for differences between means and proportions, inference about population variances, Chisquare and ANOVA, simple correlation and regression, time series and forecasting, decision theory, index numbers; Linear programming—problem formulation, simplex method and graphical solution, sensitivity analysis.
2. **Production and Operations Management:** Fundamentals of operations management; Organizing for production; Aggregate production planning, capacity planning, plant design: process planning, plant size and scale of

operations, Management of facilities; Line balancing; Equipment replacement and maintenance; Production control; Supply, chain management—vendor evaluation and audit; Quality management; Statistical process control, Six Sigma; Flexibility and agility in manufacturing systems; World class manufaturing; Project management concepts, R&D management, Management of service operations; Role and importance of materials management, value analysis, make or buy decision; Inventory control, MRP; Waste management.

3. **Management Information System:** Conceptual foundations of information systems; Information theory; Information resource management; Types of information Systems; Systems Development—Overview of Systems and Design; System Development management life-cycle, Designing online and distributed environments; Implementation and control of project; Trends in information technology; Managing data resources—Organising data. DSS and RDBMS; Enterprise Resource Planning (ERP), Expert systems, e-Business architecture, e-Governance; Information systems planning, Flexibility in information systems; User involvement; Evaluation of information systems.
4. **Government Business Interface:** State participation in business, Interaction between Government, Business and different Chambers of Commerce and Industry in India; Government's ploicy with regard to Small Scale Industries; Government clearances for establishing a new enterprise; Public Distribution System; Government control over price and distribution; Consumer Protection Act (CPA) and The Role of Voluntary Organizations in protecting consumers' rights; New Industrial Policy of the Government: liberalization, deregulation and privatisation; Indian planning system; Government policy concerning development of Backward areas/regions; The Responsibilities of the business as well as the Government to protect the environment; Corporate Governance; Cyber Laws.
5. **Strategic Cost Management:** Business policy as a field of study; Nature and scope of strategic management, Strategic intent, vision, objectives and policies; Process of strategic planning and implementa-tion; Environmental analysis and internal analysis; SWOT analysis; Tools and techniques for strategic analysis—Impact matrix: The experience curve, BCG matrix, GEC mode, Industry analysis, Concept of value chain; Strategic profile of a firm; Framework for analysing competition; Competitive advantage of a firm; Generic competitive strategies; Growth strategies—expansion, integration and diversification; Concept of core competence, Strategic flexibility; Reinventing strategy; Strategy and structure; chief Executive and Board; turnaround management; Management of strategic change; Strategic alliances, Mergers and Acquisitions; Strategy and corporate evolution in the Indian context.
6. **International Business:** International Business Environment: Changing composition of trade in goods and services; India's Foreign Trade: Policy and trends; Financing of International trade; Regional Economic Cooperation;

FTAs; Internationalisation of service firms; International production; Operation Management in International companies; International Taxation; Global competitiveness and technological developments; Global E-Business; Designing global organisational structure and control; Multicultural management; Global business strategy; Global marketing strategies; Export Management; Export-Import procedures; Joint Ventures; Foreign Investment: Foreign direct investment and foreign portfolio investment; Cross-border Mergers and Acquisitions; Foreign Exchange Risk Exposure Management; World Financial Markets and International Banking; External Debt Management; Country Risk Analysis.

38. MATHEMATICS

Paper-I

1. **Linear Algebra:** Vector spaces over R and C, linear dependence and independence, subspaces, bases, dimensions, Linear transformations, rank and nullity, matrix of a linear transformation.
   Algebra of Matrices; Row and column reduction, Echelon form, congruence's and similarity; Rankof a matrix; Inverse of a matrix; Solution of system of linear equations; Eigenvalues and eigenvectors, characteristic polynomial, Cayley-Hamilton theorem, Symmetric, skew-symmetric, Hermitian, skew-Hermitian, orthogonal and unitary matrices and their eigenvalues.
2. **Calculus:** Real numbers, functions of a real variable, limits, continuity, differentiability, mean-value theorem, Taylor's theorem with remainders, indeterminate forms, maxima and minima, asymptotes; Curve tracing; Functions of two or three variables; Limits, continuity, partial derivatives, maxima and minima, Lagrange's method of multipliers, Jacobian.
   Riemann's definition of definite integrals; Indefinite integrals; Infinite and improper integral; Double and triple integrals (evaluation techniques only); Areas, surface and volumes.
3. **Analytic Geometry:** Cartesian and polar coordinates in three dimensions, second degree equations in three variables, reduction to Canonical forms; straight lines, shortest distance between two skew lines, Plane, sphere, cone, cylinder, paraboloid, ellipsoid, hyperboloid of one and two sheets and their properties.
4. **Ordinary Differential Equations:** Formulation of differential equations; Equations of first order and first degree, integrating factor; Orthogonal trajectory; Equations of first order but not of first degree, Clairaut's equation, singular solution.
   Second and higher order liner equations with constant coefficients, complementary function, particular integral and general solution.
   Section order linear equations with variable coefficients, Euler-Cauchy equation; Determination of complete solution when one solution is known using method of variation of parameters.

Laplace and Inverse Laplace transforms and their properties, Laplace transforms of elementary functions. Application to initial value problems for 2nd order linear equations with constant coefficients.

5. **Dynamics and Statics:** Rectilinear motion, simple harmonic motion, motion in a plane, projectiles; Constrained motion; Work and energy, conservation of energy; Kepler's laws, orbits under central forces.

   Equilibrium of a system of particles; Work and potential energy, friction, Common catenary; Principle of virtual work; Stability of equilibrium, equilibrium of forces in three dimensions.

6. **Vector Analysis:** Scalar and vector fields, differentiation of vector field of a scalar variable; Gradient, divergence and curl in cartesian and cylindrical coordinates; Higher order derivatives; Vector identities and vector equation.

   Application to geometry: Curves in space, curvature and torsion; Serret-Furenet's formulae. Gauss and Stokes' theorems, Green's indentities.

Paper-II

1. **Algebra:** Groups, subgroups, cyclic groups, cosets, Lagrange's Theorem, normal subgroups, quotient groups, homomorphism of groups, basic isomorphism theorems, permutation groups, Cayley's theorem.

   Rings, subrings and ideals, homomorphisms of rings; Integral domains, principal ideal domains, Euclidean domains and unique factorization domains; Fields, quotient fields.

2. **Real Analysis:** Real number system as an ordered field with least upper bound property; Sequences, limit of a sequence, Cauchy sequence, completeness of real line; Series and its convergence, absolute and conditional convergence of series of real and complex terms, rearrangement of series. Continuity and uniform continuity of functions, properties of continuous functions on compact sets.

   Riemann integral, improper integrals; Fundamental theorems of integral calculus.

   Uniform convergence, continuity, differentiability and integrability for sequences and series of functions; Partial derivatives of functions of several (two or three) variables, maxima and minima.

3. **Complex Analysis:** Analytic function, Cauchy-Riemann equations, Cauchy's theorem, Cauchy's integral formula, power series, representation of an analytic function, Taylor's series; Singularities; Laurent's series; Cauchy's residue theorem; Contour integration.

4. **Linear Programming:** Linear programming problems, basic solution, basic feasible solution and optimal solution; Graphical method and simplex method of solutions; Duality.

   Transportation and assignment problems.

5. **Partial Differential Equations:** Family of surfaces in three dimensions and formulation of partial differential equations; Solution of quasilinear partial differential equations of the first order, Cauchy's method of characteristics; Linear partial differential equations of the second order with constant coefficients, canonical form; Equation of a vibrating string, heat equation, Laplace equation and their solutions.
6. **Numerical Analysis and Computer Programming:** Numerical methods: Solution of algebraic and transcendental equations of one variable by bisection, Regula-Falsi and Newton-Raphson methods, solution of system of linear equations by Gaussian Elimination and Gauss-Jorden (direct), Gauss-Seidel (iterative) methods. Newton's (forward and backward) and interpolation, Lagrange's interpolation.
   Numerical integration: Trapezoidal rule, Simpson's rule, Gaussian quadrature formula. Numerical solution of ordinary differential equations: Eular and Runga Kutta methods. Computer Programming: Binary system; Arithmetic and logical operations on numbers; Octal and Hexadecimal Systems; Conversion to and from decimal Systems; Algebra of binary numbers.
   Elements of computer systems and concept of memory; Basic logic gates and truth tables, Boolean algebra, normal forms.
   Representation of unsigned integers, signed integers and reals, double precision reals and long integers.
   Algorithms and flow charts for solving numerical analysis problems.
7. **Mechanics and Fluid Dynamics:** Generalised coordinates; D'Alembert's principle and Lagrange's equations; Hamilton equations; Moment of inertia; Motion of rigid bodies in two dimensions.
   Equation of continuity; Euler's equation of motion for inviscid flow; Stream-lines, path of a particle; Potential flow; Two-dimensional and axisymmetric motion; Sources and sinks, vortex motion; Navier-Stokes equation for a viscous fluid.

39. MECHANICAL ENGINEERING

Paper-I

1. **Mechanics**
   1.1 **Mechanics of Rigid Bodies:** Equations of equilibrium in space and its application; first and second moments of area; simple problems on friction; kinematics of particles for plane motion; elementary particle dynamics.
   1.2 **Mechanics of Deformable Bodies:** Generalized Hooke's law and its application; design problems on axial stress, shear stress and bearing stress; material properties for dynamic loading; bending shear and stresses in beams; determination of principle stresses and strains-analytical and

graphical; compound and combined stresses; bi-axial stresses-thin walled pressure vessel; material behaviour and design factors for dynamic load; design of circular shafts for bending and torsional load only; deflection of beam for statically determinate problems; theories of failure.

2. **Engineering Materials:** Basic concepts on structure of solids, common ferrous and non-ferrous materials and their applications; heat-treatment of steels; non-metalsplastics, ceramics, composite materials and nano-materials.

3. **Theory of Machines:** Kinematic and dynamic analysis of plane mechanisms. Cams, Gears and empicyclie gear trains, flywheels, governors, balancing of rigid rotors, balancing of single and multicy- linder engines, linear vibration analysis of mechanical systems (single degree of freedom), Critical speeds and whirling of shafts.

4. **Manufacturing Science**

   4.1 **Manufacturing Process:** Machine tool engineering - Merhant's force analysis: Taylor's tool life equation; conventional machining; NC and CNC machining process; jigs and fixtures.

   Non-conventional machining-EDM, ECM, ultrasonic, water jet machining etc.; application of lasers and plasmas; energy rate calculations.

   Forming and welding processes-standard processes.

   Metrology-concept of fits and tolerances; tools and guages; comparators; inspection of length; position; profile and surface finish.

   4.2 **Manufacturing Management:** System design: factory location—simple OR models; plant layout-methods based; applications of engineering economic analysis and break-even analysis for product selection, process selection and capacity planning; predetermined time standards.

   System planning; forecasting methods based on regression and decomposition, design and blancing of multi model and stochastic assembly lines; inventory management-probablistic inventory models for order time and order quanitity determination; JIT systems; strategic sourcing; managing inter plant logistics.

   System operations and control: Scheduling algorithms for job shops; applications of statistical methods for product and process quality control applications of control charts for mean, range, percent defective, number of defectives and defects per unit; quality cost systems; management of resources, organizations and risks in projects.

   System improvement: Implementation of systems, such as total quality management, developing and managing flexible, lean and agile Organizations.

Paper-II

1. **Thermodynamics, Gas Dynamics Turbine**
   1.1 Basic concept of First-law and Second law of Thermodynamics; concept of entropy and reversibility; availability and unavailability and irreversibility.
   1.2 Classification and properties of fluids; incompressible and compressible fluids flows; effect of Mach number and compressibility; continuity momentum and energy equations; normal and oblique shocks; one dimensional isentropic flow; flow or fluids in duct with frictions that transfer.
   1.3 Flow through fans, blowers and compressors; axial and centrifugal flow configuration; design of fans and compressors; single problems compresses and turbine cascade; open and closed cycle gas turbines; work done in the gas turbine; reheat and regenerators.
2. **Heat Transfer**
   2.1 Conduction heat transfer—general conduction equation-Laplace, Poisson and Fourier equations; Fourier law of conduction; one dimensional steady state heat conduction applied to simple wall, solid and hollow cylinder and spheres.
   2.2 Convection heat transfer—Newton's law of convection; free and forces convection; heat transfer during laminar and turbulent flow of an incompressible fluid over a flat plate; concepts of Nusselt number, hydrodynamic and thermal boundary layer their thickness; Prandtl number; analogy between heat and momentum transfer—Reynolds, Colbum, Prandtl analogies; heat transfer during laminar and turbulent flow through horizontal tubes; free convection from horizontal and vertical plates.
   2.3 Black body radiation—basic radiation laws such as Stefan-boltzman, Planck distribution, Wein's displacement etc.
   2.4 Basic heat exchanger analysis; classification of heat exchangers.
3. **Engines**
   3.1 Classification, themodynamic cycles of operation; determination of break power, indicated power, mechanical efficiency, heat balance sheet, interpretation of performance characteristics, petrol, gas and diesel engines.
   3.2 Combustion in SI and CI engines, normal and abnormal combustion; effect of working parameters on knocking, reduction of knocking; Forms of combustion chamber for SI and CI engines; rating of fuels; additives; emission.
   3.3 Different systems of IC engines-fuels; lubricating; cooling and transmission systems. Alternate fuels in IC engines.

4. **Steam Engineering:**
   4.1 Steam generation—modified Ranking cycle analysis; Modern steam boilers; steam at critical and supercritical pressures; draught equipment; natural and artificial draught; boiler fuels solid, liquid and gaseous fuels. Steam turbines—Principle; types; compounding; impulse and reaction turbines; axial thrust.
   4.2 Steam nozzles—flow of steam in convergent and divergent nozzle pressure at throat for maximum discharge with different initial steam conditions such as wet, saturated and superheated, effect of variation of back pressure; supersaturated flow of steam in nozzles, Wilson line.
   4.3 Rankine cycle with internal and external irreversibility; reheat factor; reheating and regeneration, methods of governing; back pressure and pass out turbines.
   4.4 Steam power plants—combined cycle power generation; heat recovery steam generators (HRSG) fired and unfired, co-generation plants.
5. **Refrigeration and Air-conditioning**
   5.1 Vapour compression refrigeration cycle—cycle on p-H & T-s diagrams; ecofriendly refrigerants—R 134a. 123; Systems like evaporators, condensers, compressor, expansion devices. Simple vapour absorption systems.
   5.2 Psychrometry—properties; processes; charts; sensible heating and cooling; humidification and dehumidification effective temperature; air-conditioning load calculation; simple duct design.

40. MEDICAL SCIENCE

Paper-I

1. **Human Anatomy:** Applied anatomy including blood and nerve supply of upper and lower limbs and joints of shoulder, hip and knee.
   Gross anatomy, blood supply and lymphatic drainage of tongue, thyroid, mammary gland, stomach, liver, prostate, gonads and uterus.
   Applied anatomy of diaphragm, perineum and inguinal region.
   Clinical anatomy of kidney, urinary bladder, uterine tubes, vas deferens.
   Embryology: Placenta and placental barrier. Development of heart, gut, kidney. uterus, ovary, testis and their common congenital abnormalities.
   Central and Peripheral Autonomic Nervous System: Gross and clinical anatomy of ventricles of brain, circulation of cerebrospinal fluid; Neural pathways and lesions of cutaneous sensations, hearing and vision; Cranial nerves distribution and clinical significance; Components of autonomic nervous system.
2. **Human Physiology:** Conduction and transmission of impulse, mechanism of contraction, neuromuscular transmission, reflexes, control of equilibrium, posture and muscle tone, descending pathways, functions of cerebellum, basal ganglia, Physiology of sleep and consciousness.

Endocrine System: Mechanism of action of hormones; formation, secretion, transport, metabolism, function and regulation of secretion of pancreas and pituitary gland.

Physiology of Reproductive System: Pregnancy menstrual cycle, lactation, pregnancy.

Blood: Development, regulation and fate of blood cells.

Cardio-vascular,cardiac output, blood pressure, regulation of cardiovascular functions.

3. **Biochemistry:** Organ function tests—liver, kidney, thyroid Protein synthesis. Vitamins and minerals.
   Restriction fragment length Polymorphism (RFLP).
   Polymerase chain reaction (PCR). Radio-immunoassays (RIA).
4. **Pathology:** Inflammation and repair, disturbances of growth and cancer, Pathogenesis and histopathology of rheumatic and ischaemic heart disease and diabetes mellitus. Differentiation between benign, malignant, primary and metastatic malignancies, Pathogenesis and histopathology of bronchogenic carcinoma, carcinoma breast, oral cancer, cancer cervix, leukemia, Etiology, pathogenesis and histopathology of—cirrhosis liver, glomerulonephritis, tuberculosis, acute osteomyelitis.
5. **Microbiology:** Humoral and cell mediated immunity.
   Diseases caused by and laboratory diagnosis of —
   - Meningococcus, Saimonella
   - Shigella, Herpes, Dengue, Polio
   - HIV/AIDS, Malaria, E. Histolytica, Giardia
   - Candida, Cryptococcus, Aspergillus.
6. **Pharmacology:** Mechanism of action and side effects of the following drugs:
   - Antipyretics and analgesics, Antibiotics,
   - Antimalaria, Antikala-azar, Antidiabetics,
   - Antihypertensive, Antidiuretics, General and cardiac vasodilators, Antiviral, Antiparasitic, Antifungal, Immunosuppressants,
   - Anticancer.
7. **Forensic Medicine and Toxicology:** Forensic examination of injuries and wounds; Examination of blood and seminal stains; Poisoning, sedative overdose, hanging, drowning, burns, DNA and finger print study.

Paper-II

1. **General Medicine**
   - Etiology, clinical features, diagnosis and principles of management (including prevention) of: Typhoid, Rabies, AIDS, Dengue, Kala-azar, Japanese Encephalitis.

- ♦ Etiology, clinical features, diagnosis and principles of management of: Ischaemic heart disease, pulmonary embolism. Bronchial asthma.

  Pleural effusion, tuberculosis, Malabsorption syndromes; acid peptic diseases, Viral hepatitis and cirrhosis of liver.

  Glomerulonephritis and pyelonephritis, renal failure, nephrotic syndrome, renovascular hypertension, complications of diabetes mellitus, coagulation disorders, leukaemia, Hypo and hyper thyrodism, meningitis and encephalitis.

  Imaging in medical problems, ultrasound, echo- cardiogram, CT scan, MRI. Anxiety and Depressive Psychosis and schizophrenia and ECT.

2. **Paediatrics:** Immunization, Baby friendly hospital, congenital cyanotic heart disease, respiratory distress syndrome, broncho—pneumonias, kernicterus. IMNCI classification and management, PEM grading and management. ARI and Diarrhea of under five and their management.
3. **Dermatology:** Psoriasis, Allergic dermatitis, scabies, eczema, vitiligo, Stevan Johnson's syndrome, Lichen Planus.
4. **General Surgery:** Clinical features, causes, diagnosis and principles of management of cleft palate, harelip. Laryngeal tumour, oral and esophageal tumours.

   Peripheral arterial diseases, varicose veins, coarctation of aorta. Tumours of Thyroid, Adrenal, Glands. Abscess cancer, fibroadenoma and adenosis of breast.

   Bleeding peptic ulcer, tuberculosis of bowel, ulcerative colitis, cancer stomach. Renal mass, cancer prostatie.

   Haemothorax, stones of Gall bladder, Kidney, Ureter and Urinary Bladder.

   Management of surgical conditions of Rectum, Anus and Anal canal, Gall bladder and Bile ducts.

   Splenomegaly, cholecystitis, portal hypertension, liver abscess, peritonitis, carcinoma head of pancreas.

   Fractures of spine, Colles' fracture and bone tumors. Endoscopy.

   Laprascopic Surgery.
5. **Obstetrics and Gynaecology including Family Planning**

   Diagnosis of pregnancy: Labour management, complications of 3rd stage, Antepartum and postpartum hemorrhage, resuscitation of the newborn, Management of abnormal life and difficult labour. Management of small for date or premature newborn.

   Diagnosis and management of anemia. Preeclampsia and Toxaemias of pregnancy, Management of Post-menopausal Syndrome.

   Intra-uterine devices, pills, tubectomy and vasectomy. Medical termination of pregnancy including legal aspects.

   Cancer cervix.

   Leucorrhoea, pelvic pain; infertility, dysfunctional uterine bleeding (DUB), amenorrhoea, Fibroid and prolapse of uterus.

6. **Community Medicine (Preventive and Social Medicine):** Principles, methods approach and measurements of Epidemiology. Nutrition, nutritional diseases/ diorders and Nutrition Programmes. Health information Collection, Analysis and Presentation.
   Objectives, components and critical analysis of National programmes for control/eradication of:
   Malaria, Kala-azar, Filaria and Tuberculosis, HIV/AIDS, STDs and Dengue.
   Critical appraisal of Health care delivery system.
   Health management and administration; Techniques, Tools, Programme Implementation and Evaluation.
   Objectives, Components, Goals and Status of Reproductive and Child Health, National Rural Health Mission and Millennium Development Goals.
   Management of hospital and industrial waste.

41. PHILOSOPHY

Paper-I

History and Problems of Philosophy

1. **Plato and Aristotle**: Ideas; Substance; Form and Matter; Causation; Actuality and Potentiality.
2. **Rationalism** (Descartes, Spinoza, Leibniz); Cartesian Method and Certain Knowledge; Substance; God; Mind-Body Dualism; Determinism and Freedom.
3. **Empiricism** (Locke, Berkeley, Hume): Theory of Knowledge; Substance and Qualities; Self and God; Scepticism.
4. **Kant:** Possibility of Synthetic a priori Judgments; Space and Time; Categories; Ideas of Reason; Antinomies; Critique of Proofs for the Existence of God.
5. **Hegel:** Dialectical Method; Absolute Idealism.
6. **Moore, Russell and Early Wittgenstein**: Defence of Commonsense; Refutation of Idealism; Logical Atomism; Logical Constructions; Incomplete Symbols; Picture Theory of Meaning; Sying and Showing.
7. **Logical Positivism**: Verification Theory of Meaning; Rejection of Metaphysics; Linguistic Theory of Necessary Propositions.
8. **Later Wittgenstein**: Meaning and Use; Language-games; Critique of Private Language.
9. **Phenomenology (Husserl):** Method; Theory of Essences; Avoidance of Psychologism.
10. **Existentialism** (Kierkegaard, Sarte, Heidegger): Existence and Essence; Choice, Responsibility and Authentic Existence; Being-in-the-world and Temporality.
11. **Quine and Strawson**: Critique of Empiricism; Theory of Basic Particulars and Persons.

12. **Carvaka:** Theory of Knowlegde; Rejection of Transcendent Entities.
13. **Jainism:** Theory of Reality; Saptabhanginaya; Bondage and Liberation.
14. **Schools of Buddhism:** Prat Ityasamutpada; Ksanikavada, Nairatmyavada.
15. **Nyaya—Vaiesesika:** Theory of Categories; Theory of Appearance; Theory of Pramana; Self, Liberation; God; Proofs for the Existence of God; Theory of Causation; Atomistic Theory of Creation.
16. Samkhya; Prakrit; Purusa; Causation; Liberation.
17. Yoga; Citta; Cittavrtti; Klesas; Samadhi; Kaivalya.
18. **Mimamsa:** Theory of Knowlegde.
19. **Schools of Vedanta:** Brahman; Isvara; Atman; Jiva; Jagat; Maya; Avida; Adhyasa; Moksa; Aprthaksiddhi; Pancavidhabheda.
20. **Aurobindo:** Evolution, Involution; Integral Yoga.

Paper-II

Socio-Political Philosophy

1. **Social and Political Ideals**: Equality, Justice, Liberty.
2. **Sovereignty**: Austin, Bodin, Laski, Kautilya.
3. **Individual and State**: Rights; Duties and Accountability.
4. **Forms of Government**: Monarchy; Theocracy and Democracy.
5. **Political Ideologies**: Anarchism; Marxism and Socialism.
6. Humanism; Secularism; Multi-culturalism.
7. **Crime and Punishment**: Corruption, Mass Violence, Genocide, Capital Punishment.
8. Development and Social Progress.
9. **Gender Discrimination**: Female Foeticide, Land and Property Rights; Empowerment.
10. **Caste Discrimination**: Gandhi and Ambedkar.

Philosophy of Religion

1. **Notions of God**: Attributes; Relation to Man and the World. (Indian and Western).
2. Proofs for the Existence of God and their Critique (Indian and Western).
3. Problem of Evil.
4. **Soul:** Immortality; Rebirth and Liberation.
5. Reason, Revelation and Faith.
6. **Religious Experience**: Nature and Object (Indian and Western).
7. Religion without God.
8. Religion and Morality.
9. Religious Pluralism and the Problem of Absolute Truth.
10. **Nature of Religious Language**: Analogical and Symbolic; Cognitivist and Non-cognitive.

42. PHYSICS

Paper-I

1. (a) **Mechanics of Particles:** Laws of motion; conservation of energy and momentum, applications to rotating frames, centripetal and Coriolis accelerations; Motion under a central force; Conservation of angular momentum, Kepler's laws; Fields and potentials; Gravitational field and potential due to spherical bodies, Gauss and Poisson equations, gravitational self-energy; Two-body problem; Reduced mass; Rutherford scattering; Centre of mass and laboratory reference frames.
   (b) **Mechanics of Rigid Bodies:** System of particles; Centre of mass, angular momentum, equations of motion; Conservation theorems for energy, momentum and angular momentum; Elastic and inelastic collisions; Rigid Body; Degrees of freedom, Euler's theorem, angular velocity, angular momentum, moments of inertia, theorems of parallel and perpendicular axes, equation of motion for rotation; Molecular rotations (as rigid bodies); Di and tri-atomic molecules; Precessional motion; top, gyroscope.
   (c) **Mechanics of Continuous Media:** Elasticity, Hooke's law and elastic constants of isotropic solids and their inter-relation; Streamline (Laminar) flow, viscosity, Poiseuille's equation, Bernoulli's equation, Stokes' law and applications.
   (d) **Special Relativity:** Michelson-Morely experiment and its implications; Lorentz transformations length contraction, time dilation, addition of relativistic velocities, aberration and Doppler effect, mass-energy relation, simple applications to a decay process. Four dimensional momentum vector; Covariance of equations of physics.
2. Waves and Optics
   (a) **Waves:** Simple harmonic motion, damped oscillation, forced oscillation and resonance; Beats; Stationary waves in a string; Pulses and wave packets; Phase and group velocities; Reflection and refraction from Huygens' principle.
   (b) **Geometrial Optics:** Laws of reflection and refraction from Fermat's principle; Matrix method in paraxial optic-thin lens formula, nodal planes, system of two thin lenses, chromatic and spherical aberrations.
   (c) **Interference:** Interference of light -Young's experiment, Newton's rings, interference by thin films, Michelson interferometer; Multiple beam interference and Fabry Perot interferometer.
   (d) **Diffraction:** Fraunhofer diffraction - single slit, double slit, diffraction grating, resolving power; Diffraction by a circular aperture and the Airy pattern; Fresnel diffraction: half-period zones and zone plates, circular aperture.

(e) **Polarisation and Modern Optics:** Production and detection of linearly and circularly polarized light; Double refraction, quarter wave plate; Optical activity; Principles of fibre optics, attenuation; Pulse dispersion in step index and parabolic index fibres; Material dispersion, single mode fibers; Lasers-Einstein A and B coefficients. Ruby and He-Ne lasers. Characteristics of laser light-spatial and temporal coherence; Focusing of laser beams. Three-level scheme for laser operation; Holography and simple applications.

3. **Electricity and Magnetism**

(a) **Electrostatics and Magnetostatics:** Laplace and Poisson equations in electrostatics and their applications; Energy of a system of charges, multipole expansion of scalar potential; Method of images and its applications. Potential and field due to a dipole, force and torque on a dipole in an external field; Dielectrics, polarisation. Solutions to boundary-value problems-conducting and dielectric spheres in a uniform electric field; Magnetic shell, uniformly magnetised sphere; Ferromagnetic materials, hysteresis, energy loss.

(b) **Current Electricity:** Kirchhoff 's laws and their applications. Biot-Savart law, Ampere's law, Faraday's law, Lenz' law. Self-and mutual- inductances; Mean and rms values in AC circuits; DC and AC circuits with R, L and C components; Series and parallel resonance; Quality factor; Principle of transformer.

4. **Electromagnetic Waves and Blackbody Radiation:** Displacement current and Maxwell's equations; Wave equations in vacuum, Poynting theorem; Vector and scalar potentials; Electromagnetic field tensor, covariance of Maxwell's equations; Wave equations in isotropic dielectrics, reflection and refraction at the boundary of two dielectrics; Fresnel's relations; Total internal reflection; Normal and anomalous dispersion; Rayleigh scattering; Blackbody radiation and Planck 's radiation law- Stefan-Boltzmann law, Wien's displacement law and Rayleigh-Jeans law.

5. **Thermal and Statistical Physics**

(a) **Thermodynamics:** Laws of thermodynamics, reversible and irreversible processes, entropy; Isothermal, adiabatic, isobaric, isochoric processes and entropy changes; Otto and Diesel engines, Gibbs' phase rule and chemical potential; Van der Waals equation of state of a real gas, critical constants; Maxwell-Boltzmann distribution of molecular velocities, transport phenomena, equipartition and virial theorems; Dulong-Petit, Einstein, and Debye's theories of specific heat of solids; Maxwell relations and application; Clausius-Clapeyron equation. Adiabatic demagnetisation, Joule-Kelvin effect and liquefaction of gases.

(b) **Statistical Physics:** Macro and micro states, statistical distributions, Maxwell-Boltzmann, Bose-Einstein and Fermi-Dirac Distributions, applications to specific heat of gases and blackbody radiation; Concept of negative temperatures.

Paper-II

1. **Quantum Mechanics:** Wave-particle duality; Schroedinger equation and expectation values; Uncertainty principle; Solutions of the one-dimensional Schroedinger equation for free particle (Gaussian wave-packet), particle in a box, particle in a finite well, linear harmonic oscillator; Reflection and transmission by a step potential and by a rectangular barrier; Particle in a three dimensional box, density of states, free electron theory of metals; Angular momentum; Hydrogen atom; Spin half particles, properties of Pauli spin matrices.
2. **Atomic and Molecular Physics:** Stern-Gerlach experiment, electron spin, fine structure of hydrozen atom; L-S coupling, J-J coupling; Spectroscopic notation of atomic states; Zeeman effect; Franck-Condon principle and applications; Elementary theory of rotational, vibrational and electronic spectra of diatomic molecules; Raman effect and molecular structure; Laser Raman spectroscopy; Importance of neutral hydrogen atom, molecular hydrogen and molecular hydrogen ion in astronomy. Fluorescence and Phosphorescence; Elementary theory and applications of NMR and EPR; Elementary ideas about Lamb shift and its significance.
3. **Nuclear and Particle Physics:** Basic nuclear properties-size, binding energy, angular momentum, parity, magnetic moment; Semi-empirical mass formula and applications. Mass parabolas; Ground state of a deuteron, magnetic moment and non-central forces; Meson theory of nuclear forces; Salient features of nuclear forces; Shell model of the nucleus - success and limitations; Violation of parity in beta decay; Gamma decay and internal conversion; Elementary ideas about Mossbauer spectroscopy; Q-value of nuclear reactions; Nuclear fission and fusion, energy production in stars. Nuclear reactors.

   Classification of elementary particles and their interactions; Conservation laws; Quark structure of hadrons: Field quanta of electroweak and strong interactions; Elementary ideas about unification of forces; Physics of neutrinos.
4. **Solid State Physics, Devices and Electronics:** Crystalline and amorphous structure of matter; Different crystal systems, space groups; Methods of determination of crystal structure; X-ray diffraction, scanning and transmission electron microscopies; Band theory of solids—conductors, insulators and semi-conductors; Thermal properties of solids, specific heat, Debye theory; Magnetism: dia, para and ferromagnetism; Elements of super-conductivity, Meissner effect, Josephson junctions and applications; Elementary ideas about high temperature super-conductivity.

Intrinsic and extrinsic semi-conductors- p-n-p and n-p-n transistors; Amplifiers and oscillators. Op-amps; FET, JFET and MOSFET; Digital electronics-Boolean identities, De Morgan's laws, Logic gates and truth tables. Simple logic circuits; Thermistors, solar cells; Fundamentals of microprocessors and digital computers.

43. POLITICAL SCIENCE AND INTERNATIONAL RELATIONS

Paper-I

Political Theory and Indian Politics

1. **Political Theory**: meaning and approaches.
2. **Theories of State:** Liberal, Neo-liberal, Marxist, Pluiralist, post-colonial and Feminist.
3. **Justice:** Conceptions of justice with special reference to Rawl's theory of justice and its communitarian critiques.
4. **Equality:** Social, political and economic; relationship between equality and freedom; Affirmative action.
5. **Rights:** Meaning and theories; different kinds of rights; Concept of Human Rights.
6. **Democracy:** Classical and contemporary theories; different models of democracy—representative, participatory and deliberative.
7. **Concept of Power:** hegemony, ideology and legitimacy.
8. **Political Ideologies:** Liberalism, Socialism, Marxism, Fascism, Gandhism and Feminism.
9. **Indian Political Thought**: *Dharamshastra, Arthashastra* and Buddhist Traditions; Sir Syed Ahmed Khan, Sri Aurobindo, M. K. Gandhi, B. R. Ambedkar, M. N. Roy.
10. **Western Political Thought**: Plato, Aristotle, Machiavelli, Hobbes, Locke, John S. Mill, Marx, Gramsci, Hannah Arendt.

Indian Government and Politics

1. **Indian Nationalism**
   (a) **Political Strategies of India's Freedom Struggle:** Constitutionalism to mass Satyagraha, Non-cooperation, Civil Disobedience; Militant and Revolutionary Movements, Peasant and Workers Movements.
   (b) **Perspectives on Indian National Movement:** Liberal, Socialist and Marxist; Radical Humanist and Dalit.
2. **Making of the Indian Constitution**: Legacies of the British rule; different social and political perspectives.
3. **Salient Features of the Indian Constitution**: The Preamble, Fundamental Rights and Duties, Directive Principles; Parliamentary System and Amendment Procedures; Judicial Review and Basic Structure doctrine.

4. (a) **Principal Organs of the Union Government:** Envisaged role and actual working of the Executive, Legislature and Supreme Court.
   (b) **Principal Organs of the State Government**: Envisaged role and actual working of the Executive, Legislature and High Courts.
5. **Grassroots Democracy:** Panchayati Raj and Municipal Government; Significance of 73rd and 74th Amendments; Grassroot movements.
6. **Statutory Institutions/Commissions**: Election Commission, Comptroller and Auditor General, Finance Commission, Union Public Service Commission, National Commission for Scheduled Castes, National Commission for Scheduled Tribes, National Commission for Women; National Human Rights Commission, National Commission for Minorities, National Backward Classes Commission.
7. **Federalism:** Constitutional provisions; changing nature of centre-state relations; integrationist tendencies and regional aspirations; inter-state disputes.
8. **Planning and Economic development**: Nehruvian and Gandhian perspectives; Role of planning and public sector; Green Revolution, land reforms and agrarian relations; liberalization and economic reforms.
9. Caste, Religion and Ethnicity in Indian Politics.
10. **Party System**: National and regional political parties, ideological and social bases of parties; Patterns of coalition politics; Pressure groups, trends in electoral behaviour; changing socio-economic profile of Legislators.
11. **Social Movement:** Civil liberties and human rights movements; women's movements; environmentalist movements.

Paper-II

Comparative Politics and International Relations

Comparative Political Analysis and International Politics

1. **Comparative Politics**: Nature and major approaches; Political economy and political sociology perspectives; Limitations of the comparative method.
2. **State in Comparative Perspective**: Characteristics and changing nature of the State in capitalist and socialist economies, and advanced industrial and developing societies.
3. **Politics of Representation and Participation**: Political parties, pressure groups and social movements in advanced industrial and developing societies.
4. **Globalisation:** Responses from developed and developing societies.
5. **Approaches to the Study of International Relations**: Idealist, Realist, Marxist, Functionalist and Systems theory.
6. **Key Concepts in International Relations**: National interest, security and power; Balance of power and deterrence; Transational actors and collective security; World capitalist economy and globalisation.

7. **Changing International Political Order**
   (a) Rise of super powers; Strategic and ideological Bipolarity, arms race and cold war; Nuclear threat;
   (b) Non-aligned Movement: Aims and achievements.
   (c) Collapse of the Soviet Union; Unipolarity and American hegemony; Relevance of non-alignment in the contemporary world.
8. **Evolution of the International Economic System:** From Brettonwoods to WTO; Socialist economies and the CMEA (Council for Mutual Economic Assistance); Third World demand for new international economic order; Globalisation of the world economy.
9. **United Nations:** Envisaged role and actual record; Specialized UN agencies—aims and functioning; need for UN reforms.
10. **Regionalisation of World Politics**: EU, ASEAN, APEC, AARC, NAFTA.
11. **Contemporary Global Concerns**: Democracy, human rights, environment, gender justice terrorism, nuclear proliferation.

India and the World

1. **Indian Foreign Policy**: Determinants of foreign policy; the institutions of policy-making; Continuity and change.
2. India's Contribution to the Non-Alignment Movement Different phases; Current role.
3. **India and South Asia**
   (a) Regional Co-operation: SAARC-past performance and future prospects.
   (b) South Asia as a Free Trade Area.
   (c) India's "Look East" policy.
   (d) **Impediments to regional co-operation**: River water disputes; illegal cross border migration; Ethnic conflicts and insurgencies; Border disputes.
4. **India and the Global South**: Relations with Africa and Latin America; Leadership role in the demand for NIEO and WTO negotiations.
5. **India and the Global Centres of Power:** USA, EU, Japan, China and Russia.
6. **India and the UN System**: Role in UN Peace-keeping; Demand for Permanent Seat in the Security Council.
7. **India and the Nuclear Question**: Changing perceptions and policy.
8. **Recent developments in Indian Foreign Policy**: India's position on the recent crises in Afghanistan, Iraq and West Asia, growing relations with US and Isreal; Vision of a new world order.

44. PSYCHOLOGY

Paper-I

Foundations of Psychology

1. **Introduction:** Definition of Psychology; Historical antecedents of Psychology and trends in the 21st centrury; Psychology and scientific methods; Psychology in relation to other social sciences and natural sciences; Application of Psychology to societal problems.
2. **Methods of Psychology:** Types of research: Descriptive, evaluative, diagnostic and prognostic; Methods of Research: Survey, observation, case-study and experiments; Characteristics of experimental design and non-experimental designs; quasi-experimental designs; Focussed group discussions, brain storming, grounded theory approach.
3. **Research methods:** Major steps in psychological research (problem statement, hypothesis formulation, research design, sampling, tools of data collection, analysis and interpretation and report writing); Fundamental versus applied research; Methods of data collection (interview, observation, questionnaire and case study). Research Designs (Ex-post facto and experimental). Application of statistical techniques (t-test, two-way ANOVA, correlation and regression and factor analysis) item response theory.
4. **Development of Human Behaviour:** Growth and development; Principles of development, Role of genetic and environmental factors in determining human behaviour; Influence of cultural factors in socialization; Life span development—Characteristics, development tasks, promoting psychological well-being across major stages of the life span.
5. **Sensation, Attention and Perception:** Sensation: concepts of threshold, absolute and difference thresholds, signal-detection and vigilance; Factors influencing attention including set and characteristics of stimulus; Definition and concept of perception, biological factors in perception; Perceptual organization-influence of past experiences, perceptual defence-factor influencing space and depth perception, size estimation and perceptual readiness; The plasticity of perception; Extrasensory perception; Culture and perception, Subliminal perception.
6. **Learning:** Concepts and theories of learning (Behaviourists, Gestaltalist and Information processing models). The processes of extinction, discrimination and generalisation. Programmed learning, probability learning, self instructional learning, concepts, types and the schedules of reinforcement, escape, avoidance and punishment, modelling and social learning.
7. **Memory:** Encoding and remembering; Shot-term memory, Long-term memory, Sensory memory, Iconic memory, Echoic memory: The Multistore model, levels of processing; Organization and Mnemonic techniques to improve memory; Theories of forgetting: decay, interference and retrieval failure: Metamemory; Amnesia: Anterograde and retrograde.

8. **Thinking and Problem Solving:** Piaget's theory of cognitive development; Concept formation processes; Information processing, Reasoning and problem solving, Facilitating and hindering factors in problem solving, Methods of problem solving: Creative thinking and fostering creativity; Factors influencing decision making and judgement; Recent trends.
9. **Motivation and Emotion:** Psychological and physiological basis of motivation and emotion; Measurement of motivation and emotion; Effects of motivation and emotion on behaviour; Extrinsic and intrinsic motivation; Factors influencing intrinsic motivation; Emotional competence and the related issues.
10. **Intelligence and Aptitude:** Concept of intelligence and aptitude, Nature and theories of intelligence-Spearman, Thurstone, Gulford Vernon, Sternberg and J.P. Das; Emotional Intelligence, Social intelligence, measurement of intelligence and aptitudes, concept of I Q deviation I Q, constancy of I Q; Measurement of multiple intelligence; Fluid intelligence and crystallized intelligence.
11. **Personality:** Definition and concept of personality; Theories of personality (psychoanalytical, socio-cultural, interpersonal, developmental, humanistic, behaviouristic, trait and type approaches); Measurement of personality (projective tests, pencil-paper test); The Indian approach to personality; Training for personality development; Latest approaches like big 5 factor theory; The notion of self in different traditions.
12. **Attitudes, Values and Interests:** Definitions of attitudes, values and interests; Components of attitudes; Formation and maintenance of attitudes. Measurement of attitudes, values and interests. Theories of attitude changes, strategies for fostering values. Formation of stereotypes and prejudices; Changing other's behaviour, Theories of attribution; Recent trends.
13. **Language and Communication:** Human language—Properties, structure and linguistic hierarchy, Language acquisition—predispotion, critical period hypothesis; Theories of Language development—Skinner and Chomsky; Process and types of communication—effective commu-nication training.
14. **Issues and Perspectives in Modern Contemporary Psychology:** Computer application in the psychological laboratory and psychological testing; Artificial intelligence; Psychocybernetics; Study of consciousnessleep-wak schedules; dreams, stimulus deprivation, meditation, hypnotic/drug induced states; Extrasensory perception; Intersensory perception; Simulation studies.

Paper-II

Psychology: Issues and Applications

1. **Psychological Measurement of Individual Differences:** The nature of individual differences. Characteristics and construction of standardized psychological tests. Types of psychological tests. Use, misuse and limitation of psychological tests. Ethical issues in the use of psychological tests.

2. **Psychological well being and Mental Disorders:** Concept of health-ill health positive health, well being casual factores in Mental disorders (Anxiety disorders, mood disorders; schizophrenia and delusional disorders; personality disorders, substance abuse disorders). Factors influencing positive health, well being; lifestyle and quality of life; Happiness disposition.
3. **Therapeutic Approaches:** Psychodynamic therapies. Behaviour therapies. Client centered therapy. Cognitive therapies. Indigenous therapies (Yoga, Meditation). Biofeedback therapy. Prevention and rehabilitation of the mentally ill; Fostering mental health.
4. **Work Psychology and Organisational Behaviour:** Personnel selection and training. Use of Psychological tests in the industry. Training and human resource development. Theories of work motivation. Herzberg, Maslow, Adam Equity theory, Porter and Lawler, Vroom; Leadership and participatory management; Advertising and marketing; Stress and its management; Ergonomics; consumer psychology; Managerial effectiveness; Transformational leadersip; Sensitivity training; Power and politics in organizations.
5. **Application of Psychology to Educational Field:** Psychological principles underlying effective teaching-learning process. Learning styles. Gifted, retarded, learning disabled and their training. Training for improving memory and better academic achievement. Personality development and value education. Educational, vocational guidance and Career counselling. Use of Psychological tests in educational institutions; Effective strategies in guidance programmes.
6. **Community Psychology:** Definition and concept of Community Psychology. Use of small groups in social action. Arousing Community consciousness and action for handling social problems. Group decision making and leadership for social change. Effective strategies for social change.
7. **Rehabilitation Psychology:** Primary, secondary and tertiary prevention programmes—role of psychologists. Organising of services for rehabilitation of physically, mentally and socially challenged persons including old persons. Rehabilitation of persons suffering from substance abuse, juvenile delinquency, criminal behaviours. Rehabilitation of victims of violence. Rehabilitation of HIV/AIDS victims, the role of social agencies.
8. **Application of Psychology to disadvantaged groups:** The concepts of disadvantaged, deprivation social, physical, cultural and economic consequences of disadvantaged and deprived groups. Educating and motivating the disadvantaged towards development; Relative and prolonged deprivation.
9. **Psychological problem of social integration:** The concept of social integration. The problem of caste, class, religion and language conflicts and prejudice. Nature and manifestation of prejudice between the ingroup and outgroup. Casual factors of such conflicts and prejudices. Psychological strategies for handling the conflicts and prejudices. Measures to achieve social integration.

10. **Application of Psychology in Information Technology and Mass Media:** The present scenario of information technology and the mass media boom and the role of psychologists. Selection and training of Psychology professionals to work in the field of IT and mass media. Distance learning through IT and mass media. Entrepreneurship through e-commerce.
    Multilevel marketing. Impact of TV and fostering value through IT and mass media. Psychological consequences of recent developments in Information Technology.
11. **Psychology and Economic development:** Achievement motivation and economic development. Characteristics of entrepreneurial behaviour. Motivating and Training people for entrepreneurship and economic development; Consumer rights and consumer awareness, Government policies for promotion of entrepreneurship among youth including women entreprenures.
12. **Application of Psychology to environment and related fields:** Environmental Psychology effects of noise, pollution and crowding. Population Psychology: Psychological consequence of population explosion and high population density. Motivating for small family norms. Impact of rapid scientific and technological growth on degradation of environment.
13. **Application of psychology in other fields**
    (a) **Military Psychology** Devising psycological tests for defence personnel for use in selection, Training, counseling; training psychologists to work , with defence personnel in promoting positive health; Human engineering in defence.
    (b) **Sports Psychology:** Psychological interventions in improving performance of athletes and sports. Persons participating in Individual and Team Games.
    (c) **Media influences on pro and anti-social behaviour.**
    (d) **Psychology of Terrorism.**
14. **Psychology of Gender:** Issues of discrimination, Management of diversity; Glass ceiling effect, Self-fulfilling prophesy, Women and Indian society.

45. PUBLIC ADMINISTRATION

Paper-I

Administration Theory

1. **Introduction:** Meaning, scope and significance of Public Administration, Wilson's vision of Public Administration, Evolution of the discipline and its present status. New Public Administration, Public Choice approach; Challenges of liberalization, Privatisation, Globalisation; Good Governance: concept and application; New Public Management.

2. **Administrative Thought:** Scientific Management and Scientific Management movement; Classical Theory; Weber's bureaucratic model its critique and post-Weberian Developments; Dynamic Administration (Mary Parker Follett); Human Relations School (Elton Mayo and others); Functions of the Executive (C.I. Barnard); Simon's decision-making theory; Participative Management (R. Likert, C. Argyris, D. McGregor.)
3. **Administrative Behaviour:** Process and techniques of decision-making; Communication; Morale; Motivation Theories content, process and contemporary; Theories of Leadership: Traditional and Modem:
4. **Organisations:** Theories systems, contingency; Structure and forms: Ministries and Departments, Corporations, Companies; Boards and Commissions; Ad hoc, and advisory bodies; Headquarters and Field relationships; Regulatory Authorities; Public-Private Partnerships.
5. **Accountability and Control:** Concepts of accountability and control; Legislative, Executive and judicial control over administration; Citizen and Administration; Role of media, interest groups, voluntary organizations; Civil society; Citizen's Charters; Right to Information; Social audit.
6. **Administrative Law:** Meaning, scope and significance; Dicey on Administrative law; Delegated legislation; Administrative Tribunals.
7. **Comparative Public Administration:** Historical and sociological factors affecting administrative systems; Administration and politics in different countries; Current status of Comparative Public Administration; Ecology and administration; Riggsian models and their critique.
8. **Development Dynamics:** Concept of development; Changing profile of development administration; 'Anti-development thesis'; Bureaucracy and development; Strong state versus the market debate; Impact of liberalisation on administration in developing countries; Women and development the self-help group movement.
9. **Personnel Administration:** Importance of human resource development; Recruitment, training, career advancement, position classification, discipline, performance appraisal, promotion, pray and service conditions; employer-employee relations, grievance redressal mechanism; Code of conduct; Administrative ethics.
10. **Public Policy:** Models of policy-making and their critique; Processes of conceptualisation, planning, implementation, monitoring, evaluation and review and their limitations; State theories and public policy formulation.
11. Techniques of Adminstrative Improvement: Organisation and methods, Work study and work management; e-governance and information technology; Management aid tools like network analysis, MIS, PERT, CPM.
12. **Financial Administration:** Monetary and fiscal policies: Public borrowings and public debt Budgets types and forms; Budgetary process; Financial accountability; Accounts and audit.

Paper-II

Indian Administration

1. **Evolution of Indian Administration:** Kautilya Arthashastra; Mughal administration; Legacy of British rule in politics and administration Indianization of Public services, revenue administration, district Administration, local self Government.
2. **Philosophical and Constitutional Framework of** Government: Salient features and value premises; Constitutionalism; Political culture; Bureaucracy and democracy; Bureaucracy and development.
3. **Public Sector Undertakings:** Public sector in modern India; Forms of Public Sector Undertakings; Problems of autonomy, accountability and control; Impact of liberalization and privatization.
4. **Union Government and Administration:** Executive, Parliament, Judiciary-structure, functions, work processes; Recent trends; Intra-governmental relations; Cabinet Secretariat; Prime Minister's Office; Central Secretariat; Ministries and Departments; Boards; Commissions; Attached offices; Field organizations.
5. **Plans and Priorities:** Machinery of planning; Role, composition and functions of the Planning Commission and the National Development Council; 'Indicative' planning; Process of plan formulation at Union and State levels; Constitutional Amendments (1992) and decentralized planning for economic development and social justice.
6. **State Government and Administration:** Union-State administrative, legislative and financial relations; Role of the Finance Commission; Governor; Chief Minister; Council of Ministers; Chief Secretary; State Secretariat; Directorates.
7. **District Administration since Independence:** Changing role of the Collector; Union-State-local relations; Imperatives of development management and law and order administration; District administration and democratic decentralization.
8. **Civil Services:** Constitutional position; Structure, recruitment, training and capacity building; Good governance initiatives; Code of conduct and discipline; Staff associations; Political rights; Grievance redressal mechanism; Civil service neutrality; Civil service activism.
9. **Financial Management:** Budget as a political instrument; Parliamentary control of public expenditure; Role of finance ministry in monetary and fiscal area; Accounting techniques; Audit; Role of Controller General of Accounts and Comptroller and Auditor General of India.
10. **Administrative Reforms since Independence:** Major concerns; Important Committees and Commissions; Reforms in financial management and human resource development; Problems of implementation.

11. **Rural Development:** Institutions and agencies since Independence; Rural development programmes: foci and strategies; Decentralization and Panchayati Raj; 73rd Constitutional amendment.
12. **Urban Local Government:** Municipal governance: main features, structures, finance and problem areas; 74th Constitutional Amendment; Global-local debate; New localism; Development dynamics, politics and administration with special reference to city management.
13. **Law and Order Administration:** British legacy; National Police Commission; Investigative agencies; Role of Central and State Agencies including para military forces in maintenance of law and order and countering insurgency and terrorism; Criminalisation of politics and administration; Police-public relations; Reforms in Police.
14. **Significant Issues in Indian Administration:** Values in public service; Regulatory Commissions; National Human Rights Commission; Problems of administration in coalition regimes; Citizen administration interface; Corruption and administration; Disaster management.

46. SOCIOLOGY

Paper-I

Fundamentals of Sociology

1. **Sociology - The Discipline**
   (a) Modernity and social changes in Europe and emergence of Sociology.
   (b) Scope of the subject and comparison with other social sciences.
   (c) Sociology and common sense.
2. **Sociology as Science**
   (a) Science, scientific method and critique.
   (b) Major theoretical strands of research methodology.
   (c) Positivism and its critique.
   (d) Fact value and objectivity.
   (e) Non-positivist methodologies.
3. Research Methods and Analysis
   (a) Qualitative and quantitative methods.
   (b) Techniques of data collection.
   (c) Variables, sampling, hypothesis, reliability and validity.
4. **Sociological Thinkers**
   (a) **Karl Marx**: Historical materialism, mode of production, alienation, class struggle.
   (b) **Emile Durkhteim**: Division of labour, social fact, suicide, religion and society.
   (c) **Max Weber**: Social action, ideal types, authority, bureaucracy, protestant ethic and the spirit of capitalism.

(d) **Talcolt Parsons**: Social system, pattern variables.
(e) **Robert K. Merton**: Latent and manifest functions, conformity and deviance, reference groups.
(f) **Mead:** Self and identity.

5. **Stratification and Mobility**
(a) **Concepts:** equality, inequality, hierarchy, exclusion, poverty and deprivation.
(b) **Theories of social stratification**: Structural func tionalist theory, Marxist theory, Weberian theory.
(c) **Dimensions**: Social stratification of class, status groups, gender, ethnicity and race.
(d) **Social mobility**: open and closed systems, types of mobility, sources and causes of mobility.

6. **Works and Economic Life**
(a) **Social organization of work in different types of society**: slave society, feudal society, industrial capitalist society.
(b) Formal and informal organization of work.
(c) Labour and society.

7. Politics and Society
(a) Sociological theories of power.
(b) Power elite, bureaucracy, pressure groups and political parties.
(c) Nation, state, citizenship, democracy, civil society, ideology.
(d) Protest, agitation, social movements, collective action, revolution.

8. **Religion and Society**
(a) Sociological theories of religion.
(b) **Types of religious practices**: animism, monism, pluralism, sects, cults.
(c) **Religion in modern society**: religion and science, secularization, religious revivalism, fundamen talism.

9. **Systems of Kinship**
(a) Family, household, marriage.
(b) Types and forms of family.
(c) Lineage and descent.
(d) Patriarchy and sexual division of labour.
(e) Contem porary trends.

10. **Social Change in Modern Society**
(a) Sociological theories of social change.
(b) Development and dependency.
(c) Agents of social change.
(d) Education and social change.
(e) Science, technology and social change.

Paper-II

Indian Society: Structure And Change

A. **Introducing Indian Society**

(i) **Perspectives on the Study of Indian Society**

(a) Indology (G.S. Ghure).

(b) Structural functionalism (M. N. Srinivas).

(c) Marxist sociology (A. R. Desai).

(ii) **Impact of colonial rule on Indian Society**

(a) Social background of Indian nationalism.

(b) Modernization of Indian tradition.

(c) Protests and movements during the colonial period.

(d) Social reforms.

B. **Social Structure**

(i) **Rural and Agrarian Social Structure**

(a) The idea of Indian village and village studies.

(b) Agrarian social structure: evolution of land tenure system, land reforms.

(ii) **Caste System**

(a) Perspectives on the study of caste systems: G. S. Ghurye, M. N. Srinivas, Louis Dumont, Andre Beteille.

(b) Features of caste system.

(c) Untouchability-forms and perspectives

(iii) **Tribal Communities in India**

(a) Definitional problems.

(b) Geographical spread.

(c) Colonial policies and tribes.

(d) Issues of integration and autonomy.

(iv) **Social Classes in India**

(a) Agrarian class structure.

(b) Industrial class structure.

(c) Middle classes in India.

(v) **Systems of Kinship in India**

(a) Lineage and descent in India.

(b) Types of kinship systems.

(c) Family and marriage in India.

(d) Household dimensions of the family.

(e) Patriarchy, entitlements and sexual division oflabour.

(vi) **Religion and Society**

(a) Religious communities in India.

(b) Problems of religious minorities.

C. **Social Changes in India**

(i) **Visions of Social Change in India**

(a) Idea of development planning and mixed economy.
(b) Constitution, law and social change.
(c) Education and social change.

(ii) **Rural and Agrarian Transformation in India**

(a) Programmes of rural development, Community Development Programme, cooperatives, poverty alleviation schemes.
(b) Green revolution and social change.
(c) Changing modes of production in Indian agriculture.
(d) Problems of rural labour, bondage, migration.

(iii) **Industrialization and Urbanisation in India**

(a) Evolution of modern industry in India.
(b) Growth of urban settlements in India.
(c) Working class: structure, growth, class mobilization.
(d) Informal sector, child labour.
(e) Slums and deprivation in urban areas.

(iv) **Politics and Society**

(a) Nation, democracy and citizenship.
(b) Political parties, pressure groups, social and political elite.
(c) Regionalism and decentralization of power.
(d) Secularization.

(v) **Social Movements in Modern India**

(a) Peasants and farmers movements.
(b) Women's movement.
(c) Backward classes & Dalit movements.
(d) Environmental movements.
(e) Ethnicity and Identity movements.

(vi) **Population Dynamics**

(a) Population size, growth, composition and distribution.
(b) Components of population growth: birth, death, migration.
(c) Population Policy and family planning.
(d) Emerging issues: ageing, sex ratios, child and infant mortality, reproductive health.

(vii) **Challenges of Social Transformation**

(a) Crisis of development: displacement, environmental problems and sustainability.
(b) Poverty, deprivation and inequalities.
(c) Violence against women.
(d) Caste conflicts.
(e) Ethnic conflicts, communalism, religious revivalism.
(f) Illiteracy and disparities in education.

47. STATISTICS

Paper-I

1. **Probability:** Sample space and events, probability measure and probability space, random variable as a measurable function distribution function of a random variable, discrete and continuous-type random variable, probability mass function, probability density function, vector-valued random variable, marginal and conditional distributions, stochastic independence of events and of random variables, expectation and moments of a random variable, conditional expectation, convergence of a sequence of random variable in distribution, in probability, in path mean and almost everywhere, their criteria and inter-relations, Chebyshev's inequality and Khintchine's weak law of large numbers, strong law of large numbers and Kolmogoroffs theorems, probability generating function, moment generating function, characteristic function, inversion theorem, Linderberg and Levy forms of central limit theorem, standard discrete and continuous probability distributions.
2. **Statistical Inference:** Consistency, unbiasedness, efficiency, sufficiency, completeness, ancillary statistics, factorization theorem, exponential family of distribution and its properties, uniformly minimum variance unbiased (UMVU) estimation, Rao Blackwell and Lehmann-Scheffe theorems, Cramer-Rao inequality for single Parameter. Estimation by methods of moments, maximum likelihood, least squares, minimum chisquare and modified minimum chisquare, properties of maximum likelihood and other estimators, asymptotic efficiency, prior and posterior distributions, loss function, risk function, and minimax estimator. Bayes estimators.

   Non-randomised and randomised tests, critical function, MP tests, Neyman-Pearson lemma, UMP tests, monotone likelihood ratio: similar and unbiased tests, UMPU tests for single paramet likelihood ratio test and its asymptotic distribution. Confidence bounds and its relation with tests.

   Kolmogorov's test for goodness of fit and its consistency, sign test and its optimality. Wilcoxon signedranks test and its consistency, Kolmogorov-Smirnov two sample test, run test, Wilcoxon-Mann-Whitney test and median test, their consistency and asymptotic normality.

   Wald's SPRT and its properties, Oc and ASN functions for tests regarding parameters for Bernoulli, Poisson, normal and exponential distributions. Wald's fundamental identity.
3. **Linear Inference and Multivariate Analysis:** Linear statistical models, theory of least squares and analysis of variance, Gauss-Markoff theory, normal equations, least squares estimates and their precision, test of significance and interval estimates based on least squares theory in oneway, two-way and three-way classified data, regression analysis, linear regression, curvilinear regression and orthogonal polynomials, multiple regression, multiple and partial

correlations, estimation of variance and covariance components, multivariate normal distribution, Mahalanobis's D^2 and Hotelling's T^2 statistics and their applications and properties, discriminant analysis, canonical correlations, principal component analysis.

4. **Sampling Theory and Design of Experiments:** An outline of fixed-population and super-population approaches, distinctive features of finite population sampling, propability sampling designs, simple random sampling with and without replacement, stratified random sampling, systematic sampling and its efficacy, cluster sampling, twostage and multi-stage sampling, ratio and regression methods of estimation involving one or more auxiliary variables, two-phase sampling, probability proportional to size sampling with and without replacement, the Hansen-Hurwitz and the Horvitz Thompson estimators, non-negative variance estimation with reference to the Horvitz-Thompson estimator, non-sampling errors.
   Fixed effects model (two-way classification) random and mixed effects models (two-way classification with equal observation per cell), CRD, RBD, LSD and their analyses; incomplete block designs, concepts of orthogonality and balance, BIBD, missing plot technique, factorial experiments and 2^4 and 3^2, confounding in factorial experiments, split-plot and simple lattice designs, transformation of data Duncan's multiple range test.

Paper-II

1. **Industrial Statistics:** Process and product control, general theory of control charts, different types of control charts for variables and attributes, X, R, s, p, np and charts, cumulative sum chart. Single, double, multiple and sequential sampling plans for attributes, OC, ASN, AOQ and ATI curves, concepts of producer's and consumer's risks, AQL, LTPD and AOQL, Sampling plans for variables, Use of Dodge-Romin tables.
   Concept of reliability, failure rate and reliability functions, reliability of series and parallel systems and other simple configurations, renewal density and renewal function, Failure models: exponential, Weibull, normal, lognormal. Problems in life testing, censored and truncated experiments for exponential models.
2. **Optimization Techniques:** Different types of models in Operations Research, their construction and general methods of solution, simulation and Monte-Carlo methods formulation of Linear Programming (LP) problem, simple LP model and its graphical solution, the simplex procedure, the two-phase metbod and the M-technique with artificial variables, the duality theory of LP and its economic interpretation, sensitivity analysis, transpotation and assignment problems, rectangular games, two-person zero- sum games, methods of solution (graphical and algebraic).

Replacement of failing or deteriorating items, group and individual replacement policies, concept of scientific inventory management and analytical structure of inventory problems, simple models with deterministic and stochastic demand with and without lead time, storage models with particular reference to dam type.

Homogeneous discrete-time Markov chains, transition probability matrix, classification of states and ergodic theorems, homogeneous continuous-time Markov chains, Poisson process, elements of queuing theory, M/MI, M/M/K, G/M/l and M/G/1 queues.

Solution of statistical problems on computers using well-known statistical software packages like SPSS.

3. Quantitative Economics and Official Statistics: Determination of trend, seasonal and cyclical components, Box-Jenkins method, tests for stationary series, ARIMA models and determination of orders of autoregressive and moving average components, fore-casting.

   Commonly used index numbers - Laspeyre's, Paasche's and Fisher's ideal index numbers, cham-base index number, uses and limitations of index numbers, index number of wholesale prices, consumer price, agricultural production and industrial production, test fot index numbers–proportionality, time-reversal, factor-reversal and circular.

   General linear model, ordinary least square and generalized least squares methods of estimation, problem of multi-collinearity, consequences and solutions of multi-collinearity, autocorrelation and its consequences, heteroscedasticity of disturbances and its testing, test for independence of disturbances concept of structure and model for simultaneous equations, problem of identification-rank and order conditions of identifiability, two-stage least sauare method of estimation.

   Present official statistical system in India relating to population, agriculture, industrial production, trade and prices, methods of collection of official statistics, their reliability and limitations, principal publications containing such statistics, various official agencies responsible for data collection and their main functions.

4. **Demography and Psychometry:** Demographic data from census, registration, NSS other surveys, their limitations. and uses, definition, construction and uses of vital rates and ratios, measures of fertility, reproduction rates, morbidity rate, standardized death rate, complete and abridged life tables, construction of life tables from vital statistics and census returns, uses of life tables, logistic and other population growth curves, fitting a logistic curve, population projection, stable population, quasi-stable population, techniques in estimation of demographic parameters, standard classification by cause of death, health surveys and use of hospital statistics.

Methods of standardisation of scales and tests, Z-scores, standard scores, T-scores, percentile scores, intelligence quotient and its measurement and uses, validity and reliability of test scores and its determination, use of factor analysis and path analysis in psychometry.

48. ZOOLOGY

Paper-I

1. **Non-chordata and Chordata**
   - (a) **Classification and relationship of various phyla up to subclasses:** Acoelomate and Coelomate, Protostomes and Deuterostomes, Bilateria and Radiata; Status of Protista, Parazoa, Onychophora and Hemichordata; Symmetry.
   - (b) **Protozoa:** Locomotion, nutrition, reproduction, sex; General features and life history of
     Paramaecium, Monocystis. Plasmodium **and** *Leishmania.*
   - (c) **Porifera:** Skeleton, canal system and reproduction.
   - (d) **Cnidaria:** Polymorphism, defensive structures and their mechanism; coral reefs and their formation; metagenesis; general features and life history of ***Obelia*** and ***Aurelia.***
   - (e) **Platyhelminthes:** Parasitic adaptation; general features and life history of Fasciola and Taenia and their-Pathogenic symptoms.
   - (f) **Nemathelminthes:** General features, life history, parasitic adaptation of Ascaris and ***Wuchereria.***
   - (g) **Annelida:** Coelom and metamerism; modes of life in polychaetes; general features and life history of Nereis, earthworm and leach.
   - (h) **Arthropoda:** Larval forms and parasitism in Crustacea; vision and respiration in arthropods (Prawn, cockroach and scorpion); modification of mouth, parts in insects (cockroach, mosquito, housefly, honey bee and butterfly), metapmor phosis in insect and its hormonal regulation, socialbehaviour ofApis and termites.
   - (i) **Molluscs:** Feeding, respiration, locomotion, general features and life history of Lamellidens, Pila and Sepia. Torsion and detorsion in gastropods.
   - (j) **Echinodermata:** Feeding, respiration, locomotion, larval forms, general features and life history of ***Asterias.***
   - (k) **Protochordata:** Origin of chordates; general features and life history of ***Branchiostoma*** and ***Herdmania.***
   - (l) **Pisces:** Respiration, locomotion and migration.
   - (m) **Amphibia:** Origin of tetrapods, parental care, paedomorphosis.
   - (n) **Reptilia:** Origin of reptiles, skull types, status of ***Sphenodon*** and crocodiles.
   - (o) **Aves:** Origin of birds, flight adaptation, migration.

(p) **Mammalia:** Origin of mammals, dentition, general features of egg laying mammals, pouchedmammals, aquatic mammals and primates, endocrine glands (pituitary, thyroid, parathyroid, adrenal, pancreas, gonads) and their interrelationships.

(q) Comparative functional anatomy of various systems of vertebrates. (integument and its derivatives, endoskeleton, locomotory organs, digestive system,. respiratory system, circulatory system including heart and aortic arches, urinogenital system, brain and sense organs (eye and ear).

2. **Ecology:**
   (a) Biosphere: concept of biosphere; biomes, Biogeochemical cycles, Human induced changes in atmosphere including green house effect, ecological succession, biomes and ecotones, community ecology.
   (b) Concept of ecosystem; structure and function of ecosystem, types of ecosystem, ecological succession, ecological adaptation.
   (c) Population; characteristics, population dynamics, population stabilization.
   (d) Biodiversity and diversity conservation of natural resources.
   (e) Wildlife of India.
   (f) Remote sensing for sustainable development.
   (g) Environmental biodegradation; pollution and its impact on biosphere and its prevention.
3. **Ethology:**
   (a) **Behaviour:** Sensory filtering, responsiveness, sign stimuli, learning, and memory, instinct, habituation, conditioning, imprinting.
   (b) Role of hormones in drive; role of pheromones in alarm spreading; crypsis, predator detection, predator tactics, social hierarchies in primates, social organization in insects;
   (c) Orientation, navigation, homing; biological rhythms: biological clock, tidal, seasonal and circadian rhythms.
   (d) Methods of studying animal behaviour including sexual conflict, selfishness, kinship and altruism.
4. **Economic Zoology:**
   (a) Apiculture, sericulture, lac culture, carp culture, pearl culture, prawn culture, vermiculture.
   (b) Major infectious and communicable diseases (malaria, filaria, tuberculosis, cholera and AIDS) their vectors, pathogens and prevention.
   (c) Cattle and livestock diseases, their pathogen (helminths) and vectors (ticks, mites, Tabanus, Stomoxys).
   (d) Pests of sugar cane (***Pyrilla perpusiella***), oil seed ***(Achaeajanata)*** and rice ***(Sitophilus oryzae)***.
   (e) Transgenic animals.
   (f) Medical biotechnology, human genetic disease and genetic counselling, gene therapy.
   (g) Forensic biotechnology.

5. **Biostatistics:** Designing of experiments; null hypothesis; correlation, regression, distribution and measure of central tendency, chi square, student-test, F-test (one-way & two-way F-test).
6. **Instrumentation methods:**
   (a) Spectrophotometer, phase contrast and fluorescence microscopy, radioactive tracer, ultra centrifuge, gel . electrophoresis, PCR, ELISA, FISH and chromosome painting.
   (b) Electron microscopy (TEM, SEM).

Paper-II

1. **Cell Biology:**
   (a) Structure and function of cell and its organelles (nucleus, plasma membrane, mitochondria, Golgi bodies, endoplasmic reticulum, ribosomes and lysosomes), cell division (mitosis and meiosis), mitotic spindle and mitotic apparatus, chromosome movement chromosome type ploytene and lambrush, organization of chromatin, heterochromatin, Cell cycle regulation.
   (b) Nucleic acid topology, DNA motif, DNA replication, transcription, RNA processing, translation, protein foldings and transport.
2. **Genetics:**
   (a) Modern concept of gene, split gene, genetic regulation, genetic, code.
   (b) Sex chromosomes and their evolution, sex determination in ***Drosophila*** and man.
   (c) Mendel's laws of inheritance, recombination, linkage, multiple alleles, genetics of blood groups, pedigree analysis, hereditary diseases in man.
   (d) Mutations and mutagenesis.
   (e) Recombinant DNA technology, plasmid, cosmid, artificial chromosomes as vectors, transgenics, DNA cloning and whole animal cloning (principles and methods).
   (f) Gene regulation and expression in prokaryotes and eukaryotes.
   (g) Signal molecules, cell death, defects in signaling pathway and consequences.
   (h) RFLP, RAPD and AFLF and application of RFLP in DNA finger-printing, ribozyme technologies, human genome project, genomics and protomics.
3. **Evolution:**
   (a) Theories of origin of life.
   (b) Theories of evolution; Natural selection, role of mutation in evolution, evolutionary patterns, molecular drive, mimicry, variation, isolation and speciation.
   (c) Evolution of horse, elephant and man using fossil data.
   (d) Hardy-Weinberg Law.
   (e) Continental drift and distribution of animals.

4. Systematics: Zoological nomenclature, international code, cladistics, molecular taxonomy and biodiversity.
5. **Biochemistry**
   - (a) Structure and role of carbohydrates, fats, fatty acids, cholesterol, proteins and amino-acids, nucleic acids. Bioenergetics.
   - (b) Glycolysis and Krebs cycle, oxidation and reduction, oxidative phosphorylation; energy conservation and release, ATP, cycl cyclic AMP- its structure and role.
   - (c) Hormone classification (steroid and peptide hormones), biosynthesis and functions.
   - (d) Enzymes: types and mechanisms of action.
   - (e) Vitamins and co-enzymes.
   - (f) Immunoglobulin and immunity.
6. **Physiology (with special reference to mammals)**
   - (a) Composition and constituents of blood; blood groups and Rh factor in man; factors and mechanism of coagulation; iron metabolism, acid-base balance, thermo regulation, anticoagulants.
   - (b) Haemoglobin: Composition, types and role in transport of oxygen and carbon dioxide.
   - (c) Digestion and absorption: Role of salivary glands, liver, pancreas and intestinal glands.
   - (d) Excretion: nephron and regulation of urine formation; osmo-regulation and excretory product.
   - (e) Muscles: Types, mechanism of contraction of skeletal muscles, effects of exercise on muscles.
   - (f) Neuron: nerve impulse—its conduction and synaptic transmission; neurotransmitters.
   - (g) Vision, hearing and olfaction in man.
   - (h) Physiology of reproduction puberty and menopause in human.
7. **Developmental Biology**
   - (a) Gametogenesis; spermatogenesis, composition of semen, ***in vitro*** and ***in vivo*** capacitation of mammalian sperm, Oogenesis, totipotency; fertilization, morphogenesis and morphogen; blastogeneis, establishment of body axes formation, fate map, gestulation in frog and chick; genes in development in chick homeotic genes, development of eye and heart, placenta in mammals.
   - (b) Cell lineage, cell to cell interaction, Genetic and induced teratogenesis, role of thyroxine in control of metamorphosisin amphibia, paedogenesis and neoteny, cell death, aging.
   - (c) Developmental genes in man, ***in vitro*** fertilization; and embryo transfer; cloning.
   - (d) Stem cells: Sources, types and their use in human welfare.
   - (e) Biogenetic law.

❑❑❑

9 Appendixes: II-IV

Appendix-II

INSTRUCTIONS TO THE CANDIDATES FOR FILLING ONLINE APPLICATION

Candidates are required to apply Online using the website www.upsconline.nic.in.

- Salient features of the system of Online Application Form are given hereunder:
- Detailed instructions for filling up online applications are available on the above mentioned website.
- Candidates will be required to complete the Online Application Form containing two stages viz. Part-I and Part-II as per the instructions available in the above mentioned site through drop down menus.
- The candidates are required to pay a fee of Rs.100/- Rupees One Hundred only) [excepting SC/ST/ Female/Persons with Benchmark Disability candidates who are exempted from payment of fee] either by depositing the money in any branch of State Bank of India by cash, or by using net banking facility of State Bank of India or by using any Visa/Master/RuPay Credit/ Debit Card.
- Before start filling up Online Application, a candidate must have his photograph and signature duly scanned in the .jpg format in such a manner that each file should not exceed 300 KB each and must not be less than 20 KB in size for the photograph and signature.
- The candidate should have details of one Photo ID viz. Aadhar Card/ Voter Card / PAN Card / Passport/ Driving License / Any other photo ID card issued by the State / Central Government. The details of this photo ID will have to be provided by the candidate while filling up the online application form. The candidates will have to upload a scanned copy of the Photo ID whose details have been provided in the online application by him/her. This photo ID will be used for all future references and the candidate is advised to carry this ID while appearing for the examination.

- The Online applications (Part I and II) can be filled from 19th February, 2019 to 18th March, 2019 till 18:00 Hrs.
- Applicants should avoid submitting multiple applications. However, if due to any unavoidable circumstances, any applicant submits multiple applications then he/she must ensure that the applications with higher RID is complete in all respects.
- In case of multiple applications, the applications with higher RID shall be entertained by the
- Commission and fee paid against one RID shall not be adjusted against any other RID.
- The applicants must ensure that while filling their Application Form, they are providing their valid and active E-Mail IDs as the Commission may use electronic mode of communication while contacting them at different stages of examination process.
- The applicants are advised to check their emails at regular intervals and ensure that the email addresses ending with @ nic.in are directed to their inbox folder and not to the SPAM folder or any other folder.
- Candidates are strongly advised to apply online well in time without waiting for the last date for submission of Online Applications.

Appendix-III

1. **Articles permitted inside Examination Hall:** Clip board or hard board (on which nothing is written), a good quality black ball pen for making responses on the Answer Sheet. Answer Sheet and sheet for rough work will be supplied by the invigilator.
2. **Articles not permitted inside Examination Hall:** Do not bring into the Examination Hall any article other than those specified above, e.g.,books,notes,loose sheets, electronic or any other type of calculators, mathematical and drawing instruments, Log Tables, stencils of maps. slide rules. Test Booklets and rough sheets pertaining to earlier session(s), etc.

   Mobiles phones, pagers, bluetooth or any other communication devices are not allowed inside the premises where the examination is being conducted. Any infringement of these instructions shall entail disciplinary action including ban from future examinations. Candidates are advised in their own interest not to bring any of the banned items including mobile phones/pagers/bluetooth to the venue of the examination, as arrangements for safekeeping cannot be assured.

   Candidates are advised not to bring any valuable/costly items to the Examination Halls, as safe keeping of the same cannot be assured. Commission will not be responsible for any loss in this regard. Penalty for wrong Answers

3. There will be penalty (Negative marking) for wrong answers marked by a candidate in the objective type question papers.
   (i) There are four alternatives for the answer to every question. For each question for which a wrong answer has been given by the candidate,one third (0.33) of the marks assigned to that question will be deducted as penally.
   (ii) If a candidate gives more than one answer, it will be treated as a wrong answer even if one of the given answers happens to be correct and there will be same penalty as above for that question.
   (iii) If a question is left blank i.e. no answer is given by the candidate, there will be no penally for that question.
4. **Unfair means strictly prohibited:** No candidate shall copy from the papers of any other candidate nor permit his papers to be copied nor give nor attempt to give nor obtain nor attempt to obtain irregular assistance of any description.
5. **Conduct in Examination Hall:** No candidate should misbehave in any manner or create disorderly scene in the Examination Hall or harass the staff employed by the Commission for the conduct of the examination. Any such misconduct will be severely penalised.
6. **Answer Sheet particulars**
   (i) Write in black ball pen your Centre and subject followed by test book let series (in bracket), subject code and roll number at the appropriate space provided on the answer sheet at the top. Also encode your book let series (A, B, C or D, as the case may be), subject code and roll number in the circles provided for the purpose in the answer sheet. The guidelines for writing the above particulars and for encoding the above particulars are given in Annexure. In case the booklet series is not printed on the test booklet or answer sheet is un-numbered, please report immediately to the invigilator and get the test booklet/answer sheet replaced.
   (ii) All corrections and changes in writing the roll number must be initialed by the candidates as well as by the invigilator and countersigned by the Supervisor.
   (iii) Immediately after commencement of the examination please check that the test booklet supplied to you does not have any unprinted or torn or missing pages or items etc. If so. get it replaced by a complete test booklet of the same series and subject.
7. Do not write your name or anything other than the specific items of information asked for, on the answers sheet/test booklet/sheet for rough work.
8. Do not fold or mutilate or damage or put any extraneous marking in the Answer Sheet. Do not write anything on the reverse of the answer sheet.
9. Since the answer sheets will be evaluated on computerised machines, candidates should exercise due care in handling and filling up the answer sheets. They

should use black ball pen only to darken the circles. For writing in boxes also they should use black ball pen Since the entries made by the candidates by darkening the circles will be taken into account while evaluating the answer sheets on computerised machines they should make these entries very carefully and accurately.

10. **Method of marking answers:** In the "OBJECTIVE TYPE" of examination, you do not write the answers. For each question (hereinafter referred to as "Item") several suggested answers (hereinafter referred to as "Responses") are given. You have to choose one response to each item.

    The question paper will being the Form of TEST BOOKLET. The booklet will contain item bearing numbers 1, 2, 3 .... etc. Under each item, Responses marked (a), (b), (c), (d) will be given. Your task will be to choose the correct response. If you think there is more than one correct response, then choose what you consider the best response.

    In any case, for each item you are to select only one response. If you select more than one response, your response will be considered wrong. In the Answer Sheet. Serial Nos. from 1 to 160 are printed. Against each numbers, there are circles marked (a), (b), (c) and (d). After you have read each item in the Test Booklet and decided which one of the given responses is correct or the best, you have to mark your response by completely blackening with black ball pen to i ndicate your response.

    For example, if the correct answer to item 1 is (b), then the circle containing the letter (b) is to be completely blackened with black ball pen as shown below:

    Example : (a) • (c) (d)

11. **Entries in Scannable Attendance List:** Candidates are required to fill in the relevant particulars with black ball pen only against their columns in the Scannable Attendance List, as given below:-
    (i) Blacken the circle [P] under the column [Present/Absent]
    (ii) Blacken the relevant circle for Test Booklet Series iii) Write Test Booklet Serial No.
    (iv) Write the Answer Sheet Serial No. and also blacken the corresponding circles below.
    (v) Append signature in the relevant column

12. Please read and abide by the instructions on the cover of Test Booklet. If any candidate indulges in disorderly or improper conduct, he will render himself liable for disciplinary action and/or imposition of a penality as the Commission may deem fit.

ANNEXURE

How to fill in the Answer Sheet of objective type tests in the Examination Hall

Please follow these instructions very carefully. You may note that since the answer sheets are to be evaluated on machine, any violation of these instructions may result in reduction of your score for which you would yourself be responsible.

Before you mark your responses on the Answer Sheet, you will have to fill in various particulars in it.

As soon as the candidate receives the Answer Sheet, he should check that it is numbered at the bottom. If it is found un-numbered he should at once get it replaced by a numbered one.

You will see from the Answer Sheet that you will have to fill in the top line, which reads thus :

केंद्र	विषय	विषय कोड		अनुक्रमांक	
Centre	Subject	S. Code					Roll Number									

If you are, say, appearing for the examination in Delhi Centre for the General Ability Test Papers* and your Roll No. is 0812769, and your test Booklet series is 'A' you should fill in thus, using black ball pen.

केंद्र	विषय	विषय कोड		अनुक्रमांक	
Centre Delhi	Subject Mathematics (A)	S. Code	0 1	Roll Number	0 8 1 2 7 6 9

You should write with black ball pen the name of the centre and subject in English or Hindi.

The test Booklet Series is indicated by Alphabets A, B,C or D at the top right hand corner of the Booklet.

Write your Roll Numbers exactly as it is in your e-Admission Certificate with black ball pen in the boxes provided for this purpose. Do not omit any zero(s) which may be there.

The next step is to find out the appropriate subject code from the Time Table. Now encode the Test Booklet Series, Subject Code and the Roll Number in the circles provided for this purpose. Do the encoding with black ball pen. The name of the Centre need not be encoded.

Writing and encoding of Test Booklet Series is to be done after receiving the Test Booklet and confirming the Booklet Series from the same.

For Mathematics * subject paper of 'A' Test Booklet Series you have to encode the subject code,which is 01. Do it thus:

पुस्तिका क्रम (ए)	विषय	0	1
Booklet Series (A)	Subject		
●		●	⓪
Ⓑ		①	●
Ⓒ		②	②
Ⓓ		③	③
		④	④
		⑤	⑤
		⑥	⑥
		⑦	⑦
		⑧	⑧
		⑨	⑨

All that is required is to blacken completely the circle marked ·A' below the Booklet Series and below the subject code blacken completely the Circles for "0" (in the first vertical column) and "1" (in the second vertical column). You should then encode the Roll No 0812769.Do it thus similarly :

अनुक्रमांक.
Roll Number

0	8	1	2	7	6	9
●	⓪	⓪	⓪	⓪	⓪	⓪
①	①	●	①	①	①	①
②	②	②	②	②	②	②
③	③	③	③	③	③	③
④	④	④	④	④	④	④
⑤	⑤	⑤	⑤	⑤	⑤	⑤
⑥	⑥	⑥	⑥	⑥	●	⑥
⑦	⑦	⑦	⑦	●	⑦	⑦
⑧	●	⑧	⑧	⑧	⑧	⑧
⑨	⑨	⑨	⑨	⑨	⑨	●

Important: Please ensure that you have carefully encoded your subject, Test Booklet series and Roll Number

*This is just illustrative and may not be relevant to your Examination. davp 5510411410012/1516

Appendix-IV

CERTIFICATE REGARDING PHYSICAL LIMITATION IN AN EXAMINEE TO WRITE

This is to certify that, I have examined Mr./Ms./Mrs............................... (name of the candidate with benchmark disability), a person with .... (nature and percentage of disability as mentioned in the certificate of disability), S/o/D/o......................., a resident of .... (Village/ District/State) and to state that he/she has physical limitation which hampers his/her writing capabilities owing to his/her disability.

Signature

Chief Medical Officer/Civil Surgeon /
Medical Superintendent of a Government Healt Care Institution.

Note: Certificate should be given by a specialist of the relevant stream/disability (eg. Visual Impairment – Ophthalmologist, Locomotor disability – Orthopaedic specialist/PMR).

LETTER OF UNDERTAKING FOR USING OWN SCRIBE

(To be filled by the candidates online to the Commission)

I…………………., a candidate with………………………(name of the disability) appearing for the ……………….. (name of the examination)……………….. bearing Roll No……………….. at ……….. (name of the centre) in the District ………………….., …………….. (name of the State). My qualification is …………..

I do hereby state that …………………………… (name of the scribe) will provide the service of scribe/reader/lab assistant for the undersighned for taking the aforesaid examination.

I do hereby undertake that his qualification is …………………… In case, subsequently it is found that his/her qualification is not as declared by the undersigned and is beyond my qualification, I shall forfeit my right to the post and claims thereto.

(Signature of the candidates with Disability)

Place:

Date:

❑❑❑